VIRTUE'S HOME TUTOR

. . . .

First Aid for
Happy and Successful
Schooling

VIRTUE'S

First Aid

. . . .

What will your child become . .

Farmer ?

T. V. Announcer ?

Priest ?

Shopkeeper ?

Clerk ?

Written and compiled by J and A E Fishman
Illustrated by Francis M L Barthropp

HOME TUTOR

for Happy and Successful Schooling

· ·

Engineer ? Scientist ? Nurse ?

Policeman ? Salesman ? Pilot ?

PUBLISHED BY VIRTUE AND COMPANY LTD

Ocean House, Little Trinity Lane, London, EC4

· ·

Published by Virtue & Co Ltd,
London, EC4 and Branches

Made and printed in Great Britain by
William Clowes and Sons Limited, London and Beccles

Typography by Francis M L Barthropp

Title page designed by John Payne

3rd Impression

Contents

· ·

contents (continued)

Introduction

. . . .

This book is intended to be used by a parent and child together at home. It is not a crammer in that it is not designed for any specific examination. The theory behind the book is that learning can be fun, and that the parent, provided he or she is able to do so, is often the best person to prove this to his own child. Sensible use of the book must inevitably result in a general improvement in all branches of school work for children under the age of 12 years.

Most parents have the knowledge with which (when shown how) they can aid enormously their children's education to the age of 12 or so. A few words of caution here—all parents hope for much from their children, but *please do not demand too much*. A man who works well with his hands is usually happier than an inefficient professional man—so do not worry your child if he does not take to "book-work". Happiness and peace of mind are more important than one's position on the social scale. The three R's, however, he must know for without them all future progress is impossible, and here this book will be a very real aid.

The work is split up into three main sections: English, arithmetic and general intelligence.

Preceding the exercises are several introductory chapters addressed primarily to the parent. The information and advice that they give is

1

quite as important as the exercises themselves. These preliminary chapters must be read and digested by the parent *before* any work is started with his child.

"Virtue's Home Tutor" is based on a correspondence course which has been running successfully for many years. The authors have collaborated extensively with psychologists, a medical practitioner, schoolteachers and examiners, all of whom have had wide experience in the general upbringing of children under 12 years of age.

The successful correspondence course has been put into its present form of a book so that the authors might impart their ideas and discoveries to a wider public. Their earlier work has been considerably revised and enlarged, and the form it now takes represents a total of fifteen years improvement and research. It differs widely from the ordinary text-book; for such a book is written for a schoolteacher to use with a large class of children of mixed ability. With this book, designed for the parent-child unit, individual attention is possible in the home, and is likely to achieve very successful results.

GRAMMAR SCHOOL EDUCATION

About 50 per cent of parents of 10- and 11-year-olds would like their children to enter grammar schools, unfortunately there is room for rather less than 20 per cent. A grammar school education is not only beneficial to a child's development and general outlook in life, it also opens up a whole range of careers not available to a child who has been taught at a secondary modern school (today's version of the pre-1944 senior elementary or central school). All the professions and the more important business and commercial houses prefer better-educated boys and girls for their administrative and clerical work;

they make sure of this by appointing only those who have some passes in the General Certificate of Education. For this, a grammar school education is the best preparation.

In some districts where there are more grammar school places available, a child may gain a free place with a lower I.Q.[1] than his more gifted cousin who lives in a less fortunate locality. Although the average for the country is one grammar school place for every five children, in some areas the proportion is one in eight, and in others even one in two. For instance two out of five children might be chosen for grammar schools in the County Borough of Merthyr in Wales, as against one in eleven in Kingston-upon-Hull. One important reason for this inequality is that years ago schools for "Higher Grade" education were built where parents could afford to pay the fees—and so a child's chance of getting into a grammar school today may depend on how prosperous the locality was fifty years ago. Also, because of the later development of grammar school education for girls, there are less places available for them than there are for boys. (It is interesting to note that until the age of 16 or so, girls do better than boys in English, arithmetic and intelligence tests. Later, however, in the Universities, the male takes the lead.)

THE 11 PLUS EXAMINATION

The grammar school entrance (11 Plus) or transfer examination usually decides whether your child is to have a grammar, technical or secondary modern school education (in Scotland the senior secondary

[1] Intelligence Quotient (I.Q.) $= \dfrac{\text{mental age}}{\text{actual age}} \times 100$ (mental age being accurately determined by special tests). Children selected for grammar schools usually have an I.Q. over 115.

school is the equivalent of the English grammar school).

There has been more effective scientific research about the 11 plus examination than about any other public examination. Great care is taken over each candidate and generally the system of selection is very just. It has its faults, but it does separate most sheep from most goats.

The examination varies slightly in the different counties that use it, and no syllabus is ever issued. The child will usually be given three papers; one in English, one in arithmetic and one general paper containing intelligence tests. About 45 minutes is allowed for each paper. The system of marking makes allowance for the child's age (otherwise the $11\frac{1}{2}$-year-old would have about three times as good a chance of passing as the child of $10\frac{1}{2}$ years—for children of both these ages may sit for the same examination). According to the number of vacancies in the local grammar schools, the awards are made from the top downwards, borderline cases receiving very special consideration. Account will also be taken of the primary school's report on your child's abilities and temperament—indeed of his whole primary school record. This is beginning to count for more and more in the selection of places in grammar schools. The grammar school concerned may interview or even re-examine (often orally) the prospective scholar. Since the 1950's the 11 Plus examination has caused much heartache and argument, and it is gradually being eradicated from our educational system. Some authorities have in fact already abolished it.

Many counties have rejected the 11 Plus examination and are making their awards on the child's school record. The 11 Plus has been criticised because many children—and their parents—became so tense and nervous at the prospect of this one examination, that it could make all the difference to their whole lives. Attempts are being made to find other methods of selection and several counties have decided upon a series of interviews with the child during his last year at primary school. Whatever the process of selection, this course of studies will significantly increase your child's knowledge and his chances of success.

COMPREHENSIVE SCHOOLS

Some local authorities have gone over to the comprehensive school system. Here, children over the age of 11 are not separated into grammar, secondary modern and technical schools, but are all housed in one very large building and then directed to various streams or courses. Whether your child's education is to be in a comprehensive or a grammar school, the benefits to him of guided parental aid given during his early school life will be of immeasurable value to his chances of a better education.

CHILDREN UNDER 9

. . . .

Your child's education began when he just opened his eyes, and his parents are his first natural teachers.

With the very young, impressive and important general improvements are capable of being achieved with even less "home-help" than is the case in the older groups. But the learning must on no account be forced. It must be done with great patience; the tasks set must be within his powers and yet at the same time extend him.

His curiosity, sense of observation and his imagination should all be encouraged. We must be patient with his "why, why, why?" even if it is often a call of attention rather than a genuine desire for knowledge. All questions should be taken seriously and discussed, and remember the magic sentence for adventure in learning—"let's find out." Every household should have easily available an encyclopedia, a dictionary and an atlas; they can be an aid in answering questions and stopping arguments.

The child should be encouraged to join in conversations with adults. In this way every activity, every talk widens his vocabulary and understanding of the world.

Under 5 years, letters may be learnt and the first ideas of numbers may be given. In infant schools speech training is introduced at this stage and many rhymes and jingles are taught which help the child with his elementary lessons. Some children can read and write all the numbers by the age of 4 years, and tell the time soon after. But remember—the early learning must be played as a game; it must give pleasure to the child and never, never leave him bored.

During the daily walks, at 4 years old, colours and shapes (one colour and one shape a day) can be taught—green fields, circular wheels, red pillar boxes, square or oblong or diamond window panes. Start with easy ones (triangles, for instance, are too difficult). He can also during these walks learn things like the days of the week and the seasons of the year in the correct order, or be taught left from right. During these walks, such signs as: STOP, HALT, WET PAINT, POST OFFICE, GARAGE and ICE CREAM can be pointed out, and he will learn to recognise them.

If there is a baby at home he should be involved in the weekly weighing. In going upstairs these can be counted on the way up or down. The "Magic Number Game" should be played—each day concentrate on a different single number, e.g. 5 fingers, 5 toes, 5 stairs, 5 plates, etc. While walking, houses, cars or lamp-posts can be counted so that he becomes quickly used to numbers.

If, in beginning work on the three R's with a young child, we start too early and the child finds the work boring, difficult or unenjoyable, much harm will be done in its persistence. *More must not be attempted than the child is ready to cope with.* Children develop differently. The child who teethes early or walks early is not brighter than the child who starts later; nor is a child necessarily backward if he does not talk until he is five years old. The bounds of normality are ill-defined. Some of us are slow starters. Some nations do not start formal schooling until the child is 7 years old, and this seems to work just as

7

well as with those nations who insist on compulsory education at a younger age.

READING

Reading naturally forms the basis of all education. Until a child can begin to recognise words and to read them, he will be quite unable to progress in any subject.

The books that a child encounters in his very early life are probably the most important he will read. On them will depend (for the rest of his life, very often) his attitude towards books in general. In a home where everyone reads, where books are cherished and used, where children are read to, and told stories whilst sitting on a parent's knee, or provided with attractive picture books—there, the barrier between the spoken and written word is quickly broken down. In this way, children soon begin to recognise words and phrases and find themselves reading. The importance of getting the child *wanting to read* cannot be over-emphasised. He must not be forced or he may end up by hating books. The child should, even at the nursery age of 3 years (and earlier), see beautiful picture books (bird, flower, animal books), and hear nursery rhymes and songs, read from the most attractive picture books available.

Children love a reading time before going to sleep, probably choosing to hear favourite books over and over again. Reading aloud to a child (just before bedtime or perhaps after lunch, at week-ends and holidays, but in any case regularly) should be part of every parent's life. This is probably as good for the parent as for the child.

Let your child point out to you and talk about items of interest from the pictures in the books, and make sure he thoroughly enjoys every moment. He will soon learn to associate books and reading with pleasure.

Read in a partially darkened room—the darkness helps to set up an atmosphere. It also adds to the interest and enjoyment to use different voices in imitation of different characters in the story. Act the part you are reading.

Do not start your child reading too early. Wait until he is ready. Many children can start reading at the age of 5 years but some with higher I.Q.s are reading at 4 years or even earlier—it all depends on the child. Recent research indicates that most children are not ready to read until they reach the *mental* age of 6 years, and some even later. Only 50 per cent of 6-year-olds are ready to read at that age, so do not force your child. Before he is able to read easily you should have a talk with his schoolteacher and ask his advice on how you can help. We think that such a talk is very important because the child must learn to love reading and his schoolteacher can tell you what method *he* is using and advise what books to use. Educational reading books are very cheap and perhaps he may lend you the school book, or books.

In reading with your child, you should know that the old alphabetical method is now very nearly obsolete, i.e. we no longer say, "see - ay - tee spells cat" but use instead the sound names of the alphabet, and so, "ke - a - te spells cat". In many schools now the child is taught complete words from the start. This is more interesting for him and should be combined with the ke - a - te method. In some schools the child is taught right from the beginning to learn whole sentences. Some County Authorities are experimenting with the Initial Teaching Alphabet. This is a new phonetic alphabet which may be proved to enable the child to learn to read more quickly than by traditional

9

methods. After the child has learned to read he then changes over to the ordinary alphabet.

In your practice with your child it is important that you only follow the method of spelling used in his school. Different systems will only confuse him. And remember—go slowly, he must be ready for it and enjoy it.

Recommended reading series (publisher's name is in brackets):

> *Let's Learn to Read* (Blackie)
> *Happy Venture* (Oliver and Boyd)
> *Beacon* (Ginn)
> *Janet and John* (Nisbet)

Make your child a line and word marker from thin cardboard (about 6 inches × 3 inches) so that he can concentrate on the line he is reading. Words to be revised before the next session can be listed on the marker and crossed off when they are known.

When reading with your child do not let him get stuck for too long at any word that he finds difficult—help him along so that he is able to read smoothly. It is advisable to use books that are a little easier than those he uses in school. Once your child can read easily and happily, you need only provide him with suitable books (use the public library).

10

FAIRY TALES

Some children can accept these as make-believe stories; others cannot, and get very upset by the wicked witches, dragons and other themes of cruelty. The world can be very frightening to a child of 5 years who finds that there is so much he cannot understand; so do not read to him frightening tales of wolves and witches just before he goes to bed. In any case until he is 6 years old or so, and more experienced in the way the world works, he will find them confusing.

WRITING

Your child should not at too early an age be given lessons in drawing perfectly formed letters. Let him first scribble and draw, using blackboard and chalks and pencils as playthings. Even 6-year-olds are not usually quite ready for the muscular control and co-ordination that writing entails. When they do begin, printed letters should first be copied, and of course tracing helps. Ordinary joined letter handwriting should not be practised until the child is about 8 years of age. At about 8 or 9 ink writing may be started, depending on his progress and the system used in his school. Use plain and not lined paper for early writing. Strangely enough the lines make his efforts more difficult at first.

ARITHMETIC

The right help given at the right time in the early stages of learning arithmetic is very important. Once a pupil loses a little ground in this subject, whether it be due to change of school, absence from school or emotional stresses, a snow-ball effect is obtained. Progress in arithmetic is like going upstairs—you have to go up one step at a time and if too many steps are missing, further progress becomes impossible.

Educational Authorities recommend that numbers only be learned up to the age of 6 years, and that only then should formal instruction in arithmetic begin. Here again it all depends on the child. His learning of numbers can be helped enormously in the home—when buying food, planning meals, setting the clock, measuring his height or weighing baby. From the earliest age children should be given

11

beads, bricks, sand and water to play with. They will then automatically compare, measure and weigh, and so lay a firm foundation for the more formal work to come.

Card and dice games help with an understanding of simple numbers, since dice entail the counting of dots. Dominoes and Ludo give practice in adding. Snakes and Ladders and Monopoly are also useful—as is Darts at a later age.

Later on playing at "shops" should be encouraged. Have a large toy clock face or an old broken-down clock, play at opening-time, lunch-time, tea-time and closing-time. Scales, weights and measures, money and goods should be full size and real if possible. Have him pretend he has different kinds of shops—fruit, shoe, grocery, etc. Wherever possible teach arithmetic in relation to live interests, e.g. in the post office—the buying of stamps and the saving of money; in the car—speeds, buying petrol, and miles per gallon; in the field of sport—records and averages; in church—counting the number of people. In recent years, the Cuisenaire (pieces of different coloured wood of different lengths) has given encouraging results in helping children all over the world to appreciate arithmetic. An average child should be able to count to 100 by the age of 6.

The basis of all arithmetic is a thorough understanding and mastery of numbers, addition, subtraction and multiplication. In the early stages make use of match sticks and elastic bands (to hold groups of sticks together).

In order not to confuse your child, use the same arithmetic book at home for his early work as he uses in school. His teacher should not mind it being taken home if you have explained the purpose of the Course to him and obtained his approval.

Remember, oral work is always better than letting your child find his own way through the exercises.

MULTIPLICATION

Whatever teaching systems for arithmetic are in use at your child's school, he cannot get away from the necessity of learning Tables. They need not necessarily be dull or boring if learnt at home in the right atmosphere.

They should be learnt in the following way (and *not* as for instance: 2 times 3=6):

> one two is two
>
> two twos are four
>
> three twos are six   *and so on*

Show that 3×2 is the same as 2×3 by arranging matchsticks as follows:

— — —   — —

— — —   — —

                 — —

Show your child that $4\times3=3\times4$ in the same way.

Some children learn better by seeing than by hearing—so have the Tables in front of your child whilst he is learning them, so that he can *see as well as say* the Tables.

MONEY

By playing shopping games your child will learn to use coins—$\frac{1}{2}$d, 1d, 3d, 6d and 1/-. Play with him, and get him to add and subtract with them. When necessary explain that $\frac{1}{2}$d needs another $\frac{1}{2}$d to make 1d or that 7d needs another 5d to make 1/-.

He should be taught to use 10/- and £1 notes and so be able to understand the workings of pounds, shillings and pence.

13

MEASURING

Give your child practice in using a ruler. First let him guess the length of a table, and then by using the ruler discover for himself how accurate his guess was. In the beginning use measurements to the nearest foot and later go on to feet and inches.

The measuring of milk and petrol should be discussed with and understood by your child. Use empty milk bottles to show that two half-pints make a pint, that two pints make a quart and that four quarts (or eight pints) make a gallon.

WEIGHTS AND SCALES

Weights and scales should be handled and explained. Show that a larger thing can weigh less than a smaller one. Show that four separately weighed ounces together balance a $\frac{1}{4}$-pound weight, and eight will balance against a $\frac{1}{2}$-pound weight. Use the scales also to give practice in addition and subtraction.

Interest the child in his own weight and bring in the use of the stone (14 pounds). Tons and hundredweights should be introduced in their practical aspects with regard to sacks of coals and notices on bridges and lorries.

TIME

Your child should study the clock's hands. (An old broken clock or watch makes an excellent educational toy.) He should learn the number of minutes in an hour and tell the time in hours, half-hours and quarter-hours. The meaning of quarters and halves (as in money and weights) should be explained to him. The measurement of time and the difference between a.m. and p.m. should be understood by him, and practised until he has no difficulty with it.

Your child should learn this rhyme for the days of the months:

Thirty days hath September, April, June, and November,
All the rest have thirty-one—excepting February alone—
Which hath but twenty-eight days clear,
And twenty-nine in each Leap Year.

STARTING SCHOOL

At about 5 years of age the child is usually ready and anxious for fresh worlds to conquer and is keen to start school. Do not suggest to him that he may be lonely ("you won't miss Mummy will you?"). Tell him instead that he will find new friends, new toys, new games. Make it sound like an exciting new adventure—which it is!

The early years at school are of the utmost importance to your child. During these years he will develop habits of work, concentration and study that will be of lasting value to him. Find out from him and from his teacher what his first difficulties are and help him to get over them quickly. Get to know his school-teacher and visit his school. If the school has a Parent-Teacher Association make use of it and attend its meetings.

Your child not only learns the three R's at school, but also a way of meeting success or failure in a competitive world. Furthermore, he will learn in school that his position in the world can be bettered by work and knowledge. Above all, we hope that he will learn the value of co-operation and of being a useful member of the community; and the child who is at ease with his work and happy in his home life has every chance of succeeding in this. Parental help on the lines we show here really does pay dividends.

15

YOUR CHILD'S HEALTH

. . . .

Experiments by psychologists have shown that to get the best results from your child you must first satisfy his physical needs; in food, fresh air, cleanliness, exercise, clothing, attention to eyes, ears, teeth and sleep.

DIET

Health can be bought! Not in the chemist's shop—but in the green-grocers', grocers', butchers', bakers', and fishmongers' shops. The well-fed have always been taller and heavier than the ill-fed. In the past the superior physique of the middle and upper classes has demon-strated this fact very markedly. Nowadays with better feeding for all, the modern child is generally taller and heavier than his parents. Rickets and scurvy (both diseases of wrong and under-feeding) are almost extinct in Great Britain today.

16

Although for ordinary household feeding it is not necessary to have a detailed knowledge of calory and protein values, some understanding of food values is essential.

Human food has six main components:

carbohydrate (starch, sugar, flour, oatmeal, rice, potatoes)

fats (butter, margarine, cheese, milk, eggs, lard, dripping, vegetable and fish oils) protein (meat, white of egg, fish, cheese, milk, nuts, peas, beans, lentils)

mineral salts, e.g. iron, sodium, calcium (dairy produce, fresh vegetables and fruit and fresh natural foods)

vitamins

water

All these are necessary for good health, and a well-balanced diet will contain all of these six categories of food.

A mixed diet of natural *fresh* foods is most important. Refined foods should be replaced by *natural* foods, e.g. honey is to be preferred to jam, marmalade or golden syrup. Condiments should be avoided. Some raw salad and raw fruit should be eaten daily—the fresher the better, for the protective vitamin content of vegetables and fruits decreases with storing. Most families have too many starchy and too many fried foods. Meat extracts have very little nutritive value.

Dairy products — milk, butter, eggs and cheese — are vital for your child. The value of milk is now undisputed; it contains all of our six categories of food. Every child under 16 years of age should have at least one pint daily; younger children should have more. It should be pasteurised or boiled and may be consumed in milk puddings, custards or with cocoa and other milk drinks. Cocoa is much better for children than tea or coffee.

Wholemeal bread is better for your child (and yourself!) than bread made from white over-refined flour.

All foods should be chewed thoroughly. The state of the mind affects the ability to digest well, and meals should be eaten in a pleasant unhurried atmosphere. There should be no hurried gulping down of unchewed food. A child should not be allowed to rush out of the room before he has finished his last mouthful.

2—H.T.

Your child should not be forced to eat, nor should he be coaxed or cajoled to swallow his food. Appetite is the best guide. Serve him with food that he likes, well and attractively prepared.

There must be no snacks between meals; even if he has left everything at the previous meal he must wait for the next mealtime—no harm will come to him for having missed a meal. Quite the reverse; the pangs of hunger will teach him more than words or a scene. Don't be an over-anxious fussy parent at meal time, indeed not at any time. As long as your child is fit and active, do not worry about his appetite.

IMPORTANCE OF WATER

Most people do not drink enough water. Since it is free, or almost so, its value is not consciously appreciated. The water of London, Manchester and Glasgow is as healthy to drink for the normal person as is that in Bath, Harrogate or Vichy. Encourage your child to drink half to one cupful of water between meals (meals are better taken dry). This extra water, which can be taken with a little flavouring (e.g. as lemonade or ginger beer), will help in establishing regular bowel habits.

BOWEL HABITS

The parent should help his child to establish regular habits from a very early age. A fixed daily time should be set apart for the child's sitting in the lavatory. Whether he has the desire or not, this time should be kept regularly and unhurriedly. After breakfast is probably the best time for most children. He may take a book or magazine with him. Neglecting this routine visit, drinking insufficient water, not eating fresh fruit and vegetables daily, and lack of exercise are the

18

usual causes of constipation. Laziness too, i.e. ignoring the call or postponing it, causes a weakness in the strength of ensuing calls and so upsets the natural working of the body.

The dangers of constipation have been much exaggerated in the press. The enthusiasm of advertisers of laxatives has led some people to believe that unless they have a daily bowel action, they are poisoning themselves. There is no evidence for this and it is doubtful whether such self-poisoning exists; if it does, it causes far less harm to the community than does the widespread taking of aperients.

CLOTHING

Do not over-clothe your child. The modern tendency is to wear as little clothing as possible. It is advisable, of course, to begin this in the summer so that the skin learns to adjust itself before the cold of the winter. Then, more clothing must be worn, for the body must be kept comfortably warm. Clothes should be loose enough not to restrict movement. Restricting belts or garters should not be used. Wool and flannel are not absorbent and should not be worn next to the skin. They are old-fashioned—the modern cellular material which allows for evaporation of perspiration is much better. Air is a good insulator of heat and it is not only the fibres of the clothes we wear, but the air held in our clothes, which prevents the body from losing the heat that it generates. Underclothes should be changed at least once a week. They should be completely removed at night and pyjamas or nightdress substituted.

19

Shoes for children (and for adults) should be broad enough to allow the toes to move about inside them, and should be straight from heel to toe on the inside of the foot. They should have strong shanks and fit snugly—particularly around the heels so that the foot does not slide forward. Shoes for walking should have a heel which is not too low so that it gives some support to the foot. Tennis and gym shoes are not designed for everyday use, as they do not give sufficient support at the instep and may easily give your child flat feet.

POSTURE, BREATHING AND FRESH AIR

Good posture is important, it not only expresses, but helps to form our attitude of mind. "Stick your bottom out as if you had a tail and are showing it off; hold your head high"—this is the advice to give your child. A slovenly posture is less conducive to success and happiness than a correct one.

The importance of deep and correct breathing is now generally accepted by the medical profession as a way to happiness and health. Teach your child to feel that when he breathes, all parts of his chest are being filled with fresh air. Have him practise, in the garden or by the open window, the deep breathing exercises he has learned at school. Shallow breathing must be discouraged and deep breathing encouraged.

Your child should play in the open air as much as possible. Sunlight is good for him, but it cannot pass through windows. His bedroom window should be open at night as well as during the day; night air is not injurious provided the bed is clear of any draughts. An open window with thicker bedclothes is far healthier than light bedclothes and no air.

20

SLEEP AND RELAXATION

A child learns more and learns faster than a grown-up. He is more active both mentally and physically than an adult; he therefore needs more sleep than is required by his parents.

Table of hours of sleep needed by children (obviously these may vary from one child to the next):

4 years of age. 12 hours sleep; bedtime 6.30

5–7 years of age. 11 to 12 hours sleep; bedtime 7.0

8–11 years of age. 10 to 11 hours sleep; bedtime 8.0

There should be no exciting activity just before bedtime. Noise, anxiety, cold and hunger are enemies of sound sleep. Children should be sent to bed at the same time every night—whether they are tired or not. Sleep is largely a matter of habit.

If your child wants a night-light let him have it, but a darkened room is generally more effective in bringing deep sleep. Should your child say he cannot sleep, tell him "It does not matter—just lie as relaxed as you can. If you lie relaxed it does not matter if you do not sleep." Relaxation and sleep are allied, and the one passes imperceptibly into the other.

In this world of ours, most of us wish to take all we can of what life has to offer. The increasing speed of everything—working and then playing in top gear—makes it essential that we teach our child to relax after physical or mental exertion. Watch the boxer between rounds, or the athlete after his sprint, and see how they go limp and relax. Many adults live in a perpetual state of tension and it is now generally accepted that high blood pressure, duodenal ulcers, certain heart diseases, asthma and many other serious ailments are partially caused and certainly aggravated by this inability to relax. The ability to flop out, to go loose and limp can be acquired.

Encourage your child to rest after the midday meal. After bouts of study and book-work, some outdoor activity like walking, tennis or cycling (and preferably not reading comics or watching television) can also be worth-while ways of resting effectively!

21

RECREATIONS AND ENTERTAINMENTS

Cycling, walking, swimming, tennis, singing, making things, playing a musical instrument and joining in social activities with others, are all to be encouraged. Doctors are becoming increasingly conscious of the necessity of some regular daily energetic exercise in the fresh air.

Cinema-going for the very young should not be encouraged, and parents—whatever the age of their child—should choose carefully the films they allow him to see.

Television—from the point of view of family life—is a very mixed blessing, and the parent who allows his child to spend hour after hour huddled over a television screen is probably guilty of retarding the child's mental and physical development. Listening to the radio also should not be permitted to take up too much of a child's time. "Televiewing" and radio listening should be selective.

Games played by the family around the fire are excellent. The games can be both educational and relaxing; spelling and intelligence tests, quizzes, masculines and feminines, and so forth. Evenings spent like this can be wonderful family fun and give more lasting satisfaction for the whole family than passively watching television. A few excellent family games which are both educational and enjoyable are: *Keywords*, *Lexicon* and *Scrabble*. Your newsagent will be able to get them for you.

In these days of scientific exactness about feeding, fresh air, germs, etc., do not neglect the old type of family life. It is most important for your child to be cuddled and fondled. Relaxation around the fireside, talking to your child, making things with him, playing games with him, singing and laughing with him are of the greatest importance if he is to get the best out of life. We do not measure our parents by

22

their efficiency in the home or in the world outside; we value them for their kindness, sympathy and love.

HOLIDAYS

For the ordinary town-dweller, going back to nature, where the artificialities of life are dispensed with and where personal effort is necessary for any degree of comfort to be attained—that is of infinite value. Camping, caravanning, tramping, "mucking about in a boat", living on a farm, all these things are much better for your child than going to a seaside hotel where everything is done for him.

CLEANLINESS

Dirt breeds ill-health and disease. The finger nails of young children should be kept short. Your child must always wash his hands after using the lavatory. Many physicians believe that we overdo things in our Western civilisation with the habit of taking a daily hot bath. The skin serves to protect the body and frequent washing away with hot water of its top layer may not be a good thing. A hot bath once or twice weekly is probably better than a daily one. A morning cold plunge in summer for those who enjoy it is quite another matter and may be encouraged.

PUNISHMENT

Generally speaking—praising a child when he does well is a much better method of bringing him up than blaming him after he has done wrong. Unfortunately the time does come when we have to punish our child; but we should not punish him because of the consequence of his deed, but because of his wrong motive. We do not punish him for breaking the vase in the drawing room, but for fighting in the

23

wrong place at the wrong time. If he broke the vase whilst he was trying to clean it, we do *not* punish him; we sympathise with him instead.

Although punishment should be administered at once (while the offence is still fresh in the child's mind) do not punish in anger. This precept can be difficult to keep. Once the child has been punished, forget about it. The child must be given to understand that he has done wrong, and the best punishment is to have him put right (if this is possible) the wrong he has done—for instance pay for the vase that was broken when he was fighting. For punishment in other cases, it is better to deprive him of a privilege than to beat him. Corporal punishment should be used very infrequently.

Finally, in punishing, condemn the act but not the child. Do not tell him that he is a "selfish" or "cruel child" but say "that was a selfish thing to do and not a bit like you!" It is of the utmost importance to encourage your child to think highly of himself.

Your child must feel that he is loved. That no matter what the differences of the day, the troubles, the upsets, the fights, the lost tempers, the things said and done—no matter what—that always underneath, in the family there is a continuing deep bond of love and understanding. He must know that a family disagreement is not a family crisis and that parental anger is not the end of the world.

24

SECURITY AND CONFIDENCE

The child's feeling of security must be strong. If money troubles should come (and most families have their financial "ups and downs"), they must not be allowed to interfere with the child's sense of value of human relations. Set him a good example of how to "take it". Talk it over with him. Explain to him that everyone worries about money;

that you get overworked and worried, and that you cannot help being cross at times; that he is more important to you than all the money in the world; that you still have one another and can still have fun, and that things will get better. "Let's see what we can do about it"— make do with a repaired or repainted toy while you do not have the money to purchase a new one.

A child must feel that he is held in high esteem by others. From his parents he gets a picture of himself—kind and clever or foolish and dull, which he accepts. He thrives on trust, appreciation and love, irrespective of the family's income or parental education. Have faith in him. Set him the right examples and encourage the right instincts. Love and faith are the two greatest qualities for a parent and a teacher.

If a child is continually scolded and given a low opinion of himself, then he will accept that opinion. If, on the other hand, he is rarely corrected and constantly told how wonderful he is, he will grow up with an exalted idea of his own abilities. If the happy medium cannot be struck, perhaps the second of these two prospects is the better.

This world of ours, we must recognise, is competitive—right from the start—right from the child's first contact with other human beings. From the day he is born, he begins to compete with his brothers and sisters for his parents' attention and affections. From his first day in school he competes with his fellows. It is all very well for educationists to say that children should develop at their own pace, and not in competition with each other. That would be ideal; but at school Mary hears Susan reading better than she can, and sees Jane getting credits for superior work and is of course affected by what she sees and hears. And so it will be seen that superiority and inferiority feelings are bred even in the best of class-rooms, and these begin from the very first school attendance of the child.

With just a little work with your child—conducted as play, you can obtain an advantage for him in his new world of school. This confident feeling of "being on top of things", of being able to cope adequately, will remain with him all his life in his own picture of himself as compared with the rest of the community.

Remember, *confidence* is the keynote of all successful human behaviour, so make the most of your child's successes and minimise his failures—*make him feel important*. It is curious that our happiness depends not so much upon what our friends think of us, but upon what deep in our hearts we really think of ourselves. So we repeat—make him feel important.

REPORTS

A disappointing school report can often be explained by a child's home troubles. For every problem-child there is often one or even two problem-parents! To give of his best a child must feel at peace with himself and his family.

You will, from the child's school reports, and possibly from talks with his teachers, already have some idea of his strength and weaknesses. If he does not seem to be doing well at school do not let him feel that you are disappointed in him or with his marks. Tell him that both you and he know that he can do better; that you do not love him less because of his poor report; but because you love him, you want to find his weaknesses and show him the cure. Ask him what his difficulties are and explain how you propose to help him. Never say "I hated sums as much as you do" or "I was never good at them either". Show a patient interest in all his difficulties. Become involved with him. Use the magic sentence, "Let's find out."

26

EXAMINATIONS

· ·

This chapter is intended to give help and advice to parents whose children have to sit for official examinations such as the 11 Plus.

Your child should go to the examination rested physically and mentally. The day before the examination he should do no new work, but revision of old corrections is well worth while.

Get his writing implements ready the night before, a pen, a ruler, three nicely sharpened pencils and an eraser. See that they are all in good condition and ready for immediate use.

He should go to bed early the night before, but not especially early, for a sudden change in routine will increase his nervousness. Do not fuss him. If he says he cannot sleep, tell him that it does not matter— if he relaxes he will get adequate rest and will eventually sleep.

If your child is *very* highly-strung his doctor may prescribe a mild sedative tonic.

Do not give a very nervous child heavy and fatty foods, but rather fruit, vegetables and sweet fruit-drinks. Much parental anxiety over a child's lack of appetite can be spared by noting which meal he enjoys most—breakfast, lunch or dinner, and giving him his main meal of the day then—even if it means giving him cold meat for breakfast! Most children like raw vegetables—carrots, lettuce, tomatoes, peas, beans and raw fruits. Let your child have these, they are better for him than stodgy puddings and rich pastry.

Get him to the examination 10 minutes before time. This is important. Last-minute hurry leads to confusion and may cause silly mistakes. If he has time to spare on "The Day", avoid "examination nerves" by keeping him busy with some routine household job.

ADVICE TO THE CHILD

Listen carefully to any instructions given you by the supervisor, read the instructions on the examination paper, make sure you understand what they mean (by asking if necessary), and carry them out properly.

When you get the word to start, go to it. The questions will tell you just what you have to do. Read them very carefully and answer them as best you can. Do *exactly* as you are told.

Begin with the first question and go straight on. Try each question as you come to it, do not waste too much time on those you are uncertain of, but go straight on to the next question. You can always come back to unfinished work when you have finished the rest of the paper. Cross out each question as you finish it; you will then know which questions, if any, you have left undone or unfinished.

The pages of the examination papers are numbered, be careful to turn over no more than one page at a time.

Should you wish to make an alteration, draw a line neatly through your mistake.

Do not make the silly mistake of mis-spelling words which are *already printed* on the examination papers—boys and girls often do!

If you come across anything unforeseen or have any doubts ask the teacher in charge.

28

AFTER THE EXAMINATION

Help your child over the reaction in the first few days after the examination. If he thinks that he has failed, encourage him by reminding him that probably 90 per cent of those that have passed, think they have failed too. Amusements and treats may be indicated here.

If, in spite of your joint efforts, your child does not gain entrance to a grammar school, he will almost certainly be much happier without the arduous grind of bookwork which it would have entailed and for which he would not be suited. The technical or secondary modern school will find and train those skills which he has, and make a useful and successful citizen of him.

THE INTERVIEW

In certain districts, some children may be called for an interview. The interviewing committee, the grammar school headmaster, and representatives from the education committee—often including their psychologist—decide which children from those called up for interview would most benefit from what the school has to offer. Send your child along clean and tidy (*not* in a new suit or dress) and tell him not to worry for he will probably be going with some of his school friends, and the committee will be kind to him.

Try to show your child that you are not over-anxious, and do *not* stress the importance of the day to him. Tell him not to talk too much, just to answer their questions briefly and to the point. Explain the routine of the interview to him. He will have to wait in a room where he can read or talk with his friends and if the committee is efficient this waiting period will not be too long. He will be ushered into the committee room where he will be made to feel at ease. Here the

29

chairman will usually have a confidential report of the child's work, play and character from his present school. He will probably be asked about his interests; do not coach him into saying good music or good literature—if this is not true. The committee is too well versed in this sort of deception and wily enough to get the truth out of him. Some children will have to be turned down—more are called up for interview than there are available grammar school places.

If your child does not gain a free place—*hide your disappointment.* Talk about the luck in examinations. The importance of Luck in a written examination is a very real thing and it is an even more important factor in oral examinations and interviews. His sense of failure must be minimised.

LATE DEVELOPERS

Some children who do not gain a place in a grammar school at 11 years of age make rapid progress in their secondary modern school and if Education Authorities feel that the child at 12 or 13 years has become grammar school material, they are usually anxious to find him a place then. Discuss the matter with his headmaster and if he agrees he will make the arrangements for another chance. The formalities of further chances vary from one district to another. Accept guidance from your child's headmaster and teacher on this matter. If you are dissatisfied with your child's school and want to go over the heads of the teachers there, you should consult the Education Officer at your local County Hall.

METHOD OF WORKING

. . . .

These are the most important factors involved in the process of learning :

Ability

Interest

Technique

His ability (his I.Q.) is what the child is born with. This is the limiting factor in any person's mental development and what we are doing here is to make the most of what the child already has. We are of course also concerned in this book with developing his interest and technique.

The normal human being will only give his full attention to what he is interested in and to what he considers worth while. One of the prime requirements of learning is keen interest, therefore it is of considerable importance that you convince your child of the value of education.

First, make your explanation in terms of what he wants to be : whether it be a Doctor, Business Man, Teacher, Engine Driver or Film Star, the benefits of a good education are manifold. Elaborate on this and point out to him that quite apart from helping him to pass the examination he will benefit all his life from the work you are going to do with him.

Secondly, put it to him in terms of what he wants : the extra personal benefits gained if he works hard enough to make the grade—

e.g. the money saved in school fees could then be used to purchase a bicycle or model train or something else that he desires. The incentive should not be the bicycle if he passes but *the bicycle if he works hard consistently*. This is to obviate any sense of failure should he not pass.

Make the subject as attractive as possible to him. Work in the best possible conditions. A cheerful atmosphere, the room quiet and well heated, the desk or table well lighted with the light coming over the left shoulder, or the right shoulder in the case of a left-handed person, the chairs comfortable but not too relaxing, and with perhaps some toffees or chocolates available. No background noise of radio or television. Keep other children out of the way and keep them quiet. His own bedroom could be ideal. Finish by joining with him if you can in a game or hobby of his own liking, table tennis, draughts, Meccano, etc.

The work you are going to do with your child is not cramming in the old sense of the word; that would be of little help to your child. Examinations are now very different from what they were when we were 11 years of age. Today a multiplicity of questions are set as against the few only of bygone days. Even if the examination at 11 has been stopped perhaps because of a local Comprehensive school or for some other form of selection, streaming (i.e. some sort of separation of the sheep from the goats) is inevitable. Your active interest in your child will still pay off. The parent is advised to be loyal to his child's schoolteacher and respect his greater knowledge and make use of it. A talk with him, if necessary, can often save you both a lot of time and labour. The teacher will be able to give you a very good idea of your child's strengths and weaknesses, and so you will not need to waste time on the subjects which he has already mastered.

THE TIME-TABLE

No two children develop along the same lines in exactly the same way. Therefore, it is neither practical nor possible for us to set out a hard-and-fast time-table for the course. Much will obviously depend upon how much time you, the parent, think you will have available to devote to your child. The most important thing is that neither he nor you should ever become bored by the work. The moment his interest fades you should stop immediately.

We suggest that ideally you should try to have three sessions a week with your child. No session should last more than half-an-hour unless he is clearly enjoying every moment of it and continuing to learn. Sometimes if the subject is difficult you may find that fifteen minutes is enough. The number of sessions you have and the length of time you spend on them will also depend very much on whether he is preparing for an examination, whether his teacher says that he is backward in any particular subject, and how much enjoyment he derives from the work with you.

You might decide that for your very first session you should concentrate entirely on the list of 3-letter words on pages 45–46. For the second session you might turn to Arithmetic, and go through with your child the table of measurements on page 262, and then start looking at the numbers on page 263. Then in the third session you could go back to Spelling and revise the 3-letter words before going on to new spelling exercises.

Try to have your sessions as early in the evening as possible. Certainly well before bed-time, for children (as well as adults) should go to bed relaxed and not with their minds still pondering over problems and difficulties. The work must be done regularly. To miss one week and then to do a double ration the next week is a poor alternative to a

3—H.T.

regular time-table. Either parent is undoubtedly the best teacher for the course, and it does not matter which. The average child will enjoy being tested by someone whom he knows and loves. Always try to finish on an easy and happy note.

Insist on every question being answered exactly as required, for it is essential to develop correct habits. The examiner wants to know whether your child is bright enough to follow the simple directions given in the question. If the question is "how many pence ?" do not accept shillings and pence in the answer. Slipshod work must be discouraged. He must follow the instructions carefully.

During work sessions *concentration* must be the order of the day. A "couldn't care less" attitude must be strongly discouraged. The key to success in any sphere of life is concentration, and in the examination itself it is of paramount importance. Never merely read this book with him. Have a pencil and paper beside you to make notes of his errors (to be gone over again in revision periods).

AIDS FOR THE PARENT

You the parent, will sometimes find that you do not know the answer to a question. Tell your child the truth. Say to him—"I do not know, but let us find out". Even the most educated man will not know all the answers, but he will know where to find them. Your sources of information are :

34

Our answers.

Your own dictionary.

Your child's schoolteacher.

Your child's own school text-books (most schools allow them to be taken home).

Your local Public Library. The Librarian there is eager to help you to obtain information on any subject that interests you.

Speed is important, for during an examination each paper has to be done in a limited time, so encourage your child not to dawdle over his answers. It is doubtful if *any* candidate finishes all the papers in the time allotted, so do not worry if he seems slow in finishing them now. But let the child sometimes compete against himself and see how many questions he can answer correctly in a given time, or for how long he can go without making a mistake.

Encourage your child to talk about his school and to bring home his school difficulties. Ask him in a casual way how he has been getting on. Do not overdo this apparently casual interest—do not make a cross-examination of it. Your child may perhaps be allowed to take home his school exercise books. Go over the errors his teacher has corrected in them and make sure he has learned the lesson. Whenever you find some subject that he does not understand, keep working on it unhurriedly with him *until you are quite sure he has mastered it.*

IMPORTANCE OF REVISION

Remember the importance of repetition and revision, and start each session with the things learnt in the last session or two. When your child learns something new that he did not understand before, then repeat it in the next few sessions so that he gets to know it really well. Keep a note in your diary or in a special notebook of the items to be revised, i.e. the new knowledge gained and the errors which were corrected in previous sessions.

Do not hesitate to make notes and to keep a check on your child's progress in these exercises. Write down the items to be gone over again, so that you will not need to waste time revising things your child already knows well. Be as lavish as you can with ticks and marks of approval on your child's worksheets. But do most of your work

35

orally and use the word "good" frequently, for encouragement will improve his self-confidence. Praise your child in public and criticise him (sparingly) in private. Never invent mistakes in order to correct them. Above all never, never lose your temper with him during difficult patches. It may not be easy for you to refrain from doing so, but your restraint is most important.

Never allow a child to lose heart, for once he has lost heart, he has lost everything. A child who feels that his parents are standing by to help him and not to punish or scold him, will work with greater confidence and meet with more success.

You will very soon realise the enormous benefit that your child is deriving from your work together. Working through these questions together is not just testing him. You must necessarily be imparting knowledge all the time, when and where it is required. The English part of this Course, as with the Intelligence Tests, if put in the correct way, i.e. with cheerfulness and as a game, can really be enjoyed by both child and parent. We suggest that the parent himself will learn not a little during this work. He will get to know much about his child. In this Course he will find an intimacy and knowledge of his child that he possibly never experienced before. He may also (let us whisper it!) even relearn some aspects of English grammar that he had long forgotten.

In doing the following exercises some words will by association of ideas open new vistas. These vistas can with much profit be explored. Do not stick to the beaten path, you can always return to it very easily. Be adventurous and your work together will be more pleasant and more profitable. If these exercises make it necessary for you to refer to an encyclopaedia or public library, or even to buy books—so much the better. You have no wiser way of spending your money than in buying books for your child.

Avoid the impulse that many ambitious parents have, to push their child beyond his powers. Your child should not be demoralised by being given too difficult work too early. On the other hand, although he should start off with the elements of each subject, he should not for long be given work which he fully understands and which is too easy for him. Provided that your child is well fed, and has adequate sleep and exercise, you need not, generally speaking, be afraid of over-working him. It is worry rather than overwork which causes break-downs; so be careful not to be over-ambitious for him. If you have a nervous highly-strung child, who in spite of your help, is just not up to standard, encourage him but do not push him too hard.

If your child just cannot achieve the standard you would like now, remember that some children are late starters and may be able to go on *later* to attain academic distinction. The talents of many are artistic rather than in being knowledgeable in the three R's. Our Education Authorities do not give art scholarships at 11 years of age. A child has a right to grow up naturally—not to have impossible goals of perfection set by frustrated parents who want to relive their lives through him. If, however, he is not up to scratch because of laziness, too many out-ings to the cinema or too much "televiewing", extra discipline and some organised work are just what he needs.

THE EXAMINATION PAPERS

Before starting on the English section, please read the note on page 331, which will help you to make the most of the Examination Papers that you will find in the blue folder accompanying this volume.

37

English

. . . .

Good English means a good vocabulary well used—using the right word at the right time and place. A reasonably wide vocabulary, effectively displayed, is a tremendous factor for success and happiness. All other aspects of English that your child learns at school (formal grammar, punctuation, spelling, etc.) are only subsidiary. Yet not only are they of importance in the grammar school examination, but mistakes of grammar in speech or in writing are handicaps socially and professionally and have kept many an otherwise bright person from rising in the world. We must therefore strive to see that such errors are kept to a minimum.

From the point of view of your child's grammar and vocabulary, even the type of child he plays with matters, and the parent should be selective in the friendships he encourages his child to develop.

BOOKS

What your child reads is obviously of great importance. Give him books at Christmas and for his birthday—and if you can afford it, give him books at other times too. Books will be kept and valued by a child, long after toys given at the same time are broken or put aside.

Encourage your child to use the local library. Do not be afraid that he will pick up infections from soiled books he may borrow. Local

Councils ensure that books exposed to infectious diseases are dis-infected adequately. Have your child make friends with the librarian who will help him to select books that he will enjoy.

In the Junior sections of local public libraries, gaily illustrated nursery rhymes, fairy tales, Bible stories, worth-while educational, adventure and school story books may be borrowed. These are a few of the better books for children, which most libraries will have:

Enid Blyton's school and adventure stories
books by Alison Uttley
books by Beatrix Potter
books by A. A. Milne
Munro Leafe's "Can be Fun" series
Jean de Brunhof's "Babar" books
Hugh Lofting's "Dr. Doolittle" books
H. L. Rey's "Zozo" books
Katherine Tozer's "Mumfie" books
Kathleen Hale's "Orlando" adventures
Traver's "Mary Poppin" and "Milly Molly Mandy" series

Many schools have their own library, and some have class libraries. Encourage your child to make use of them.

If your child "takes to" children's classics—such as Lewis Carroll, Charles Kingsley, Edward Lear—so much the better. Encourage him if you can by buying for him well-illustrated copies of these.

We suggest that if possible you have in the home a well-illustrated bird book and a book giving the names and descriptions of flowers and trees. If your child is interested in nature-studies he will find much enjoyment in identifying the different birds and flowers and trees that he sees around him.

A child loves repetition and will read a favourite book over and over

39

again. In this he is perhaps more sensible than his elders, who too
often fly from one popular novel to another.

Do not forget—it is much better for a child to be happy reading an
easy book, than for him to struggle with a difficult one.

Here are a few really worth-while books which might make a start
towards your child's own personal library:

"Aesop's Fables"

"Grimm's Fairy Tales"

"Andersen's Fairy Tales"

The Faber Book of Childrens' Verse

Kipling's "Jungle Books" and "Just So Stories"

Charles Kingsley's "The Water Babies"

Lewis Carroll's "Alice in Wonderland"

The Oxford Book of Verse for Juniors

Daniel Defoe's "Robinson Crusoe"

Jonathan Swift's "Gulliver's Travels"

Edward Lear's "Book of Nonsense"

James Barrie's "Peter Pan"

R. L. Stevenson's "Treasure Island"

Charles and Mary Lamb's "Tales from Shakespeare"

Kenneth Graham's "Wind in the Willows"

Always buy the best illustrated copies you can afford. Good illustra-
tions together with clear printing and attractive binding can make a
vast difference to a child's enjoyment of a book.

If you cannot afford the books we recommend, remember that they
can almost certainly be found in your local library.

Have your child acquire the dictionary habit. Whenever he is not
absolutely sure of the meaning of a word, *he must look it up*. We have
all at times used words we were not sure of, and have wondered—are

40

we using the wrong word and showing our ignorance? The constant use of a dictionary will make such moments less frequent and will also hasten progress in spelling.

POETRY

Read poetry to your child. He will enjoy poems like "The Ancient Mariner" and "The Pied Piper". Encourage the reading of poetry aloud. Wordsworth said that poetry is the first and last of all knowledge. Certainly there is nothing like poetry for giving a child an appreciation of the beauty of words and of using them effectively.

COMICS

Do not be intolerant in your attitude towards "comics". The average comic will quite definitely enlarge a child's vocabulary and help his sense of composition. Most of them do no harm morally, although some of American type or origin should be strongly discouraged.

Children grow out of comics eventually; we can all recall how our own tastes in literature have matured.

A publication much to be recommended is "Look and Learn". Unfortunately, children will usually not take to it as readily as they will to a "penny dreadful".

HANDWRITING

41

Some psychologists believe that handwriting is an expression of the whole individual and that nicely patterned writing is produced by healthy people with good personal adjustment. However, what is obvious is that writing should be read easily. Your child must be able to write at a fair speed—one page of an ordinary exercise book in under 15 minutes.

In practising writing do not work your child for more than 10 minutes at a time. It is forming the letters as perfectly as possible—and not the speed—that matters. Although it is undoubtedly an advantage to write quickly and legibly, the content of what is written is more important than the style of writing.

PEN-FRIENDS

42   *Encourage your child to correspond with someone of his own age and interests; he will enjoy it and derive great benefit from it.*

From about the age of $9\frac{1}{2}$ years find a pen-friend for your child. A good pen-friend could be a cousin or other relative of your child's age. If this is not possible, an advertisement in a religious or other paper will almost certainly bring enquiries. Corresponding with a pen-friend is most enjoyable, worth while and educational.

SPELLING

· ·

Although some authorities maintain that correlation of spelling ability with intelligence is quite high (i.e. people with higher I.Q.s usually spell better), this view is not generally accepted. A well-educated man is not necessarily a good speller and many eminent and talented people are bad spellers. Shakespeare spelt his own name in four different ways! Much spelling consists merely of remembering a convention. Modern English spelling is chaotic; it is so often unrelated to the way it sounds in speech. However, to be able to spell is today an advantage in life. Indifferent spelling is a bad habit and forms a bad impression. Where all other things are equal, the examiner, as well as the employer, must be biased in favour of the better-spelt paper.

You will find that only a relatively small number of words are responsible for most of the spelling mistakes your child makes. Therefore, studying the words in which spelling mistakes have already been made, is the most economical method of working.

Use the spelling lists which follow to find your child's individual weaknesses. See how long he can go without making a mistake. See how many he can get right in a given time. Use the spelling lists as a name. Give him one point for each word he spells correctly and let him compete against himself in next week's spelling session. (You will of course verify that he knows the meaning of each word on the

43

list. If you have any doubts, have him make up a sentence containing the word.)

Remember—make written notes of his mistakes, for these are the words to revise. The notes you keep will save you from wasting time in the all-important revision periods.

When your child asks you how to spell a word—don't tell him. He must say, "This is how I would spell 'necessary', is it right?" Get him to look it up in his dictionary. All learning should be active.

Many national papers publish children's crossword puzzles with pictorial or verbal clues. Some newspapers and magazines have other interesting, enjoyable and educational word-games. Encourage him to do these—he will love them. Keep two lists—one of the new words he learns and the other of his spelling mistakes, and use these lists for revision periods. Mark the finished result for accuracy and for neatness.

Teaching in spelling gives more impressive results than does teaching in any other subject.

Your child's vocabulary is of paramount importance. This book is full of words and phrases that educated people use in everyday speech. These he must learn and understand. You and your child will have a great deal of fun working as a game through the course. "What does 'at arm's length' mean?" "As black as what?" "What is the plural of child?" Keep a list of the words that he finds hard so that you will know what to revise; new knowledge gained must always be revised if it is to be retained. Not only your child's, but also your own vocabulary will grow in both words and phrases you recognise and in those that you retain and will be using. All of us recognise more than we use.

spelling list A

· ·

This list is composed of three-letter and four-letter words in common use. Hundreds of longer words can be made from them by adding suffixes or prefixes or by using the short words in combinations, one with another. Like every other subject, spelling is more easily learnt if interest is aroused. Have your child put the word into an interesting sentence. Ask him for other words having the same meaning or opposite meaning or similar spelling.

Your child will probably know most of these words already—make sure *he knows them all* before proceeding with List B.

THREE-LETTER WORDS

these should have been mastered by the age of 7–8 years

travel across lines, and not down the columns

act	add	age	ago	aid	aim	air	all
any	are	arm	art	ash	ate	bad	bag
bar	bed	bee	beg	bid	big	bit	bow
box	boy	but	buy	can	cap	car	cat
cow	cry	cup	cut	day	did	dig	dog
due	dry	ear	eat	egg	end	eye	fan
far	fat	few	fit	fix	fly	for	fun
fur	gay	get	God	got	gun	had	hat
hen	her	hid	him	his	hit	hot	how
hut	ice	ill	ink	jar	job	joy	key
kid	lad	law	lay	led	leg	let	lie
lip	log	low	lot	mad	man	map	may
men	met	mix	mow	mud	new	nod	nor

45

not	now	nun	nut	oak	odd	off	old
one	our	out	owe	own	pan	pay	pea
pen	pie	pig	pin	pot	ran	raw	red
rob	rub	sad	sat	saw	say	sea	see
set	she	sin	sir	sit	six	sky	sob
son	sun	sum	tea	thy	tie	tip	ton
too	top	toy	try	two	use	van	vex
way	wet	wit	who	why	win	won	wan
web	wag	war	was	yet	you	yew	yes

 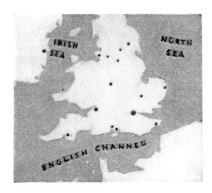 

These three pictures illustrate different words in the three-letter word list; can you find each of them? (Answers at foot of page 54.)

FOUR-LETTER WORDS

go through this and succeeding spelling lists at your child's most comfortable pace

able	acre	also	area	army	aunt	away	baby
back	bake	ball	band	bare	barn	bath	bear
beat	been	bell	belt	bend	bent	best	blew
bill	blow	bird	blue	boat	body	boil	bold
book	boot	bone	born	both	bowl	bull	burn

bury	bush	busy	cage	cake	call	calm	came
camp	card	care	case	cash	cast	cell	city
clad	club	coal	coat	cold	coin	come	cook
cool	copy	cost	crew	crop	cure	damp	dare
dark	dash	date	dawn	dead	deal	dear	debt
deck	deed	deep	deny	desk	dish	does	done
door	down	drag	draw	drew	drop	drum	duck
duke	dull	dust	duty	each	ease	edge	else
even	ever	evil	fact	fail	fall	fair	fame
fare	farm	fast	fate	fear	feed	feel	feet
fell	felt	fill	find	fine	firm	fish	five
flag	flat	flew	flow	folk	fond	food	fool
foot	form	four	free	from	full	gain	game
gate	gave	gaze	gift	girl	give	glad	goat
goes	gone	good	grew	grey	grow	hair	hale
half	hand	hang	hard	harm	hate	have	head
hear	heat	heel	held	help	here	hero	high
hill	hire	hold	hole	holy	home	hook	hope
horn	hour	huge	hung	hurt	idea	idle	into
inch	iron	join	July	jump	June	just	keep
kept	knee	knew	knot	kick	kill	kind	king
kiss	know	lack	lady	laid	lake	lamb	lamp
land	lane	last	late	lawn	lead	leap	left
less	life	lift	like	line	lion	list	live
load	loan	long	look	loss	lost	love	luck
made	mail	maid	main	make	mark	many	mass
meal	mean	meat	meet	milk	mild	mine	mind
miss	moon	more	most	move	much	must	nail
name	navy	near	neck	need	nest	news	next

47

nice	nine	none	noon	nose	note	obey	once
only	open	over	pack	page	paid	pair	pale
park	part	pass	past	path	peep	pick	pile
pink	pipe	pity	plan	play	poem	poet	pole
pond	port	post	pour	pray	pull	pure	push
rage	rail	rain	rank	rare	rate	read	real

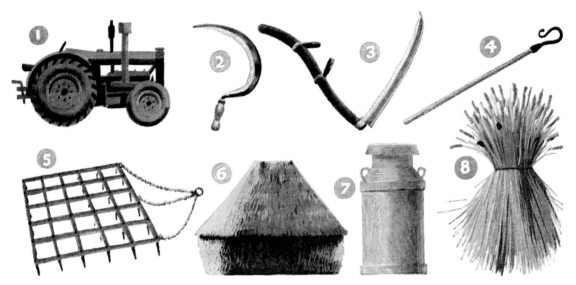

Here are some things that you might see on a farm. Write on a slip of paper their correct names (answers at foot of page 50).

rear	rest	ride	rich	ring	risk	road	roar
rock	rode	roll	roof	room	root	rope	rude
ruin	rule	sack	safe	said	sail	sake	sale
salt	same	sand	sank	save	seat	seed	seek
seem	seen	self	send	sent	shed	ship	shop
shot	show	shut	sick	side	sign	silk	sing
sink	size	skin	snap	soap	soft	soil	sold
some	song	soon	soul	sore	sort	spot	star

stay	step	stir	stop	such	suit	sure	tail
take	talk	tall	task	team	tear	tell	tent
term	test	than	that	thee	them	then	they
thin	this	thou	thus	tide	till	tiny	toil
tone	took	toss	town	tree	trip	true	type
ugly	unto	urge	upon	vain	very	view	vote
wage	wake	wait	walk	wall	want	warm	wash
wear	week	weep	well	went	were	west	what
when	whom	wide	wife	wild	will	wine	wing
wipe	wire	wish	with	wolf	wood	wool	word
wore	work	worm	wrap	yard	year	your	yolk

spelling list B

. . . .

Composed of five-, six-, seven-, eight- and nine-letter words in most common use. Care has been taken as far as possible to omit all words which could be formed as described in the note on List A (page 45), except where pronunciation of the longer word differs from its components written by themselves. Your child might learn a group of five-letter words one week, and a group of eight-letter words the next. Don't waste time on words he already knows. Again, keep notes of his mistakes, for those are the words to go over again and again in revision times until he has been cured of his misunderstandings.

    These lists contain everyday words (which should be part of your child's vocabulary) and not the unusual and difficult words which are rarely used by children and for which the modern examiner has no use.

49

4—H.T.

FIVE-LETTER WORDS

allow	admit	above	along	about	alive	again	agree
awake	aside	avoid	awful	apply	alone	alarm	apart
anger	angry	apple	after	April	arose	bless	being
block	broke	bread	break	beast	bring	black	bough
bound	below	birth	brave	bathe	brook	brick	broad
burst	bench	brain	build	boast	bride	brief	blame
blood	brown	beach	board	blind	class	cross	chill
cloud	could	clock	chain	chair	catch	carry	child
close	cover	cream	crash	charm	chose	cabin	creep
crept	clean	count	cried	court	clear	cheek	cheer
coast	cruel	crime	curse	cause	cheap	crowd	crown
carol	chase	canal	cease	cloth	climb	chief	china
claim	chest	coach	cough	drink	drunk	dress	dream
dozen	devil	death	doubt	depth	drive	drove	dying
daily	delay	dance	dough	enjoy	enter	every	exist
empty	early	earth	equal	event	flash	frost	front
flock	feast	fight	funny	found	float	field	fancy
fixed	first	forth	fault	false	frame	fleet	faint
flour	floor	fence	faith	fresh	final	flesh	flame
flood	fully	force	fruit	fifth	fifty	glass	grass
given	grand	green	giant	guard	guess	guest	guide
glory	glove	grant	grave	grown	grain	globe	grief
grace	great	group	going	heard	house	happy	horse
habit	hedge	heart	hurry	human	heavy	haste	issue
ideal	joint	judge	known	knife	knock	least	large
leave	lodge	lower	loose	limit	lying	light	learn

Answers to quiz on page 48: 1. tractor   2. sickle   3. scythe   4. shepherd's crook
5. harrow or rake   6. haystack   7. milk-churn   8. wheatsheaf.

linen	level	laugh	local	mouse	money	might	match
marry	month	metal	merry	march	motor	mount	major
model	music	night	never	noble	north	nurse	noise
order	ocean	other	ought	occur	organ	plant	plain
party	pound	patch	paper	penny	place	plate	prove
proof	power	pride	press	plane	pitch	porch	prize
proud	point	pence	piece	pupil	pause	pearl	peace
price	peril	quick	quite	quiet	queen	queer	robin
right	round	river	royal	ready	roast	reply	raise
reign	rough	reach	shall	spoon	start	sweep	sleep

Can you find these objects in the list of five-letter words?
(Answers at foot of page 54.)

sheep	steep	smell	swell	spell	shell	still	swept
slept	slain	stain	sweet	sheet	stiff	speak	smile
sight	sound	shook	space	spoke	since	state	steam
shade	story	south	stick	spend	spent	saint	stuff
stand	stone	shout	stole	stout	shock	stock	shoot
short	shift	swift	stuck	speed	spear	sport	stood
skirt	shirt	sense	seven	shame	shake	shape	share
sharp	sword	style	slice	slide	stamp	score	store

51

shore	slope	smoke	strip	stage	stare	scare	spare
shine	shone	stove	scene	scale	swing	storm	straw
sugar	spoil	smart	spite	serve	sorry	steel	study
slave	steal	seize	table	those	these	there	teach
threw	throw	thing	tight	track	think	tower	thick

More pictures of words in the five-letter word list for you to find.
(Answers at foot of page 54.)

truly	trace	trail	tried	trick	train	three	trade
tooth	teeth	trust	truth	taste	treat	twice	title
tribe	troop	today	their	tired	third	total	twist
tough	thank	trial	touch	utter	upper	uncle	union
under	until	visit	value	voice	would	white	woman
women	watch	waist	whole	waste	wheat	write	wrote
wrong	whose	widow	wound	world	worth	weigh	wreck

52

SIX-LETTER WORDS

across	animal	always	afraid	asleep	around
admire	arrive	afford	affect	attack	attend
August	amount	advise	advice	answer	avenue
accept	autumn	almost	action	active	artist
affair	appear	appeal	actual	behind	better

broken	basket	battle	before	bridge	butter
bitter	beyond	branch	beauty	border	burden
bottom	bottle	breast	breath	borrow	bought
coming	clever	cattle	corner	candle	change
choose	choice	create	cousin	copper	colour
common	caught	cheese	centre	castle	compel
church	credit	couple	custom	course	circle
column	clothe	cotton	county	coffee	charge
chance	detail	demand	double	desert	divide
direct	doctor	danger	defeat	defend	depend
decide	desire	during	easily	enough	employ
except	expect	excuse	escape	eleven	entire
effect	effort	empire	engine	either	engage

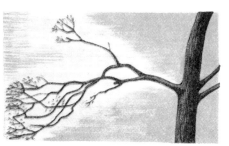  

Three pictures of six-letter words; can you spot them in the list?
(Answers at foot of page 54.)

future	fellow	family	fairly	former	figure
Friday	flight	friend	famous	finger	fourth
finish	French	gather	garden	ground	gentle
glance	golden	happen	hollow	herald	handle
honest	honour	hardly	health	heaven	hungry
hunger	height	invite	intend	income	island
knight	latter	lawyer	lesson	letter	little

listen	leader	lovely	length	labour	likely
method	modern	memory	murder	Monday	meadow
minute	mother	muddle	mighty	moment	motion
manner	mirror	master	matter	market	nation
nature	narrow	nearly	notice	number	native
object	oppose	obtain	occupy	o'clock	orange
oblige	person	pocket	parson	poison	police
people	powder	palace	public	prison	profit
prefer	permit	plenty	prayer	proper	please
period	partly	prince	praise	remind	relief
record	rubber	reason	report	rocket	result
reader	return	regard	reward	rabbit	remove
refuse	repair	rather	rattle	really	reduce
remain	repeat	remark	sudden	suffer	summer
supper	string	sister	strain	savage	Sunday
square	sailor	street	strong	steady	should
shadow	saddle	school	scream	silver	stable
supply	seldom	season	simple	select	speech
source	salary	surely	simply	safety	spirit
system	second	spring	search	smooth	sorrow
silent	slight	sought	single	secret	spread
secure	stream	twelve	travel	temple	thread
thrown	though	tongue	throne	treaty	throat
ticket	toward	temper	thrill	tailor	terror
twenty	thirty	tender	taught	useful	upward

Answers to the picture quizzes : p. 46, bag, map, top ; p. 51, cabin, chest, guard ; p. 52, plane, shell, tower ; p. 53, branch, column, rocket.

FACING-PAGE QUIZ. *Who wear the clothes that you can see in this picture? Write your answers on a slip of paper and make sure that you can spell them correctly (answers at foot of page 56).*

wealth	window	wisdom	worthy	wooden	wonder
walrus	weapon	wander	winter	writer	within
wicked	wobble	warble	wigwam	weaver	yellow

SEVEN-LETTER WORDS

against	article	account	already	advance	appoint
anxious	address	arrange	attempt	between	brother
beneath	British	balance	breathe	believe	benefit
brought	because	Britain	careful	conduct	correct
certain	chicken	cottage	consist	consent	content
clearly	command	central	connect	compare	citizen
company	capital	chapter	college	curtain	courage
contain	curious	chamber	council	century	country
control	concern	destroy	darling	display	dessert
declare	disease	deliver	diamond	disturb	descend
develop	delight	defence	evening	exclaim	English
England	exactly	explain	examine	expense	express
example	further	fashion	failure	freedom	foreign
fifteen	factory	feeling	furnish	fortune	general
hundred	harvest	husband	history	holiday	improve
instead	inquire	include	journey	kitchen	kingdom
liberty	leather	library	leading	machine	married
message	meeting	morning	million	mention	mistake
measure	meaning	nothing	neither	natural	opinion
observe	officer	perhaps	provide	protect	proceed
promise	prepare	present	passage	parents	picture
popular	pattern	private	produce	possess	prevent

Answers to quiz on previous page: 1. jockey 2. mayor 3. miner 4. butcher
5. bullfighter 6. ballet dancer 7. bus conductor 8. cricketer 9. diver.

perform	payment	perfect	purpose	problem	quickly
quarter	quality	recover	regular	realise	require
request	reserve	receive	respect	surface	scatter
stretch	support	station	suppose	shelter	soldier
someone	society	serious	swallow	strange	several
suggest	savings	succeed	success	special	student
silence	similar	servant	service	subject	satisfy
teacher	thunder	thought	tonight	tremble	trouble
uniform	usually	unknown	various	variety	village
vehicle	worship	western	weather	witness	without
whistle	whisper	written	welcome	whether	worship

EIGHT-LETTER WORDS

accident	although	approach	addition	business
children	clothing	complete	consider	continue
cupboard	describe	discover	district	darkness
distance	division	daughter	elephant	electric
entrance	exchange	exercise	familiar	glorious
guardian	handsome	hospital	increase	interest
magazine	material	mountain	medicine	minister
majority	marriage	merchant	national	opposite
occasion	ordinary	physical	purchase	probably
property	printing	position	pleasure	possible
preserve	practice	question	quantity	relation
remember	shepherd	scarcely	straight	splendid
Saturday	stranger	standard	strength	struggle
surround	shoulder	sentence	separate	surprise
tomorrow	training	threaten	thousand	terrible
telegram	together	treasure	thorough	yourself

57

NINE-LETTER WORDS

attention	advantage	according	brilliant
beautiful	behaviour	Christian	Christmas
companion	condition	dangerous	different
difficult	embarrass	encourage	endeavour
excellent	furniture	important	immediate
judgement	knowledge	necessary	neighbour
naturally	passenger	privilege .	prejudice
recommend	substance	sometimes	telephone
therefore	vegetable	Wednesday	yesterday

TEN-LETTER WORDS

afterwards	connection	department	expression
experience	especially	gramophone	invitation
impossible	marvellous	particular	production
speciality	subsequent	television	veterinary

ELEVEN- AND TWELVE-LETTER WORDS

acknowledge	accommodate	association
independent	information	mischievous
opportunity	Switzerland	nevertheless
preparation	scholarship	examination

58

spelling rules

. . . .

When adding *ing* or *y* to words ending with *e,* first leave out the *e*:

      save — saving   love — loving

      shine — shiny   stone — stony

Put *i* before *e* except immediately after *c*:

　　ceiling　receipt　niece　chief

but

　note the following important exceptions:

　　weight　height　seize　neighbour　reign

The second *l* of *full* is dropped, when *full* is added to another word:

　　cheerful　hopeful　thankful

The sound *j*.

In *Jane* we get the true sound for *j*, but *g* and *d* can sound the same, as for instance in:

en.ine — engine	mana.er — manager	pa.e — page
sol.ier — soldier	ju..e — judge	.in.er — ginger

Some letters can hold their tongues and be silent:

　　k　l　t　p　n　w

Read out to your child the following sentences containing words with silent letters. Make sure that he can spell the words which are in bold type:

　Sir George is a **knight** and lives in a **castle**.

　A **knife** is used for cutting.

　Knitting is done with needles.

　Do you **know** the answer?

　Knock on the door.

　In string you may find a **knot**.

　The **knuckle** is part of your hand and the **knee** is part of your leg.

　Dates grow on a **palm** tree.

　The opposite of a rough sea is a **calm** sea.

　Teacher **writes** with **chalk**.

59

The yellow part of an egg is the **yolk**.

The young of a cow is a **calf**.

In church you may hear **psalms** and **hymns**.

A **salmon** is a large red-fleshed fish.

One of the seasons of the year is **autumn**.

Land surrounded by water is **known** as an **island**.

A referee blows a **whistle** (here the *t* is silent—the *h* should influence the pronunciation).

In the olden days **swords** were used as weapons.

Which are the silent letters in:

heard (a)	search (a)	hour (h)	fight (g, h)
island (s)	carriage (a)	meant (a)	scene (c)
tongue (u)	Wednesday (e)	sign (g)	sword (w)
honour (h)	weather (a)	write (w)	school (h)

The silent *b*.

Ask your child for the missing word and its spelling:

A small portion of bread is called a c—.	(crumb)
To mend a burst pipe you need a p—.	(plumber)
One who cannot speak is d—.	(dumb)
Near your forefinger is the t—.	(thumb)
For your hair you need a c—.	(comb)
Arms and legs are known as l—.	(limbs)
In very cold weather your fingers feel n—.	(numb)
When you are not sure you are in d—.	(doubt)
To get to the top you have to c—.	(climb)
When you owe money you are in d—.	(debt)
L— are born very early in the year.	(lambs)

When S and H play together they make the noise that we use when we want someone to be quiet.

The silent *c* (coming after *s*):

    For cutting you use sc——.   (scissors)

    To go up is to asc——.   (ascend)

    To go down is to desc——.   (descend)

    Another word for view is sc——.   (scene)

    Another word for perfume is sc——. (scent)

gh and *ph* pronounced as *f*:
61

    The opposite of smooth is r——.   (rough)

    The opposite of tender is t——.   (tough)

    You l—— when you are amused.   (laugh)

    —— is as good as a feast.   (enough)

    You c—— with a cold on the chest. (cough)

    You use a camera for taking ——. (photographs)

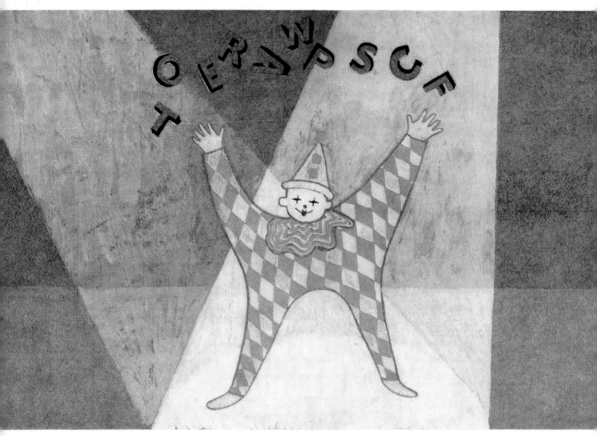

Friendly H likes to play with most letters, especially W, T, S, and C.

62

An — has no parents.   (orphan)

An — is a very large animal with a trunk.   (elephant)

A radio announcer speaks into a — and   (microphone,

plays records on a —.   gramophone)

f can also sound like *v*, e.g. of.

c and *k*.

After a short-sounding vowel the letter *c* likes to be followed by *k* :

back   brick   rock   suck

but remember the important exceptions:

attic	comic	music	magic
across	picture	practise	declare

After a long-sounding vowel, k can stand alone, as in:
bake fake sake seek hike look
c can also sound like s:
acid ice centre juice niece

Friendly *h*.
h likes to play with his friends *w*, *t*, *s* and *c*. Sometimes he likes to play with two of his friends together, as in:
patch ditch Dutch stitch
In these examples the *t* is not pronounced—but it must be written in!
When *h* plays with *w* as in:
when where which
you should be able to hear both the *w* and the *h*. You don't always when some people speak!

n has two great friends, *g* and *k*:
bang bank sang sank sing sink sling slunk

e the magician.
When he follows a word he can change it:
win — wine   mat — mate
but when he is followed by a greater magician (any other vowel) he disappears:
like — liking   bottle — bottling
but a lesser magician—like a consonant—cannot harm *e* the magician:
use — useful

63

q, the prisoner, must never go out alone. Warder *u* must always be with him: quick   equal   liquid   quantity

Here is prisoner Q trying to run away from U his warder

Plurals with *s*. Sometimes they hiss, and sometimes they buzz:

    hats (the *s* has a hissing sound)

    dogs (the *s* has a buzzing sound)

    boys and *toes* sound as if they end with a *z*.

Jolly old pals together, *g*, *h* and *t*.

Let your child supply the missing words, they all end in *ght* :

He hurried and only just c— the train. (caught)

His parcel was heavy but mine was l—. (light)

Baby's w— was seven pounds at birth. (weight)

As a result of the f— he had a black eye. (fight)

Have you b— your lunch with you ? (brought)

His h— was 5 feet 3 inches. (height)

The shortest distance between two points is a
— line. (straight)

65

Some difficult spellings :

ending in *able* — likeable, probable, valuable

ending in *ible* — horrible, possible, visible

a or *e* :

pleasant   assistant   *but* innocent   impudent   intelligent

distance   attendance *but* evidence   presence

words pronounced similarly but spelt differently

. . . .

Make sure that your child knows when to use each different spelling:

ALL   *the whole*   All is lost.

AWL   *a tool for making holes in leather*   The cobbler uses an awl.

AIL   *to be ill*   Children ail if they do not eat and sleep regularly.

ALE   *a drink*   Ale is made from hops.

ALTAR   *a table in church on which offerings are placed*   The priest went to the altar.

ALTER   *to change*   He will never alter.

AIR   { *a tune or melody*   He played an old English air on the flute.
            { *atmosphere*   Air is clean and pure on mountain-tops.

HEIR   *inheritor*   His son is heir to his fortune.

ERE   *before*   Ere we go.

e'er *ever*, like ere, is a word used in poetry.

ALLOWED   *permitted*   He allowed the pony to trot.

ALOUD   *not in a whisper*   Say it aloud so that I can hear.

ALMS   *charity*   He gave alms to the beggar.

ARMS   *limbs*   We have two arms and two legs.

ARMS   *weapons*   Spears and rifles are arms.

ANTE-   *prefix meaning before*   Ante-natal— before birth (natal means birth).

ANTI-   *prefix meaning against*   Anti-aircraft guns are used to shoot down aircraft.

ARC	*part of a circle* An arc can be drawn with a compass.
ARK	*vessel* The animals went into the Ark two by two.
ASCENT	*the climb* The first successful ascent of Everest was made in 1953.
ASSENT	*agreement* The father gave his assent for the marriage to take place.
ATE	*past tense of verb to eat* I ate my supper.
EIGHT	*the number* 8 There are eight oarsmen in the Oxford boat.
BAIL	*part of cricket stumps, or money paid in Court to free someone temporarily* The ball hit the bail. He was released on bail.
BALE	*a bale of material, or to get rid of unwanted water* He carried the bale of wool. They had to bale or the boat would have sunk.
BAIT	*material to attract fish* The bait used to catch trout may be a fly.
BATE	*lessen* With bated breath the boys listened to the story.
BAY	*inlet* The bay was dangerous for shipping. *shrub or tree* Bay leaves are useful for cooking. *bark* The bay of a hound is frightening to many animals.
BAYS	*the plural form of bay above*
BAIZE	*cloth* Billiard tables are covered with green baize.
BALL	*dance* Cinderella went to the ball. *anything round* Wool may be wound into a ball.
BAWL	*shout* Ruffians bawl at each other.
BANS	*forbids* The dictator bans freedom.
BANNS	*of marriage* The banns were read in church.
BASE	*wicked* A man with a base mind is disliked.
BASS	*deep sounding* Bass music is written for men to sing.

67

BARE   *naked*   Kilts are worn with bare knees.

BEAR   *carry*   Sometimes one has to grin and bear one's troubles.
animal   The bear often lives in a cave.

BIER   *a wooden stand for carrying the dead to the grave*   The coffin was on the bier.

BEER   *a drink*   Beer is a popular drink in many countries.

BIRTH   *to be born*   The cat gave birth to four kittens.

BERTH   *a sleeping place on a train or ship*   His berth was reserved for him.

BE   *exist*   What is to be, will be.

BEE   *insect*   The bee makes honey.

BEECH   *tree*   Beech-wood is useful for making carpenters' tools.

BEACH   *shore*   The beach was covered with seaweed.

BEAN   *vegetable*   The bean is found in a pod.

BEEN   *part of the verb to be*   Have you been to the seaside?

BEAT   *strike*   Do not beat a dog severely.

BEET   *vegetable*   Sugar is made from beet, as well as from the sugar-cane.

68

BOW	*salute*	A bow is an old-fashioned way for a gentleman to greet a lady.
BOUGH	*branch*	The bough was heavy with fruit.
BELL	*object for ringing*	The bell chimed six times.
BELLE	*beauty*	She was the belle of the ball.
BERET	*cap*	A beret is a round cap for men or women.
BERRY	*fruit*	A berry is sometimes good to eat, but some are poisonous.
BURY	*cover*	Bury the body in the grave.
BI	*prefix meaning two*	A bi-cycle has two wheels.
BY	*prefix meaning by the way*	A by-pass is a road that skirts a town.
BUY	*exchange for money*	Please buy me some stamps.
BYE	*cricket term*	The wicket-keeper let through a bye.
BLUE	*a colour*	The sky is blue.
BLEW	*past tense of verb to blow*	He blew out the light.
BOAR	*pig*	The boar is a male pig.
BOER	*a South African of Dutch descent*	The Boers live in South Africa.
BOOR	*clumsy or ill-mannered person*	A boor is a rude man.
BORE	*pierce*	To bore a hole we may use a drill.
	weary by tedious talk	Witty people do not bore.
	past tense of verb to bear	He bore himself well. (His posture was good.)
BOLD	*courageous*	Drake was a bold seaman.
BOWLED	*cricket term*	He bowled well in the Test Match.
BOY	*a male child*	The boy ran faster than his sister.
BUOY	*an anchored float*	The ship passed the buoy.
BOLDER	*more bold*	The bolder of the two boys saved the drowning dog.
BOULDER	*rock*	The boulder was dislodged from the cliff causing a small landslide.

69

BOARDER	*lodger*	A landlady is paid by her boarders.
BORDER	*edge*	The border was planted with primroses.

The dividing line between two countries   He escaped over the border into Mexico.

The robber escapes over the boarder/border. *Which is correct?*
(Answer at foot of page 96.)

BREACH	*gap*	There is a breach in the wall where the bomb fell.
BREECH	*back part of a gun*	The soldier loaded a shell into the breech of the gun.
BREAD	*food made from flour*	Bread is a very common food.
BRED	*born*	He was a well bred dog.
BROACH	*open*	In fear and trepidation he broached the subject.
BROOCH	*ornament*	She admired the brooch on the lapel of her friend's coat.
BUT	*only*	You may go to the ball Cinderella, but you must be home by 12 o'clock.
BUTT	*target*	That unfortunate boy was the butt of our jokes.
	a large barrel	Beer is often kept in a butt.
CANDID	*sincere*	The prisoner's candid defence swayed the jury.
CANDIED	*sugared*	Candied honey is sugary, not smooth.

CARAT	*gold measure*	The boy was given a fountain pen with a 14 carat gold nib.
CARROT	*vegetable*	Donkeys like to eat carrots.

CAUGHT   *captured*   The police caught the burglar.

COURT   *enclosed space*   The children played in the court.
We also speak of law courts, royal courts, courting a lady (trying to please).

CEILING   *top limit*   The ceiling was painted white. The bomber had a ceiling of 70,000 feet.

SEALING   *close tightly*   She was sealing the parcel for registered post.

CEREAL   *a food*   We eat cereal for breakfast.

SERIAL   *a story published in instalments*   We read the new episode of the serial.

CHECK   *prove by comparison*   Check your answers with mine.

CHEQUE   *money order*   A cheque was accepted in payment by the store.

CZECH   *nationality*   A native of Czechoslovakia is called a Czech.

CHOIR   *group of singers*   The choir sang the anthem.

QUIRE   *measure for paper* (24 *sheets*)   The printer counted the quires of paper.

CHORD   *musical term*   She played the chord of C Major on the piano.

CORD   *rope*   The prisoners were bound tightly with strong cord.

CELL   *a prison room*   He was alone in his tiny cell.

SELL   *to exchange something for money*   Will you sell me your bicycle?

CLIMB   *ascend*   Will you climb the ladder?

CLIME   *climate*   A poetical word for climate.

71

CITE	*quote* He could cite the law to prove his point.
SIGHT	*vision* His sight was impaired by constant reading in bed at night.
SITE	*position* A hotel will be built on the site of the old tavern.
CLAUSE	*part of a sentence* We went out when the rain stopped. (*When the rain stopped* is a clause.)
CLAWS	*birds' feet, also cats' etc.* The eagle grasped the bird with its claws.
COARSE	*rough* The gamekeeper was wearing a jacket made of coarse tweed cloth.
COURSE	*way* The Captain set the ship on a northerly course.
COLONEL	*military rank* The soldiers saluted the Colonel, who was their commanding officer.
KERNEL	*part of a nut* The kernel is the softer part inside the hard shell of a nut.
COMPLIMENT	*praise* The Headmaster paid a high compliment to the boy's work.
COMPLEMENT	*full number* The addition of two boys to the class made up its full complement.
CREAK	*grating noise* The hinges of a door creak when they need oiling.
CREEK	*inlet* The oil tanker glided slowly up the creek until it arrived at the landing jetty.
CURRANT	*raisin made from grapes, or a berry which grows on a bush* Currants are often used in cakes and puddings.
CURRENT	*a flow of air, water or electricity* There are dangerous currents in the water by the bridge.
CYMBAL	*musical instrument* The clash of the cymbals could be heard as the band marched past.
SYMBOL	*sign* The olive branch is a symbol of peace.

72

DEAR   *costly or loved*   She is very dear to me.

DEER   *animal*   In the park were many deer.

DEW   *condensed vapour*   In the early morning you may find drops of dew on the grass.

DUE   *owing*   The builder paid the money due to the labourer for work done.

The lawyer can cite/sight/site *every point of the law. Which do you think is the correct spelling?* (*Answer at foot of page 96.*)

DIE   *to stop living*   He is very ill and may die.

DYE   *to colour something with a stain, or another name for the stain itself*   I am going to dye my old dress brown.

DYED   *past tense of verb to dye*   The grey coat was sent to the cleaners to be dyed brown.

DIED   *past tense of verb to die*   The Black Knight died from his wounds received in battle.

DOE   *female rabbit, hare or deer*   The doe gave birth to four baby rabbits.

DOUGH   *kneaded flour*   Dough is used in making bread.

DRAFT   *a plan*   The architect made a rough draft of the new building before deciding on the final sketch.

DRAUGHT   *current of air*   The living room door was left open and this caused a draught.

73

The currant/current *is flowing under the bridge. Which of these do you think is the correct spelling?* (*Answer at foot of page 96.*)

DUAL	*of two* The car had dual controls, one for the learner and the other for the instructor.
DUEL	*combat* The count and the captain fought a duel with pistols in a deserted wood.
EARN	*gain by labour* The labourer will earn £9 weekly by working for the builder.
URN	*vessel* A large urn was used for making tea.
EWER	*water jug* A ewer is a bowl or jug specially made to hold water or some other liquid.
HEWER	*cutter* The hewer cut the tree trunk into logs.
FAINT	*weak* At the sight of blood some people are inclined to faint.
FEINT	*pretence* The boxer made a feint with his left hand and struck his adversary with the right.

74

FAIR	*just, average, a market with sideshows* In view of the foul, the referee made a fair decision by giving a penalty. John and James were going to the fair to ride on the roundabouts.
FARE	*travel charge, food* The man paid my fare when I travelled on the bus. The fare at the hotel was good.
FATE	*one's lot or fortune* It was always John's fate to be caught when he was late for school.
FETE	*festival* A garden fete was held at the Manor House.
FAUN	*woodland god* A faun was a Roman god that looked like a man, but had the ears, horns and tail of a goat.
FAWN	*deer, colour* A fawn is a light yellowish deer less than a year old. One also speaks of a colour as being fawn (i.e. light yellowish).
FEET	*measure, lower part of legs* The height of the tree was twenty feet. His feet were tired from walking so far.
FEAT	*deed* He performed an amazing feat when he jumped 6 feet 3 inches.
FIND	*discover* If you find the treasure you will be rewarded.
FINED	*past tense of verb to fine* The magistrate fined the motorist for speeding.
FIR	*tree* A Christmas tree is generally a fir tree.
FUR	*animal coat* Their Persian kitten had a beautiful soft fur.
FLEA	*insect* The flea is an insect which feeds on the blood of animals, or human beings.
FLEE	*run away* The enemy tried to flee, but was caught.
FLEW	*past tense of verb to fly* When winter came many birds flew to a warmer country.
FLUE	*passage in a chimney* A flue is a passage for smoke or hot air.

75

FOOL	*a stupid person*	He is a fool.
FULL	*room for no more*	His cup was full.
FOR	*preposition*	He went to the shops for some sweets.
FORE	*at the front*	It is usually the more educated man who comes to the fore.
FOUR	*number*	A hand has four fingers and a thumb.
FORMALLY	*ceremoniously*	The agreement was formally signed and sealed.
FORMERLY	*in the past*	He was formerly the office boy, but is now the general manager.
FLOUR	*fine meal*	Flour is made from grinding grain and is used for bread and cakes.
FLOWER	*plant*	The daffodil is a flower which sometimes grows wild in woods.
FORTH	*out*	Come forth!
FOURTH	*next after third*	He came fourth in his class examination.
FOUL	*vile*	We opened the door to let out the foul air.
FOWL	*bird*	We decided to have a fowl for Christmas.
FREES	*liberates*	The jailer frees the prisoners after they have served their sentences.
FREEZE	*turn into ice*	The temperature is so low I think the pond will freeze overnight.
GAIT	*style of walking*	The man with the injured leg had a peculiar gait.
GATE	*an entrance*	The lodgekeeper opened the gate so that the car could enter the drive.
GRATE	*part of a fire*	She cleaned the ashes from the grate.
	to rub	The chef grated the cheese.
GREAT	*important, huge*	The Spanish Armada was a great fleet of ships.

76

GRISLY	*horrible* It was a grisly sight to see the elephants dying for lack of water.
GRIZZLY	*greyish* The man had a grizzly beard.
GROWN	*past participle of verb to grow* The tree has grown very tall.
GROAN	*sigh* A groan of despair was uttered by the prisoner when he heard his sentence passed by the judge.
GUESSED	*past tense of verb to guess* He guessed the correct answer to the question.
GUEST	*visitor* I am going away to the seaside as a guest of friends of mine.
GUILT	*sin* The prisoner admitted his guilt.
GILT	*covered with gold or silver* The cutlery was silver gilt.
HAIR	*of head* The hair on men's heads is usually cut when it grows too long.
HARE	*animal* A hare is an animal like a rabbit but larger.
HALL	*passage way* Wipe your feet on the mat before entering the hall.
HAUL	*to pull* A tractor is sometimes used to haul logs from the forest to the saw-mills.
HAIL	*to call, or frozen rain* The weather changed and it began to hail.
HALE	*strong* The old man was hale and hearty.
HEAL	*cure* The doctor will help you heal your injury.
HEEL	*part of the foot* The heel is the rear part of the foot below the ankle.
HEAR	*listen* We are waiting to hear the headmaster talk.
HERE	*in or to this place* We will come back here in the spring.
HEARD	*past tense of verb to hear* We heard the clock strike six.
HERD	*a number (usually of cattle)* A herd of cows passed us on their way to be milked.

77

HEW	*cut down*	The job of a lumber-jack is to hew the trees.
HUE	*colour*	The boy was admiring the hues of the rainbow.

HIM   *pronoun*   Give him a new cricket bat.

HYMN   *religious song*   In church, hymns are sung in praise of God.

HOLE   *open place*   You must mend the hole in your sock.

WHOLE   *complete*   The whole town was on holiday.

HOUR   *sixty minutes*   The batsman batted for an hour.

OUR   *belonging to*   He came in our car.

ISLE   *island*   They went to the Isle of Wight for their holiday.

AISLE   *part of church leading to altar*   The bride and bride-groom came down the aisle.

IN   *a preposition*   He is in his room.

INN   *a public house where food and drink can be bought*   We stopped for food at the inn.

KNEAD   *to mix into a smooth mass*   You must knead dough to make bread.

NEED   *require*   I need your help.

KEY   *locks and unlocks doors*   As I am not going out, I will give you my key.

QUAY   *landing place*   The passengers disembarked from the liner on to the quay.

KNIGHT   *honourable rank*   Sir Galahad was a knight of King Arthur's round table.

78   NIGHT   *opposite of day*   The night begins at sunset and ends at sunrise.

KNOW   *conscious of*   Do you know where your grandmother lives ?

NO   *negative*   No trespassers are allowed.

KNOWS   *conscious of*   The headmaster does not guess, he knows the answer.

NOSE	*part of face* You should breathe through your nose.
LED	*past tense of verb to lead* He led the horse by the reins.
LEAD	*a metal* Lead is a heavy metal.
LESSEN	*decrease* If we lessen our pull on the rope it will go slack.
LESSON	*unit of learning* The new teacher will give his first lesson tomorrow.
LOOSE	*not tight* A screw was loose, so I tightened it.
LOSE	*to be beaten in a contest* You will lose the match if you do not practise.
LOAN	*something that is lent and not given* The money was to be a loan and not a gift.
LONE	*alone* We saw a lone wolf in the distance.
LUTE	*a musical instrument* She played well on the lute.
LOOT	*plunder* The robbers got away with the loot.
MADE	*past tense of verb to make* The cook made an iced cake.
MAID	*servant* She asked the maid to bring in the tea.
MAIL	*post* If you catch the mail your letter will arrive to-morrow.
MALE	*man* Boys and men are males, girls and women are females.
MAIN	*most important* The main industry of Lancashire is cotton.
MANE	*long hair on the neck of a lion* The lion's mane consists of long, heavy hair on its neck.
MANNER	*way* The manner in which he spoke was offensive.
MANOR	*country house* The Manor house was for sale.
MEAT	*food* A vegetarian is one who does not eat meat.
MEET	*encounter* I will meet you at 8 o'clock.
METE	*measure* The magistrate will mete out justice.

79

METAL	*copper, tin, etc.* The ash-tray was made of metal.
METTLE	*being ready to do one's best* She was told to be on her mettle for the match.
MEDAL	*a reward* His bravery earned him a medal.
MEDDLE	*to interfere* Do not meddle in the affairs of others.
MIGHT	*strength* Work with all your might.
MITE	*coin used in Bible times, or a small child* The widow gave her mite to the beggar.
MINER	*occupation* The miner went down the coal mine to bring up the coal.
MINOR	*unimportant* It was a minor mistake, so it did not matter. *under* 21 A boy or girl is a minor until reaching the age of 21.
MISSED	*past tense of verb to miss* He ran fast, but missed the train.
MIST	*foggy cloud* There was a heavy mist over the downs.
MOAN	*sound of suffering* A low moan came from the injured man.
MOWN	*past tense of verb to mow* The gardener has mown the front lawn.
MUSCLE	*of the body* The wrestler flexed his muscles to show his strength.
MUSSEL	*shell fish* A mussel is a shell fish which lives in fresh or sea water.

80

Here is a strong man flexing his muscles/mussels; *which do you think is the correct spelling?*   (*Answer at foot of page 96.*)

NAVAL	*of the navy* The Home Fleet was anchored at Spithead for the naval review.
NAVEL	*part of the body* The navel is a mark on the surface of the body, often referred to by children as "tummy button".
NOT	*negative* You must not cross the road without first looking both ways.
KNOT	*fastening* The postman tied a knot in the string. *nautical measure (miles per hour)* The steamer had a speed of 10 knots.
KNEW	*past tense of verb to know* He knew what he was doing.
NEW	*fresh* John was given a new suit for his birthday.
GNU	*animal* A gnu is an antelope with an ox-like head and long tail, which lives in Africa.
NONE	*not any* He had none.
NUN	*a religious woman who lives in a convent* The nun attended the service.
OAR	*for rowing* The crew of the life-boat manned the oars.
OR	*conjunction* We can either go by bus or train.
ORE	*crude mineral* Ore, such as gold, is mined in South Africa.
ONE	*singular* There was a vacancy for one only.
WON	*past tense of verb to win* Our team has won three matches out of four.
PAIL	*bucket* Jack and Jill went up the hill to fetch a pail of water.
PALE	*without colour* The child's face was pale from the shock of the fall.
PAST PASSED	*different tenses of verb to pass* It was half *past* four when we *passed* him. He dribbled *past* me and then *passed* the ball to Tom.

81

6—H.T.

| PAIN | *suffering* | The boy who broke his leg was in great pain. |
| PANE | *of glass* | The window pane was broken by a cricket ball. |

"Who has broken my window pain/pane*?" asks the old man. Which is the correct spelling?* (*Answer at foot of page 96.*)

PAIR	*set of two*	He bought a pair of shoes.
PEAR	*fruit*	A pear is a sweet juicy fruit which grows on trees.
PARE	*cut or trim*	I will pare your apple.
PAUSE	*interval*	There was a short pause before the new programme started.
PAWS	*of animals*	The dog had both paws bandaged and found it difficult to walk.
PEAS	*vegetable*	We had duck and green peas for dinner.
PEACE	*quiet*	We all enjoy peace and quiet.
PIECE	*part or portion*	I would like a piece of cheese.
PEAL	*of bells*	The peal of the church bells was heard for miles around.
PEEL	*pare*	The cook will peel the potatoes for lunch.
PEER	*equal*	The manager is so good at his job that it would be

82

	hard to find his peer.
	a man of title A duke is a peer of the realm.
PIER	*landing stage* The pier was only used for small fishing boats.
PILLAR	*support* The main pillar of the building was three feet in circumference.
PILLOW	*head-rest* As soon as he laid his head on the pillow he fell asleep.
PLACE	*a particular locality* If things are not kept in their proper place they will be difficult to find.
PLAICE	*fish* Plaice is a flat, salt-water fish.
PLANE	*a tool for smoothing wood* The carpenter uses a plane.
PLAIN	*flat country* There are no hills on Salisbury Plain.
	without decoration Her frock was plain, but very smart.
POOR	*not rich* He is so poor that he has no money at all.
PORE	*one of the many holes in the skin* We sweat through our pores.
POUR	*to flow* Will you please pour the tea?
PAW	*animal's foot* The dog has hurt its paw.
PRACTICE	*noun* Practice makes perfect.
PRACTISE	*verb* He will practise bowling and batting every day to become a good cricketer.
PRAISE	*commend* The master gave praise to the cleverest boy in the form.
PRAYS	*asks earnestly* The minister prays to God for the peace of the world.
PREYS	*troubles heavily* Worry preys on his mind.
PRIZE	*reward* The prize will be given to the top boy of the form.
PRISE	*break open* The locksmith will have to prise open the door if we cannot find the key.

83

PRINCIPAL   *chief or head*   The principal of the school was interviewing new pupils.

PRINCIPLE   *basic truth*   It is a good principle never to tell lies.

PROFIT   *gain*   The business made a good profit.

PROPHET   *seer*   The prophet hinted at a forthcoming disaster.

RAIN   *condensed moisture*   Continuous rain flooded the countryside.

REIGN   *rule*   The Queen's reign was a happy one.

REIN   *the strap controlling a horse's movements*   She held the horse's reins.

RAISE   *to lift*   Raise the lid of the box.

RAYS   *a line of light or heat*   Some of the health-giving rays from the sun do not penetrate ordinary glass.

RAZE   *to destroy*   The enemy would raze the town.

RAP   *knock*   There was a rap on the door.

WRAP   *cloak*   Wrap yourself up well before you go out.

RAW   *uncooked*   Raw meat is not usually considered good to eat.

ROAR   *loud noise*   The roar of the lion was frightening.

READ   *present tense of verb to read*   We read books for pleasure and learning.

REED   *water plant*   A reed grows in wet places.

READ   *past tense of verb to read*   I have read this book many times.

RED   *colour*   Red is a colour often used to denote danger.

RIGHT   *opposite of wrong*   As the boy gave the right answer he was given full marks.

      opposite of left   In France you drive on the right of the road.

WRITE   *inscribe*   Please write your name and address on this piece of paper.

RITE	*a solemn ceremony* The coronation rites were very impressive.
ROE	*eggs of a fish* Cod's roe may be bought at the fishmonger's shop.
ROW	*a line of people or things, or a way of propelling a boat* Will you row the boat?
ROES, ROWS	*the plurals of the above.*
ROSE	*a beautiful flower* The rose is the queen of flowers.
RING	*circle* They all joined hands and made a ring round the Christmas tree. *sound* Did the bell ring?
WRING	*squeeze out* Wring out the washing before you put it on the clothes line. (also rung and wrung; past tenses of verbs to ring and to wring).
ROAD	*track* The Romans built the first road in Britain.
RODE	*past tense of verb to ride* We rode on our bicycles for ten miles.
ROWED	*past tense of verb to row* He rowed for Cambridge in the boat race.
ROUTE	*way to go* Which route will you take from London to Cornwall?
ROOT	*base of a plant* The root of the carrot plant is the part we eat.
SALE	*act of selling* The sale of the furniture brought £97.
SAIL	*of a boat* A fishing boat sometimes has brown sails.
SAUCE	*a condiment* Sauce can make some food taste better.
SOURCE	*beginning* The source of a river is where it begins.
SCULL	*a method of moving a boat* He was learning to scull.
SKULL	*the bony case of the brain* His skull was fractured.

85

SCENE   *view*   A lovely scene met his eyes when he reached the top of the hill.

                      part of a play   The actors played the scene with great emotion.

SEEN   *past tense of verb to see*   I have seen the new moon.

SEA   *salt water*   The British Isles are surrounded by sea.

SEE   *perceive*   I see that you have hurt your leg.

                      area of a bishop's authority   The bishop is head of the clergy in his own see.

86   *The* surfs/serfs *are carrying salt from the salt mines. Which do you think is the correct spelling?*   *(Answer at foot of page 96.)*

SEAM   *a sewing join*   A coat usually has a seam at the back.

SEEM   *appear*   You seem to be ill.

SEES   *present tense of verb to see*   The boy sees the train coming.

SEAS   *plural of sea*   Rivers nearly always flow into seas.

SEIZE	*take hold of*	Be careful, the dog may seize it.

SCENT   *smell*   The scent of the flowers was fragrant.

SENT   *past tense of verb to send*   Have you sent the letter?

CENT   *hundred, or American coin*   The interest rate is 5 per cent.

SERF   *slave*   The serfs were put to work in the mines of Siberia.

SURF   *waves*   The boat came in through the surf.

SHEAR   *to cut*   The farmer is going to shear his sheep.

SHEER   *absolute*   The boxer won by the sheer speed of his punching.

SELLER   *one who sells something*   He was the seller of the car.

CELLAR   *an underground room*   Wine and coal were kept in a cellar.

SHORE   *edge of the sea*   The boys collected shells on the shore.

SURE   *certain*   Are you sure you are right?

SIDE   *edge*   The boy walked by the side of the canal.

SIGHED   *past tense of verb to sigh*   The girl sighed because she was alone.

SITE   *situation*   They chose the site of their new house because of the view.

SIGHT   *act of seeing*   As her sight was poor she had to wear glasses.

SIZE   *extent of volume*   You can tell by the size of the tree that it must be old.

87

SIGHS   *present tense of verb to sigh, also plural of the noun*   Her sighs could be heard at the other end of the room.

SLAY   *kill*   Slay them! cried the Romans.

SLEIGH   *sledge*   The sleigh is used when the snow is thick on the ground.

SLOE	*fruit*	Gin may be made from the sloe berry.
SLOW	*not fast*	He is too slow to win.

SO	*thus*	And so they lived happily ever after.
SEW	*stitch*	Sew a seam in that coat.
SOW	*scatter seed*	The farmer sows seed in the early spring.

What a funny hat the old lady is wearing! No wonder the children stare/stair *at her. Which is the correct spelling? (Answer at foot of page 96.)*

88

SOLE	*part of a shoe*	A sole of a shoe is usually made of leather.
	single	The sole occupant of the carriage was a sailor.
	fish	A dover sole is thought to be the best fish of its kind.
SOUL	*spirit*	She put her heart and soul into the work.
SOAR	*rise*	Larks soar into the clouds.
SORE	*painful*	I have a sore elbow.

SOME	*several*	Some men wear moustaches.
SUM	*total*	The sum of money amounted to one hundred pounds.
SON	*male child*	His son was called Robert.
SUN	*heavenly body*	The sun shines longer and more brightly in summer.
STAIR	*step*	There were forty-six stairs to climb.
STARE	*gaze at*	It is impolite to stare at people.
STAKE	*risk*	How much will you stake on the horse?
	post	The plot was marked by four stakes in the ground.
STEAK	*meat*	Beef-steak is delicious when grilled.

STATIONARY *not moving* The car is stationary.

STATIONERY *writing material* The newsagent sometimes sells stationery too.

STEAL	*rob*	"Thou shalt not steal" says the Commandment.
STEEL	*metal*	Chisels are usually made from steel.
STALK	*to pursue without being seen*	Hunters often stalk wild animals.
	stem	Bluebells have long stalks.
STORK	*a bird*	A stork is a water bird with long legs.
STOREY	*horizontal division of a building*	The house has four storeys.
STORY	*tale*	"Moby Dick" is a story about a whale.
STILE	*step over a fence*	You can cross the field when you have climbed over the stile.
STYLE	*manner*	A good batsman usually has a good style.
SUITE	*group*	A suite of furniture usually includes two chairs and a couch.
SWEET	*opposite to sour*	Sugar is sweet.
TALE	*story*	Bob liked the tale his father read to him.
TAIL	*part of an animal*	It is cruel to pull a cat's tail.

89

| TAUT | *tightly drawn*   The cable between the ships was taut. |
| TAUGHT | *past tense of verb to teach*   The boy had been taught to read. |

| TEA | *beverage*   Tea is grown in India and China. |
| TEE | *golf term*   A golf ball is placed on a tee. |

The house has four storeys/stories. *Which is the correct spelling?*
(Answer at foot of page 96.)

| TEAM | *group*   Our football team won the cup. |
| TEEM | *abundant*   The pond teems with fish. |

| THEIR | *belonging to them*   They took their clothes. |
| THERE | *in (or to) that place*   There is a rabbit. I go there. |

| THROUGH | *conjunction*   The man went through the gate. |
| THREW | *past tense of verb to throw*   He threw a stone into the water. |

| THROES | *violent pangs*   She was in the throes of agony. |
| THROWS | *hurls*   He throws the ball to his team-mates. |

| THROWN | *past tense of verb to throw*   The ball was thrown back over the wall. |

THRONE   *seat of royalty*   The Queen sat on the throne.

TEAR   *when crying*   She shed tears because she was unhappy.

TIER   *row or layer*   A wedding cake may have three tiers.

Here is a wedding-cake with three tiers/tears; *which is correct?*
(Answer at foot of page 96.)

TIDE   *the rise and fall of the sea*   The tide is going out.

TIED   *fastened together*   They were tied together.

91

TO   *preposition*   He went to school.

TOO   *also*   She too went to school.

TWO   *number*   Two boys went to school.

TOE   *part of foot*   Corns sometimes form on toes.

TOW   *pull*   Old cars sometimes need a tow to start in cold
          weather.

TOLD	*past tense of verb to tell* I told you not to get your frock dirty.
TOLLED	*to sound* The bell tolled the hours.
VANE	*weathercock* The weather vane showed that the wind was blowing from east to west.
VAIN	*proud* He was as vain as a peacock.
VEIN	*blood vessel* Veins carry blood back to the heart.
VALE	*valley* The Vale of the Thames is very lovely.
VEIL	*face covering* Eastern women often wear a veil.
WAIL	*cry* The wail of the cats disturbed the night.
WHALE	*mammal* The whale is the largest living animal.
WAIVE	*forego* He waived his claim to the inheritance.
WAVE	*signal* Wave your hand when you say goodbye.
	sea-wave The wave swept over the promenade.
WERE	*verb* Were you there?
WARE	*goods for sale* Staffordshire is famous for pottery ware.
WEAR	*to dress* Eskimos wear furs.
WHERE	*adverb* Where are you going?
WADE	*walk through water, etc.* Fishermen have to wade out far when prawning.
WEIGHED	*past tense of verb to weigh* The grocer weighed a pound of rice.
WAIST	*part of body* You fasten a belt round your waist.
WASTE	*not to make good use of* Waste not want not.
WAIT	*attend* Please wait for me, I shall not be long.
WEIGHT	*amount* Sugar is sold by weight.
WAY	*path* Tell me the way to school.
WEIGH	*fix the weight* The grocer must weigh many of his wares.
WHEY	*part of curdled milk* When milk turns sour the watery part is called whey.

92

WEAK	*feeble*	The strong should protect the weak.
WEEK	*seven days*	There are seven days in a week.
WEATHER	*climate*	Winter weather is usually cold.
WHETHER	*conjunction*	You must go to school whether it is wet or fine.

This is a piece of china wear/ware; *which spelling is correct?*
(*Answer at foot of page 96.*)

WET	*watery*	The pavements were wet with rain.
WHET	*sharpen*	The delicious aromas whet my appetite.
WHICH	*pronoun*	Which of the two was to blame?
WITCH	*woman sorcerer*	In the fairy tale the witch rode a broomstick.
WOOD	*timber*	Mahogany is a reddish-coloured wood.
WOULD	*past tense of verb to be*	Would you behave in the same way?

93

YEW	*wood*	Yew wood is used to make bows. ✓
EWE	*female sheep*	The ewe protects her lambs from harm.
YOU	*pronoun*	You are a good pupil.

94 There/their *parents* where/wear/were there/their *to meet them. Which are the correct spellings in this sentence?* (*Answers at foot of page 96.*)

YOKE	*wooden harness*	A yoke is a wooden crosspiece fastened over the necks of two beasts of burden.
YOLK	*yellow part of an egg*	In cooking, the yolk and the white of an egg are often separated.

AN EXERCISE IN SPELLING

Here is a useful exercise for your child. Have him go through these sentences and write down the correct spelling on a piece of paper. The correct words to use are at the end of the exercise.

1. The **DUE|DEW** glistened on the grass.

2. The bird hopped on to the **BOW|BOUGH** and seemed to **BOW|BOUGH** to us.

3. Would you like a **PIECE|PEACE** of **STAKE|STEAK** to eat?

4. A **GRATE|GREAT** fire blazed in the **GRATE|GREAT**.

5. From which firm did you **HIRE|HIGHER** the car?

6. He found the **KEY|QUAY** near the **KEY|QUAY**.

7. **WOULD|WOOD** you please cut the **PAIR|PEAR OFF|OF ITS|IT'S STALK|STORK** with the **PAIR|PEAR** of scissors?

8. I like swimming in the **SEA|SEE** on my holidays.

9. It was **NIGHT|KNIGHT** in the days when **NIGHTS|KNIGHTS** were bold.

10. It caused him much **PANE|PAIN** when he broke the **PANE|PAIN** of glass.

11. **YOU|EWE|YEW** can see the **YOU|EWE|YEW** near the **YOU|EWE|YEW** tree.

12. He **THREW|THROUGH** the **BALL|BAWL** into the **BLEW|BLUE** sky.

13. Your **SUN|SON WOULD|WOOD** write describing the **SCENE|SEEN**.

14. Can you draw the **NOSE|KNOWS** of the **HARE|HAIR**?

15. Do not **SEIZE|SEAS** the **WEAK|WEEK** dog by **ITS|IT'S SORE|SAW TALE|TAIL**.

16. Joan of Arc was burnt at the **STEAK|STAKE**.

17. He sold the car for a huge **PROFIT|PROPHET**.

95

18. The furnace was smelting the iron **ORE|OAR|OR**.

19. The man held the horse's **REIGNS|RAINS|REINS**.

20. **THERE|THEIR** parents were **THERE|THEIR** to meet them.

21. The boys **WERE|WHERE|WEAR** told to **WERE|WHERE| WEAR** their colours **WHERE|WERE|WEAR** they could be **SEEN|SCENE**.

22. **ITS|IT'S TOO|TWO|TO** late for the **TWO|TOO|TO** of us **TO|TOO|TWO** go.

23. The school **WITCH|WHICH** you **SEA|SEE** is **QUITE| QUIET** large.

24. The **TWO|TOO MALE|MAIL** stewards on the **MALE|MAIL** train were **BORED|BOARD** because they were not **ALOUD| ALLOWED** to **HEAR|HERE** the music.

25. He **PASSED|PAST** me and then he ran **PAST|PASSED** my brother **TOO|TWO**.

26. **ALTER|ALTAR** the flowers on the **ALTAR|ALTER**.

Answers: **1** *dew* **2** *bough, bow* **3** *piece, steak* **4** *great, grate* **5** *hire* **6** *key, quay* **7** *would, pear, off, its, stalk, pair* **8** *sea* **9** *night, knights* **10** *pain, pane* **11** *you, ewe, yew* **12** *threw, ball, blue* **13** *son, would, scene* **14** *nose, hare* **15** *seize, weak, its, sore, tail* **16** *stake* **17** *profit* **18** *ore* **19** *reins* **20** *their, there* **21** *were, wear, where, seen* **22** *it's, too, two, to* **23** *which, see, quite* **24** *two, male, mail, bored, allowed, hear* **25** *passed, past, too* **26** *alter, altar*

Answers to the picture quizzes: p. 70, border; p. 73, cite; p. 74, current; p. 80; muscles; p. 82, pane; p. 86, serfs; p. 88, stare; p. 90, storeys; p. 91, tiers, p. 93, ware; p. 94, their, were, there.

Some words, although spelt alike, have more than one meaning:

> *Spring* comes in March
> My watch *spring* is broken

Now use these words in more than one way:

> chest   lean   ring   round   sore   ball   bowl

GRAMMAR

. . . .

sentences

A sentence is a group of words which makes sense and contains a verb. It must express a complete thought.

> Tom hit the ball.

Make interesting sentences (not questions) containing the following words (your child should be encouraged to use the words in an interesting manner, showing his command of language. e.g. escape. "The prisoner's escape was unsuccessful"):

accept	consent	imagine	tolled
advise	decrease	inferior	what
agree	deny	prefer	which
although	dose	prey	who
ancient	encounter	request	whom
annual	except	soar	whose
artful	fairies	stake	while
borne	gracious	that	why
client	gratitude	there's	

97

phrases

· ·

A phrase is a group of words which does not make sense by itself, but is just part of a sentence. (In the field, up the lane.) Ask your child to say which of the following are sentences and which are phrases:

A string of beautiful, coloured beads.	(phrase)
At the break of day.	(phrase)
He came quickly.	(sentence)
At home, by the fireside.	(phrase)
The man was kind.	(sentence)
The rain came pouring down.	(sentence)
Holding onto his hand.	(phrase)
It can be useful.	(sentence)

The *subject* of a sentence is the person or thing spoken about:
in "Tom hit the ball" *Tom* is the subject.

The *predicate* is what you say about the subject:
Hit the ball is the predicate in the sentence "Tom hit the ball".

punctuation

· ·

CAPITALS

A capital letter is normally used in writing:

For the first letter of the first word at the beginning of every sentence

For the first letter of proper nouns (George), countries (France), towns (London), and titles (the Kings).

For the first letter of the names of the days (Tuesday), months (April), festivals (Easter).

For the first letter of the names of houses, ships, streets, newspapers, books, play-titles (King Street).

For a person's initials (A. T. Smith).

For the *word* I.

For the first letter of a sentence inside a new set of inverted commas.

At the beginning of each line of a poem.

Have your child write out the following sentences, putting in the capital letters :

> was charles, king of england, imprisoned in the tower of london ?
>
> the daily times' reporter, a. b. brown, was present on tuesday at the opening of shakespeare's play "the taming of the shrew" at stratford-on-avon.
>
> (*Was Charles, King of England, imprisoned in the Tower of London?*
>
> *The Daily Times' reporter, A. B. Brown, was present on Tuesday at the opening of Shakespeare's play "The taming of the shrew" at Stratford-on-Avon.*)

99

COMMAS

Commas are used in a sentence to mark a pause (He hit the ball, not a run was scored). "And" may take the place of a comma (In my pocket

I have a penny, a penknife and a handkerchief). Young writers tend to use too many commas and not enough full stops. Look out for this failing in your child's essays.

Young writers tend to use too many commas.

FULL STOPS

A full stop is used at the end of a sentence, unless the sentence calls for a question mark (?) or an exclamation mark (!). It is also used after initials (J. A. Smith) and after abbreviations (Jan. 1st).

100

EXCLAMATION MARKS

An exclamation mark is used after expressions of surprise, emotion, fear and delight:

　　　Oh! Ah! Look! Hurrah!

　　　What a superb innings May played at Lords!

　　　I did not know you were here!

　　　How fierce he looks!

QUESTION MARKS

A question mark is always placed at the end of a question.

> What are you doing?

But a question mark is *not* used in:

> I asked him what he was doing.

APOSTROPHES

An apostrophe is a mark (') used to indicate (a) the possessive case, or (b) the omission of a letter or letters.

(a) The possessive case.

If the word does not end in *s*, add *'s*:

> The book of the boy — the boy's book
>
> The books of the children — the children's books

If the word ends in *s* and is singular, add *'s*:

> The book of Charles — Charles's book

If the word ends in *s* and is plural, add *'*:

> The books of the girls — the girls' books

Can your child explain the difference between sentences (a) and (b):

(a) The girls' books are missing. (The books of many girls are missing).

(b) The girl's books are missing. (The books of one girl are missing).

101

Have your child write out these sentences, putting in apostrophes:

a girls school	(girls')
childrens toys	(children's)
Jacks hat was missing	(Jack's)
Jack goes to a boys school	(boys')

the babys cot was empty   (baby's)

the babies ward was full   (babies')

the womans gloves were lost   (woman's)

the teachers desk contained the childrens books

(teacher's, children's)

(b) The omission of a letter or letters.

In speaking we often join two words together by leaving out a letter or two. In writing this we use an apostrophe:

I'm — I am   I'll — I will   couldn't — could not

I've — I have   one's — one is   it's — it is

he's — he is   can't — cannot   we'll — we will

In speech you might say "My father's a doctor". But you should *write*, "My father is a doctor". Similarly, although you might say "How's your rheumatism?", you would *write* "How is your rheumatism?"

When *its* and *your* are used in the sense of belonging, we use no apostrophe:

It's natural for a dog to use *its* tail.

You're not to take *your* books with you.

Hers, ours, theirs, yours (The book is *yours*).

102

Putting an apostrophe in *its*, when it should not have one, is a very common fault.

Use the following in sentences:

ladies'   men's   enemy's   ships'   towns'

QUOTATION MARKS (INVERTED COMMAS)

Words quoted are put into quotation marks. The boy said, "He has the book". Note the comma before the quotation mark and that since the words inside the marks form a complete sentence, the first letter is a capital letter.

Titles are put into quotation marks :

I have read "David Copperfield".

The whole meaning of a sentence can be changed if the quotation marks are put in different positions :

The master said, "The boy is a fool."

"The master", said the boy, "is a fool." (note that the *i* in *is* is not a capital letter).

The boy said, "He has the book."

"The boy", said he, "has the book."

Some exercises in punctuation

Write out the following, putting in punctuation marks :

The dog said John is naughty.

"The dog", said John, "is naughty."

Every lady in the land
Has twenty nails on each hand
Five and twenty on hands and feet
This is true and no deceit.
Every lady in the land has twenty nails.
On each hand five, and twenty on hands and feet.
This is true and no deceit.
Note the spelling of *deceit,* but *receipt* has a silent *p.*

103

Write the following correctly:

Hello he exclaimed youre soon back i forgot my ticket said jimmy and they wouldnt let me in you are a duffer laughed mrs smith youll forget to eat your dinner one day

"Hello!" he exclaimed, "You're soon back."

"I forgot my ticket," said Jimmy, "and they wouldn't let me in."

"You are a duffer," laughed Mrs. Smith. "You'll forget to eat your dinner one day."

Insert capital letters, commas, full stops, quotation marks, and exclamation marks in this nursery rhyme:

little jack horner sat in the corner

eating a christmas pie

he put in his thumb and took out a plum

and said what a good boy am I

104

Little Jack Horner sat in a corner,
Eating a Christmas pie.
He put in his thumb, and took out a plum,
And said, "What a good boy am I!"

A and An

. . . .

An is used before words beginning with a vowel or a silent *h*:

an apple	an odd	an eager	an iris	an uncle
an hour	an honest	an honourable		an heir

A is used before all other words:

a crab   a pail   a horrible   a face   a car

Some words beginning with the letter *u* sound as if they begin with *you* (as in unicorn—*you*-nicorn). Such words must be preceded by *a*:

a unit   a union   a university

Words beginning with *x* sound as if they begin with a vowel, we therefore use *an* before them:

an X-ray

Have your child use *a* or *an* before the following words:

aeroplane	book	cloud	egg-spoon	high building
oil-can	obedient	girl	tall tree	usual sight

105

Ask your child which he would use (a or an) to complete these sentences:

She is —— heroine.	(a)
He is —— honest man.	(an)
I can see —— helicopter.	(a)

nouns

. . . .

A noun is the name of a person, place or thing (e.g. Tom, London, pencil). If we can put *a, an* or *the* before a word then it is a noun (e.g. a boy, an hour, the leg). There are four kinds of nouns.

PROPER NOUNS

These name individual persons, places or things (e.g. George, London, Easter). A proper noun should begin with a capital letter.

COMMON NOUNS

These name one or more of a group of objects that are alike (e.g. girl, lion, cat, world, sun, giant). Even if they are plural (girls, lions, cats, etc.), they are still common nouns.

COLLECTIVE NOUNS

These name a collection of objects (e.g. flock, herd, committee, crowd, dozen).

ABSTRACT NOUNS

These indicate things we cannot see, hear or touch (e.g. anger, hope, truth, pity, faith).

Although proper nouns begin with a capital letter, the others do not. Which of the following should begin with a capital letter (read the list to your child and have him tell you the answer):

107

tuesday — *yes*   easter — *yes*   swallow — *no*

FACING-PAGE QUIZ. *On the opposite page a number of well-known objects are illustrated. Ask your child to guess what the objects are and tell you whether A or AN should be used before each of them (answers are at the foot of page 108).*

susan — *yes*	rainfall — *no*	master — *no*
host — *no*	glasgow — *yes*	thomas — *yes*
football — *no*	may (the month) — *yes—otherwise, the answer is "no"*	

Now have your child tell you the letters that should be in capitals (make sure the answers are covered):

london is the largest town in england   (*London, England*)

i am j. a. brown of 21 sidcup lane, dover   (*I, J. A. Brown, Sidcup Lane, Dover*)

Read the following sentences to your child and let him tell you which are the nouns (they are underlined):

The <u>classroom</u> contains the <u>teacher</u> and the <u>pupils</u>.

The <u>fire</u> was burning brightly in the <u>grate</u>.

Now ask your child to form nouns from the following (the answers are in italics), and point out any difficult spellings to him:

able	*ability*	absent	*absence*
accept	*acceptance*	accurate	*accuracy*
advise	*advice*	anxious	*anxiety*
achieve	*achievement*	announce	*announcement*
ascend	*ascent*	advertise	*advertisement*
angry	*anger*	arrive	*arrival*
amuse	*amusement*	beautiful	*beauty*
begin	*beginning*	carry	*carriage*
confuse	*confusion*	cowardly	*cowardice*
choose	*choice*	childish	*child*

108

Answers to quiz on previous page: 1. an aeroplane   2. a bucket   3. an apple   4. an engine or a locomotive   5. a cow   6. an egg cup   7. a spanner   8. a car or an automobile   9. a lamp standard or lamp post   10. an ice cream   11. an orange   12. a mallet   13. a ship, steamer or cargo boat   14. an umbrella (sometimes affectionately called a "brolly").

examples of different kinds of nouns

Proper noun (ALGERNON)

Common noun (PIG)

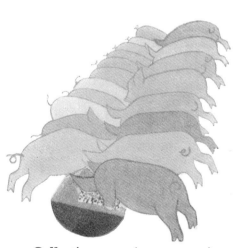

Collective noun (A LITTER)

Abstract noun (ANGER)

correct	*correction*	curious	*curiosity*
cruel	*cruelty*	clean	*cleanliness*
dark	*darkness*	captive	*captivity*
depart	*departure*	describe	*description*
defend	*defence*	deep	*depth*
decide	*decision*	deny	*denial*
do	*deed*	discreet	*discretion*
desperate	*despair*	die	*death*
difficult	*difficulty*	disappear	*disappearance*
enjoy	*enjoyment*	excite	*excitement*
expensive	*expense*	excellent	*excellence*
exhaust	*exhaustion*	encourage	*encouragement*
fail	*failure*	famous	*fame*
free	*freedom*	fragrant	*fragrance*
friend	*friendship*	frightened	*fright*
grand	*grandeur*	grieve	*grief, or grievance*
grow	*growth*	happy	*happiness*
hate	*hatred*	heroic	*hero, or heroism*
hinder	*hindrance*	honest	*honesty*
ignorant	*ignorance*	high	*height*
imagine	*imagination*	introduce	*introduction*
invite	*invitation*	impudent	*impudence*
innocent	*innocence*	infant	*infancy*
injure	*injury*	just	*justice*
know	*knowledge*	laugh	*laughter*
long	*length*	lose	*loss*
loyal	*loyalty*	lunatic	*lunacy*
man	*manhood*	move	*movement*
noisy	*noise*	obedient	*obedience*

perform	*performance*	pure	*purity*
peaceful	*peace*	please	*pleasure*
popular	*popularity*	prove	*proof*
poor	*poverty*	proud	*pride*
receive	*receipt*	rapid	*rapidity*
reveal	*revelation*	remember	*remembrance*
refuse	*refusal*	secure	*security*
serve	*service*	responsible	*responsibility*
silent	*silence*	skilful	*skill*
see	*sight*	sit	*seat*
strong	*strength*	simple	*simplicity*
satisfy	*satisfaction*	speak	*speech*
splendid	*splendour*	true	*truth*
timid	*timidity*	think	*thought*
ugly	*ugliness*	vain	*vanity*
warm	*warmth*	weigh	*weight*
wise	*wisdom*		

verbs

· ·

A verb is a doing or telling word. It says something about the subject:

In "Tom *hit* the ball" the verb is *hit*.

In "The ball *was hit*" the words *was hit* form the verb.

In "The ball *will be hit*" the words *will be hit* form the verb.

111

Read the following phrases to your child and ask him to fit suitable verbs into the blank spaces—give him a clue by telling him the first syllables of each verb:

to in—— a fortune	(inherit)
to un — an operation	(undergo)
to re—— a seat in a train	(reserve)
to re—— a secret	(reveal)
to ab—— a sinking ship	(abandon)
to de—— a war	(declare)

A verb is a doing *or* telling *word. She* shouts *because the old lady is very deaf.* (shouts *is a verb.*)

112

"To turn", a verb with many friends.

Use the verb "to turn" in interesting sentences with each of the following words:

down   back   in   off   on   out   over   round   up   to

Here are a number of verbs used in their different tenses. Use the list in this way:

1. Read out to your child a line from column (a) e.g. "Today I am".

2. Run your eye further along the line and read out the first two words of column (b) "Yesterday I —" and get your child to give you the correct verb (printed in italic).

3. Continue across the page, and see if your child can complete the entire line correctly.

(a)	(b)	(c)	(d)
Today I am	yesterday I *was*	I shall *be*	I have *been*
Today I arise	yesterday I *arose*	I shall *arise*	I have *arisen*
Today I awake	yesterday I *awoke*	I shall *awake*	I have *awakened*
Today I bear	yesterday I *bore*	I shall *bear*	I have *borne*
Today I begin	yesterday I *began*	I shall *begin*	I have *begun*
Today I blow	yesterday I *blew*	I shall *blow*	I have *blown*
Today I break	yesterday I *broke*	I shall *break*	I have *broken*
Today I bring	yesterday I *brought*	I shall *bring*	I have *brought*
Today I bite	yesterday I *bit*	I shall *bite*	I have *bitten*
Today I buy	yesterday I *bought*	I shall *buy*	I have *bought*
Today I catch	yesterday I *caught*	I shall *catch*	I have *caught*
Today I choose	yesterday I *chose*	I shall *choose*	I have *chosen*
Today I come	yesterday I *came*	I shall *come*	I have *come*
Today I creep	yesterday I *crept*	I shall *creep*	I have *crept*
Today I cry	yesterday I *cried*	I shall *cry*	I have *cried*
Today I do	yesterday I *did*	I shall *do*	I have *done*
Today I draw	yesterday I *drew*	I shall *draw*	I have *drawn*
Today I drink	yesterday I *drank*	I shall *drink*	I have *drunk*
Today I drive	yesterday I *drove*	I shall *drive*	I have *driven*
Today I eat	yesterday I *ate*	I shall *eat*	I have *eaten*
Today I fall	yesterday I *fell*	I shall *fall*	I have *fallen*

8—H.T.

113

Today I feel   yesterday I *felt*   I shall *feel*   I have *felt*
Today I fight   yesterday I *fought*   I shall *fight*   I have *fought*
Today I find   yesterday I *found*   I shall *find*   I have *found*
Today I fly   yesterday I *flew*   I shall *fly*   I have *flown*
Today I forget   yesterday I *forgot*   I shall *forget*   I have *forgotten*
Today I freeze   yesterday I *froze*   I shall *freeze*   I have *frozen*

114

Tom hit the ball. Name the proper noun, noun and verb in this sentence.
(Answers at foot of page 130.)

Today I give	yesterday I *gave*	I shall *give*	I have *given*
Today I go	yesterday I *went*	I shall *go*	I have *gone*
Today I grow	yesterday I *grew*	I shall *grow*	I have *grown*
Today I have	yesterday I *had*	I shall *have*	I have *had*
Today I hide	yesterday I *hid*	I shall *hide*	I have *hidden*
Today I hurt	yesterday I *hurt*	I shall *hurt*	I have *hurt*
Today I keep	yesterday I *kept*	I shall *keep*	I have *kept*
Today I kneel	yesterday I *knelt*	I shall *kneel*	I have *knelt*
Today I know	yesterday I *knew*	I shall *know*	I have *known*
Today I lay	yesterday I *laid*	I shall *lay*	I have *laid*
Today I leave	yesterday I *left*	I shall *leave*	I have *left*
Today I lie	yesterday I *lay*	I shall *lie*	I have *lain*
Today I lend	yesterday I *lent*	I shall *lend*	I have *lent*
Today I make	yesterday I *made*	I shall *make*	I have *made*
Today I pay	yesterday I *paid*	I shall *pay*	I have *paid*
Today I ride	yesterday I *rode*	I shall *ride*	I have *ridden*
Today I read	yesterday I *read*	I shall *read*	I have *read*
Today I ring	yesterday I *rang*	I shall *ring*	I have *rung*
Today I rise	yesterday I *rose*	I shall *rise*	I have *risen*
Today I run	yesterday I *ran*	I shall *run*	I have *run*
Today I say	yesterday I *said*	I shall *say*	I have *said*
Today I see	yesterday I *saw*	I shall *see*	I have *seen*
Today I sell	yesterday I *sold*	I shall *sell*	I have *sold*
Today I shake	yesterday I *shook*	I shall *shake*	I have *shaken*
Today I sing	yesterday I *sang*	I shall *sing*	I have *sung*
Today I show	yesterday I *showed*	I shall *show*	I have *shown*
Today I sleep	yesterday I *slept*	I shall *sleep*	I have *slept*
Today I speak	yesterday I *spoke*	I shall *speak*	I have *spoken*
Today I swim	yesterday I *swam*	I shall *swim*	I have *swum*

115

Today I tear	yesterday I *tore*	I shall *tear*	I have *torn*
Today I teach	yesterday I *taught*	I shall *teach*	I have *taught*
Today I take	yesterday I *took*	I shall *take*	I have *taken*
Today I think	yesterday I *thought*	I shall *think*	I have *thought*
Today I wear	yesterday I *wore*	I shall *wear*	I have *worn*
Today I win	yesterday I *won*	I shall *win*	I have *won*
Today I write	yesterday I *wrote*	I shall *write*	I have *written*

See if your child can form verbs (in italic) from the following:

admission	*admit*	assembly	*assemble*	choice	*choose*
composition	*compose*	critic	*criticise*	defiance	*defy*
explanation	*explain*	health	*heal*	life	*live*
moisture	*moisten*	sale	*sell*	fat	*fatten*
comparison	*compare*	dark	*darken*	entrance	*enter*
description	*describe*	pleasure	*please*	sight	*see*
solution	*solve*	studious	*study*	food	*feed*
grief	*grieve*	long	*lengthen*	obedience	*obey*
sharp	*sharpen*	strong	*strengthen*	simple	*simplify*
strife	*strive*	terror	*terrify*	soft	*soften*
thought	*think*	trial	*try*	black	*blacken*

Some difficult ones:

friend	*befriend*	danger	*endanger*	peril	*imperil*

116

The same word can be a different part of speech in different circumstances:

(a) a man who minds the trains

(b) a man who trains the minds

In (a) "minds" is the verb and "trains" is the noun. In (b) their roles are reversed.

adjectives

· ·

An adjective is a word used to describe a noun or pronoun:

  kind boy *large black* knife *lucky* me!

Adjectives are tell-tales, informers, gossips. They can be used before or after the noun:

  the *tall, strong* man *or* the man is *tall and strong*

An adjective formed from a proper noun is spelt with a capital letter:

  English American Christian

117

The kind Boy Scout is helping the old blind man across the road. Which are the adjectives in this sentence?　(Answer at foot of page 130.)

Have your child add suitable adjectives to the following nouns (try to get adjectives which are frequently associated with the noun, e.g. industrious beaver, brave rescuer, dainty dancer):

beaver	fairy	rescuer	giant	dancer
rose	road	breeze	parcel	villain

Now ask your child what nouns he associates with these adjectives (the words in italic are good replies, but anything suitable will do):

an ancient	*city, cathedral*	a brave	*soldier*
a dainty	*fairy, dancer*	a hearty	*laugh*
a famous	*general, actor, politician*		
a haughty	*lady*	a graceful	*dancer, swan*
a juicy	*orange*	a perilous	*journey*
a rosy	*apple*	a rippling	*brook*
a silvery	*laugh*	a stern	*teacher, parent*
a busy	*street, bee*	a curious	*statement, child*
a huge	*giant*	a muddy	*river, street*
a wise	*man, teacher*	a faithful	*dog, friend*

Let your child form adjectives from the following words. The adjectives are the words in italic:

ability	*able*	alarm	*alarming*
adventure	*adventurous*	amuse	*amusing*
angel	*angelic*	affection	*affectionate*
anger	*angry*	anxiety	*anxious*
athlete	*athletic*	attract	*attractive*
beauty	*beautiful*	Britain	*British* (note
care	*careful*		capital B)
caution	*cautious*	cheer	*cheerful*
circle	*circular*	comfort	*comfortable*

comic	*comical*	coward	*cowardly*
cruelty	*cruel*	curiosity	*curious*
custom	*customary*	danger	*dangerous*
deceive	*deceitful*	desire	*desirable*
disaster	*disastrous*	disgrace	*disgraceful*
distance	*distant*	doubt	*doubtful*
energy	*energetic*	expense	*expensive*
faith	*faithful*	fame	*famous*
father	*fatherly*	fortune	*fortunate*
friend	*friendly*	France	*French* (note
giant	*gigantic*		capital F)
girl	*girlish*	glory	*glorious*
gold	*golden*	grace	*graceful*
heat	*hot*	hero	*heroic*
honour	*honourable*	imagine	*imaginary*
industry	*industrious*	joy	*joyous*
justice	*just*	length	*long*
luxury	*luxurious*	love	*lovely* or *loving*
man	*manly*	mischief	*mischievous*
mountain	*mountainous*	muscle	*muscular*
mystery	*mysterious*	music	*musical*
nature	*natural*	nation	*national*
number	*numerous*	patriot	*patriotic*
patience	*patient*	peril	*perilous*
picture	*picturesque*	pity	*pitiful*
please	*pleasant*	poison	*poisonous*
power	*powerful*	pride	*proud*
profit	*profitable*	prosper	*prosperous*
quarrel	*quarrelsome*	rag	*ragged*

119

sense	*sensible* or *senseless*	science	*scientific*
sheep	*sheepish*	silence	*silent*
skill	*skilful*	slave	*slavish*
sympathy	*sympathetic*	strength	*strong*
succeed	*successful*	talk	*talkative*
terror	*terrible*	trouble	*troublesome*
truth	*truthful*	triumph	*triumphant*
vacancy	*vacant*	value	*valuable*
villain	*villainous*	victory	*victorious*
width	*wide*	winter	*wintry*
wonder	*wonderful*	youth	*youthful*

Ask your child to think up suitable adjectives to be used *before* the following nouns (good answers are in italic; accept anything suitable, and encourage him to use his imagination).

apple	*rosy*	mistake	*serious*
alarm	*false*	mother	*loving*
brook	*babbling*	nook	*sheltered*
clouds	*fleecy*	sea	*calm, rough, salt*
corn	*golden*	sky	*blue, clear*
day	*fine*	sums	*difficult, easy*
fields	*green*	sunshine	*brilliant*
mule	*stubborn, obstinate*	torrent	*raging*

Now ask him to supply other adjectives, in place of those in italic:

a *rotten* attempt (poor)

an *awful* shock (a severe)

a *dry* book (an uninteresting)

a *poor* show (an unenjoyable)

lovely weather	(fine)
a *terrible* downpour	(severe)
beastly luck	(bad)
a *nasty* trick	(an unkind)

SHE WAS WEARING A SHABBY SKIRT WITH A DREADFUL BLOUSE AND YET SHE HAD A LOVELY NECKLACE.......

The lady gossiping over the garden fence is using several adjectives; can you spot them all? (*Answers at foot of page 130.*)

Adjectives may be used in a special way. Ask your child what we mean by the following expressions (answers in italic):

a heavy heart	*sad*
a bright face	*glad*
a firm manner	*determined*
hard work	*difficult*
a stormy meeting	*noisy*
honeyed words	*flattering*

121

pronouns

. . . .

A pronoun is a word (such as I, he, it, they) used instead of a noun so that sentences can be of reasonable length:

My brother John picked up the cup and then *he* dropped *it*.

Here; *he* is used instead of *my brother John*, and *it* for *cup*. They are pronouns, and by using them we avoid tiresome repetition of the nouns.

John picked up the cup and then he *dropped* it.

See if your child can join these sentences by using the correct pronoun:

John is his name, and John lives near us.

(John is his name, and *he* lives near us.)

They are good children, and we like good children.

(They are good children, and we like *them*.)

122

Now, see if your child can use who, whom, whose, which, or what, correctly. Keeping the answers hidden, let him tell you the word he thinks is the correct one.

example : (Who, Whom, Whose, Which, What) did that ?

It was you (who, whom, whose, which, what) did it.   who

To (who, whom, whose, which, what) are you taking that ?

whom

She is the girl (who, whom, whose, which, what) book I borrowed.   whose

Here is the car (who, whom, whose, which, what) is for sale.

which

(Who, Whom, Whose, Which, What) is the matter ?   What

Ride the horse (who, whom, whose, which, what) you find there.   which

conjunctions

· ·

A conjunction is a joining word. The most commonly used is "and".

bread *and* butter   pepper *and* salt   milk *and* sugar

123

A conjunction is a joining word. Here you can see Miss Conjunction joining Miss Word One with Miss Word Two.

Here are two sentences which can be run into one, by the use of a conjunction:

>Jack fell down. He hurt himself.
>
>Jack fell down, *and* he hurt himself.

When two sentences are joined, a comma is needed before the conjunction, but one does not otherwise use a comma before "and". Children use "and" too frequently. Many other words can be used instead, for instance:

after	although	as	because
before	but	for	so
while	yet	if	when

Let your child use them in joining the following sentences:

>I went home. I had finished work.   (when)
>
>I am not thirsty. I have just had a lemonade.   (for, because)
>
>Give my book back to me. I shall need it.   (as)
>
>Helen came into the room. She gave me the book. She had just finished reading.   (and, which)
>
>He laughed happily. He had just scored a goal. The referee said he was offside.   (for, but)

adverbs

· ·

124

An adverb describes the verb (it is a gossip, like its relative the adjective!). It tells us how, when, or where:

>Tom ran *swiftly* up the stairs

An adverb can also go before the verb:

>*Swiftly* Tom ran up the stairs

Most adverbs are formed from corresponding adjectives by adding ly:

slow*ly*   beautiful*ly*   angri*ly*

The girl had a sweet voice — The girl sang sweet*ly*

They made a quick start — They started quick*ly*

Ask your child to do this with:

The slow horse galloped home — (The horse galloped home slowly)

Ask your child to change the following adjectives into adverbs (in italic):

| easy | *easily* | frequent | *frequently* |
| safe | *safely* | simple | *simply* |

Change the following nouns into adverbs (in italic):

ability	*ably*	happiness	*happily*
joy	*joyfully*	faith	*faithfully*
fury	*furiously*	insolence	*insolently*
folly	*foolishly*	accident	*accidentally*
silence	*silently*	depth	*deeply*
humility	*humbly*	vigour	*vigorously*

Ask your child to write three sentences, in all of which the word "light" must be used:

In the first sentence, as a verb (e.g. Please *light* the fire).

In the second sentence, as a noun (e.g. Please give me a *light*).

In the third sentence, as an adjective (e.g. The boy could only lift the *light* weight).

125

See if your child can add adverbs to the following verbs (suitable adverbs in brackets):

to run (quickly)   to see (clearly)

to arrive (punctually)   to shout (loudly)
to shine (brightly)   to write (neatly)
to dance (gracefully)   to hate (intensely)
to contribute (generously)   to ignore (completely)

prepositions

A preposition shows the relationship between two things. Here are two examples:

Tom is *on* the field.   Tom called *for* the cricket bag.

Your child must learn to use the correct preposition (e.g. similar *to* but different *from*):

His pen is similar *to* yours.
His school is different *from* yours.

Another common mistake in choosing a preposition is in confusing *with* and *at*. They should be used as follows:

He was impatient *with* her. (*with* goes with a person)
He was impatient *at* the delay. (*at* goes with a thing)

Test your child by reading aloud the following list and getting him to tell you the correct preposition (in italic) to use with each word:

agree	*with*	hope	*for*	associate	*with*
to be fond	*of*	look	*at*	confide	*in*
differ	*from*	contrast	*with*	liking	*for*
decide	*upon*	prepare	*for*	resign	*from*
rely	*on*	speak	*to*	submit	*to*
attracted	*to* or *by*	tinker	*with*	repelled	*by*
at break	*of* day		*through* thick and thin		

singulars and plurals

· ·

A singular noun refers to one thing and a plural refers to more than one—*hat* is singular and *hats* is the plural; similarly *ox* and *oxen*. There are no set rules for forming the plural from the singular. As in spelling, one follows, as it were, a convention and learns by experience. The following tabulated list is however very comprehensive (for an 11-year-old) and will help your child to remember all that he needs on this subject.

To form the plural we usually just add an *s* to the singular:

top	*tops*	book	*books*	day	*days*
valley	*valleys*	girl	*girls*	picture	*pictures*
cake	*cakes*	pencil	*pencils*		

Words ending in x, s, sh, or ch. To these words we add es:

fox	*foxes*	box	*boxes*	tax	*taxes*
hiss	*hisses*	glass	*glasses*	wish	*wishes*
watch	*watches*	church	*churches*		

Words ending in f or fe. We usually change the f to v and add es or s:

life	*lives*	knife	*knives*	half	*halves*
leaf	*leaves*	loaf	*loaves*	calf	*calves*
shelf	*shelves*	wolf	*wolves*		

The exceptions are:

dwarfs	roofs	chiefs	reefs
proofs	gulfs	strifes	

Some have two plurals:

scarfs and scarves	turfs and turves
wharfs and wharves	hoofs and hooves

127

Words ending in y. Where the y is preceded by a vowel we just add an s:

| day | *days* | boy | *boys* | key | *keys* |

Where the y is preceded by a consonant, we change the y to i and add es:

baby	*babies*	lady	*ladies*	fly	*flies*
army	*armies*	city	*cities*	reply	*replies*
daisy	*daisies*	family	*families*		

penny has two plurals—*pennies* and *pence*

On the left is a glass *(singular); for the plural we add* -es *and get* glasses. *How many glasses can you see here altogether?* (*Answer at foot of page 130.*)

Words ending in o. Add es:

| cargo | *cargoes* | potato | *potatoes* | hero | *heroes* |
| negro | *negroes* | echo | *echoes* | | |

The exceptions are pianos, banjos, halos, solos. There are no hard and fast rules in this group. We just have to remember.

Some words have old English or foreign plurals:

| man | *men* | child | *children* | radius | *radii* |

With nouns needing a hyphen, we make the more important word the plural:

paint-brush	paint-*brushes*	hat-box	hat-*boxes*
goal-kick	goal-*kicks*	carving-knife	carving-*knives*
commander-in-chief	*commanders*-in-chief	fighter-bomber	fighter-*bombers*
sister-in-law	*sisters*-in-law	hanger-on	*hangers*-on
maid-servant	maid-*servants*		

Note: man-servant   *men-servants* (both words change)

Miss Smith   *The Misses* Smith

Words ending in "ful" form the plural by adding s to the end of the word:

cupfuls   handfuls   housefuls

Unusual plurals:

louse	*lice*	tooth	*teeth*	goose	*geese*
foot	*feet*	mouse	*mice*	ox	*oxen*

Sometimes the same word is used for the plural:

deer   sheep grouse fowl   corps   mackerel fish
cod   salmon trout   swine dozen (we say: four dozen,
                                             but: there are dozens!)

Some nouns only have a plural. They have no singular:

riches	tongs	trousers	scissors	billiards
bellows	thanks	means	measles	shears
pliers	pincers	gallows	goods	

Yet we talk of *trouser-button* and *billiard-ball.*

Some nouns have no plural:

advice   news   furniture

e.g. The news *is* good (singular)

9—H.T.

129

Some words change their meaning in plural form:

| manner | *manners* | brace | *braces* | spectacle | *spectacles* |
| copper | *coppers* | force | *forces* | air | *airs* |

Have your child make up interesting sentences showing that he understands both meanings.

Ask your child to change all the nouns to plural in:

His foot hurt him — *Their feet hurt them*

He robbed the men's shop — *They robbed the men's shops*

Have him give the singular of (and make sure that he can spell them):

carriages	*carriage*	ditties	*ditty*	geese	*goose*
leaves	*leaf*	mice	*mouse*	times	*time*
theirs	*his*	we	*I*	halves	*half*

and the plural of:

myself	*ourselves*	baby	*babies*	calf	*calves*
church	*churches*	city	*cities*	knife	*knives*
motorcar	*motorcars*	valley	*valleys*		
sister-in-law	*sisters*-in-law	passer-by		*passers*-by
man-eater	man-*eaters*	that		*those*
himself	*themselves*	this		*these*

Certain terms are used in connection with some particular plurals. For instance; instead of saying, "a lot of soldiers" or "a lot of ships", we say "an army of soldiers", "a fleet of ships". Have your child learn the following:

130

an anthology of poems

an army of soldiers

(know and spell; bayonets, battalion, troops, regiment. A soldier who has just enlisted is known as a *recruit*)

Answers to quizzes: p. 114, Tom, ball, hit; p. 117, kind, old, blind; p. 121, shabby, dreadful, lovely; p. 128, 8.

Which caption fits which illustration? Write on a slip of paper the correct caption from the list below for each picture (answers at the foot of page 132). a duet — a trio — a solo — a quartet

a bale of cotton, or wool

a battery of guns

a band, or orchestra of musicians

a bench of magistrates, or bishops

a batch, or sheaf of papers

a bevy of ladies

a block of houses

a board of directors

a bouquet of flowers

a brood of chicks

a bunch of grapes, keys, or bananas

a bundle of rags, clothes, rubbish or sticks

a catch or haul of fish

a chest of drawers

a choir of singers

A —— of magistrates; what is the missing word?

a class of scholars

a clod of earth

a clump of trees

a cluster of stars, grapes, trees, shrubs or diamonds

Answers to quiz on previous page: 1. a solo   2. a duet   3. a trio   4. a quartet.

a clutch of eggs

a collection of stamps or pictures

a company of actors

a crate of goods, or fruit

a crew of sailors

a crowd of people

a family of relatives

a fleet of ships, or motorcars

a flight of steps, or birds

a flock of sheep

a forest, or spinney of trees

a formation of aeroplanes

a gang, or team of labourers

a gaggle of geese

a galaxy of stars

a herd of cattle (e.g. cows, deer)

a hoard of money

a horde of savages

a host of angels

a library of books

a litter of cubs, pups, pigs, or kittens

a load of trouble, worries, or hay

a mob of disorderly people (robbers, thieves, gangsters)

an orchard of fruit trees

a pack of cards, wolves, hounds, or asses

a party of people, or friends

a peal of bells

a plague of insects (particularly locusts)

a posy of flowers (also bouquet)

A —— of houses; what is the missing word?

a rope of pearls

a row of hills

a school of whales

a set of golf clubs, or tools

a sheaf of corn

a shoal of fish (e.g. herring)

a shock of hair

a skein of silk or wool

a squad of recruits, or soldiers

a stack of hay, wood or corn

a staff of servants, teachers or workers

a string of beads, or pearls

a suit of clothes

a suite of furniture, or rooms (distinguish from a suit of clothes)

a swarm of insects (bees, locusts, etc.)

a team of players, oxen or horses

a tribe of natives

a troop of horsemen (known in the army as cavalry)

a troupe of dancers or performers (but a company of actors)

a truss of hay

a tuft of grass, or hair

a volley of shots

a village of cottages (a small group would be a hamlet)

a zoo of wild animals

A — of drawers; what is the missing word?

When we are speaking of a number of people, we use the following words:

at church — *a congregation*

at a concert, theatre or cinema — *an audience*

at a football or cricket match — *spectators*

(remember, a *referee* at football and *umpires* at cricket)

in a public hall — *an assembly*

in a riot — *a mob*

rowdy people — *a rabble*

135

in a street — *a crowd*, or *throng*

thieves — *a gang*, or *a pack*

Let your child tell you what the following are known as (answers in italic):

a single eyeglass	*monocle*
a cycle with two wheels	*bicycle*
a cycle with three wheels	*tricycle*
a period of 100 years	*century*
a creature with a hundred legs	*centipede*

genders (distinction of sex)

Whilst in forming plurals the English language is more complicated than most other languages, in the matter of genders it is usually simpler. There are four genders.

MASCULINE

This denotes the male sex (e.g. man).

FEMININE

This denotes the female sex (e.g. woman).

COMMON

This denotes either sex (e.g. child, cousin)

NEUTER

This denotes an object without sex (e.g. chair, house, picture).

The feminine is formed from the masculine in one of three ways.

1. *Changing masculine to feminine by a change of word*

These are common examples which your child should know. Read out the masculine words to him, and see if he can give you the correct feminines :

bachelor	*spinster*	boar	*sow*
boy	*girl*	brave	*squaw*
brother	*sister*	buck	*doe*

A — of aeroplanes; what is the missing word?

bullock or steer	*heifer*	bull	*cow*
cock	*hen*	colt	*filly*
dog	*bitch*	drake	*duck*
drone	*bee*	earl	*countess*
fox	*vixen*	he	*she*
gentleman	*lady*	man	*woman*
master	*mistress*	nephew	*niece*
king	*queen*	Adam	*Eve*

137

sir	*madam*	son	*daughter*
stag	*doe*	stallion	*mare*
hart	*hind*	uncle	*aunt*
ram	*ewe*	wizard	*witch*
father	*mother*	monk	*nun*
gander	*goose*	husband	*wife*

A —— of furniture; what is the missing word?

2. *Changing masculine to feminine by adding a prefix* (before the word):

goat (or billy-goat   *nanny-goat*
     or he-goat)   *she-goat*

bear	*she-bear*	manservant	*maidservant*
bird (or cockbird)	*hen-bird*		

3. *Changing masculine to feminine by adding a suffix* (after the word), *or by altering the last syllable*:

abbot	*abbess*	actor	*actress*
author	*authoress*	baron	*baroness*
count	*countess*	duke	*duchess*

emperor	*empress* (note the spelling of empress)	giant	*giantess*
		governor	*governess*
		heir	*heiress*
hero	*heroine*	instructor	*instructress*
Jew	*Jewess*	lion	*lioness*
manager	*manageress*	masseur	*masseuse*
poet	*poetess*	prince	*princess*
negro	*negress*	sultan	*sultana*
tiger	*tigress*	traitor	*traitress*
waiter	*waitress*		

Note (in reverse):

bridegroom	*bride*	widower	*widow*

A — of hair; what is the missing word?   **139**

Ask your child to change the sexes in these two sentences:

    The bull attacked the milkmaid.

    (The *cow* attacked the *milkman*.)

    His master's heir is a manservant who is a bachelor.

    (*Her mistress's heiress* is a *maidservant* who is a *spinster*.)

Masculine (A COCK)   Feminine (A HEN)

examples of the different genders

Common (A STUDENT)   Neuter (A CHURCH)

Now give the masculines of:

cow	*bull*	doe	*buck*
duck	*drake*	ewe	*ram*
heifer	*young bull,*	sow	*boar or pig*
	bullock or		
	steer		

Some peculiar sexes: We speak of *Mother Nature* and *Father Time*. A ship and car are referred to as *she*, and we sometimes call a child, dog or cat *it*. We also speak of "The Motherland"—although Germans describe their country as "The Fatherland". What genders are the following:

companion	*common*	doctor	*common*
landlord	*masculine*	child	*common*
actor	*masculine*	widow	*feminine*
student	*common*		

degrees of comparison

· ·

SHORT ADJECTIVES

We say "David is *tall*", "John is *taller*", and that "Simon is the *tallest* of the three".

ONE	TWO (add *er*)	THREE OR MORE (add *est*)
tall	taller	tallest
short	shorter	shortest
sweet	sweeter	sweetest
sour	sourer	sourest

Note how we use *as,* *than* and *of*:

> David is *as* tall *as* Henry
> John is taller *than* Henry
> Cecil is the tallest *of* them all

David is tall, *John is* taller, *but Simon is the* tallest *of the three.*

If there is a silent *e* at the end of the adjective it is omitted:

| nice | nicer | nicest |
| fine | finer | finest |

A *y* at the end of a word is changed to *i*:

jolly	jollier	jolliest
dry	drier	driest
pretty	prettier	prettiest

A consonant following a short sounding vowel (i.e. the *i* in big, not the *i* in ice) is usually doubled:

| fit | fitter | fittest |
| big | bigger | biggest |

LONG ADJECTIVES

With some adjectives of two syllables, and with all adjectives containing more than two syllables, we use *more* and *most*:

ONE	TWO	THREE OR MORE
handsome	more handsome	most handsome
beautiful	more beautiful	most beautiful

Alice in Wonderland said "curiouser and curiouser", but that was because she was so surprised that she spoke bad English!

ADVERBS

These are compared in the same way as adjectives. Since most adverbs are of two or more syllables, we frequently use *more* and *most* (quickly, *more* quickly, *most* quickly), but there are exceptions, for which there are no definite rules, and your child will have to remember these:

ONE	TWO	THREE OR MORE
badly	worse	worst
well	better	best
much	more	most
near	nearer	nearest
little	less	least
far	{ farther / further	{ farthest / furthest

143

prefixes

· ·

A word may be changed by adding a prefix; here are some of them:

| BY | *near, or extra* | bystander, byproduct |
| DE | *down, or away* | depress, depose |

DIS	*not*	disagree, discuss
FORE	*in front of*	foreman, foreground
IG	*not*	ignoble
IM	*not*	impossible, improbable
IN	*not*	incapable, inescapable
MIS	*not*	mistrust, misunderstood
OFF	*from*	offspring, offshoot
OVER	*too much*	overgrow, overheat
POST	*after*	postscript, post-war
PRE	*before*	prefix, predict
RE	*again*	regain, reread, relive
SUB	*under*	submarine
UN	*not*	unhelpful, unhealthy
UNDER	*below*	underdog, underpaid
DEMI	*half*	demigod
HEMI	*half*	hemisphere
SEMI	*half*	semicircle
MONO	*one*	monoplane, monotone
BI	*two*	bicycle, bisect
TRI	*three*	tricycle, triangle
DEC	*ten*	decimal
CENTI	*a hundred*	centipede, centigrade
MULTI	*many*	multiple
POLY	*many*	polytechnic

Some prefixes go even further in changing the meanings of words and cause them to mean their opposites. Ask your child to give the opposites of these words by using the correct prefixes, and use them in suitable sentences (the answers are printed in italic):

able	*unable*	appear	*disappear*
accurate	*inaccurate*	attentive	*inattentive*
agreeable	*disagreeable*	available	*unavailable*
avoidable	*unavoidable*	beaten	*unbeaten*
behave	*misbehave*	believe	*disbelieve*
breakable	*unbreakable*	capable	*incapable*

This shows how a prefix changes a word. On the left is fit, *and then by adding three small letters we have* misfit.

conscious	*unconscious*	content	*discontent*
continue	*discontinue*	count	*miscount*
comfort	*discomfort*	curable	*incurable*
direct	*indirect*	deniable	*undeniable*
exact	*inexact*	easy	*uneasy*
educated	*uneducated*	equal	*unequal*
faithful	*unfaithful*	famous	*infamous*
forgivable	*unforgivable*	fold	*unfold*

145

fit	*unfit*	fit	*misfit*
happy	*unhappy*	honour	*dishonour*
honest	*dishonest*	human	*inhuman*
important	*unimportant*	just	*unjust*
justice	*injustice*	lead	*mislead*
legal	*illegal*	legible	*illegible*
logical	*illogical*	like	*unlike*
manage	*mismanage*	moral	*immoral*
mortal	*immortal*	natural	*unnatural*
noble	*ignoble*	own	*disown*
place	*displace* or	polite	*impolite*
	misplace	proper	*improper*
perfect	*imperfect*	please	*displease*
pleasant	*unpleasant*	possible	*impossible*
regular	*irregular*	reliable	*unreliable*
responsible	*irresponsible*	selfish	*unselfish*
safe	*unsafe*	sense	*nonsense*
sufficient	*insufficient*	trust	*distrust*
truthful	*untruthful*	twist	*untwist*
understand	*misunderstand*	usual	*unusual*
visible	*invisible*	wrap	*unwrap*

What do we mean by:

pro-American	*for, or on the side of, the Americans*
anti–Russian	*against the Russians*
semi-detached house	*detached on one side only*
post-war credit	*after-the-war credit*
pre-war standards	*before-the-war standards*
auto-biography	*self-written life story*

146

More examples of prefixes and suffixes (additions after a word)
altering the meaning of words:

thought	*after*thought *fore*thought thought*ful* thought*less*
sense	*non*sense sense*less* sens*ible*
print	*mis*print *re*print

some common grammatical mistakes

· ·

IS AND ARE

The following mistake is often heard:

> The father and his son is here.

This sentence is bad because the wrong verb (is) has been used. It should be spoken—or written—in this way:

> The father and his son *are* here.

When two singular nouns (father, son) are joined by *and*, the verb (is) must be plural (are).

Now examine these sentences:

> The father with his son is here.
>
> John like his father is tall.

In both these sentences two singular nouns (father, son — John, father) are used, but as they are joined by *with* and *like* the verb (is) in each case is singular. The singular verb (is) would also be used if **147** *as well as* linked the two nouns, as in "The butcher as well as the baker is delivering today".

Have your child select the correct verb for each of these sentences:

> The father, as well as his son is/are coming.   (is)
>
> The father and his son is/are coming.   (are)

One of them are sure to come should be : One of them *is* sure to come.
The *is* refers to one, and not them. With: *each, neither, anybody,
everybody and nobody, every, either, none* the verb is in the singular :

> Everybody was there.
>
> Neither of the girls is here.
>
> Nobody is to leave.

Get your child to point out the wrong words in these sentences; the
correct word is given in brackets after each sentence.

> Neither Dick nor Joan is/are coming.   (is)
>
> Each of them is/are coming by car.   (is)
>
> If one of your chums is in trouble, you should not hesitate to
> help him/them.   (him)

IT'S AND ITS

It's means *it is* :

> It's a fine day, it's not going to rain.

Its is used to denote possession :

> The beast raised its head.

Have your child point out the wrong word in each of these sentences :

> The dog wagged it's/its tail.   (its)
>
> This is good but it's/its not cheap.   (it's)
>
> It's/Its a long lane that has no turning.   (It's)

148

Very few people use the words : "It is I". Practically everyone these
days would say, "It is me". Although—strictly speaking—"It is I"
is correct, "It is me" is now accepted. The same applies to the
following :

> It is she (not *It is her*)   It is they (not *It is them*)
>
> It is he (not *It is him*)   It is we (not *It is us*)

YOU, ME AND I

Between you and I should be: between you and me.

you run faster than me should be: you run faster than I (do), the *do* being understood, but not spoken.

HIM AND HE

Not *she is as rich as him* but: she is as rich as he.

HER AND ME

Not *he gave her and I sweets* but: he gave her and me sweets. (This will be more easily remembered if one thinks of the sentence *He gave sweets to her and to me.*)

NEITHER AND EITHER

Neither is followed by *nor*, and *either* is followed by *or*.

> Neither you nor your friend is allowed.
>
> Either Tom or you is guilty.
>
> (Note: *is* and not *are* is used here.)

AS AND HAS, IS AND HIS

These may be confused by children because they forget to sound the *h*:

> He *has* no money but is *as* proud *as* a peacock.
>
> The boy *is* playing with *his* father.

LIE AND LAY

These words are often confused, remember:

149

you lie down now yesterday you lay down	} you have lain down
you lay a book down I lay the book down	} I have laid the book down
the hen lays an egg	yesterday the hen laid an egg
I tell a lie	yesterday I lied

Use the appropriate form of the verb *lie* or *lay* in the following:

I — in bed and listened to the radio.	(lay)
Who is going to — the table.	(lay)
The naughty boy — to the teacher.	(lied)
The dog was — asleep by the fire.	(lying)

PRACTICE AND PRACTISE

The verb (practise) is spelt with an *s* and the noun (practice) with a *c*:

The doctor has a large practice.

Practise what you preach.

I BEFORE E EXCEPT AFTER C

believe   receive

The exceptions to this rule are:

seize   neighbour   reign

FROM AND TO (see under PREPOSITIONS page 126)

Different from, but similar to. Be sure to use the right preposition. The preposition *from* goes with different, and *to* goes with similar.

CAN AND MAY

Can means: it is possible. *May* means: it is permitted.

You can fight in school, but you may not.

RISE AND RAISE

I rise at 7 a.m.

Yesterday I rose at 7.15 a.m. *but*

I raised the lid yesterday.

LIKE AND AS

Like is followed by a noun or pronoun, and *as* by a sentence:

She looks like you.

She looks as I would like to do.

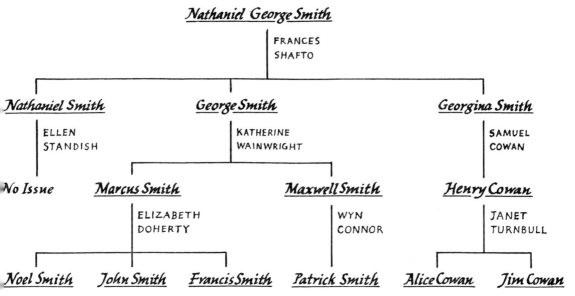

Here are some questions for your child about this family tree (the answers are at the foot of page 152).

1. How many grandchildren has George Smith and who are they? 2. What is the name of John Smith's aunt by marriage? 3. What is the name of George Smith's brother-in-law? 4. If Wyn Connor dies, who becomes a widower? 5. What was the name of Marcus Smith's grandmother before she was married?

BETWEEN AND AMONG

Between is used for two people or things, and *among* for more than two:

> She is between June and Ann.
> She is among a lot of girls.

Do not use: *between you and I,* but: *between you and me.*

Ask your child to point out the wrong words in the following sentence:

> The nuts were divided among/between the two girls, and the apples among/between the three boys. (*between, among*)

151

ALRIGHT

There is no such word as *alright*. The two words are *all* and *right*:

> He is quite all right.

We do not however recommend using this expression. "He is quite well." is better.

AIN'T

There is no such word as *ain't*. *Aren't I* is also wrong. *Am I not* is correct.

LOTS OF

Instead of "a lot of" or "lots of", use such words as; *many, much,* or *a great deal*. Do not say, "We have lots of trouble." but "We have a great deal of trouble."

LOSE AND LOOSE

Lose is a verb. Loose is an adjective

> Did they lose the match?
> I have a loose collar.

WHO, WHOM AND WHOSE

are used for people, and *that* and *which* for animals, and things.

> the girl, *who* was in front to *whom* I was talking and *whose*
> > father is my friend
> the donkey *which* was leading
> the house *that* was very large

152

TEACH AND LEARN

A teacher teaches. A pupil learns.

> I am going to learn to swim.
> My father is going to teach me.

Answers to quiz on previous page: 1. Four; Noel, John, Francis and Patrick Smith
2. Wyn Connor 3. Samuel Cowan 4. Maxwell Smith 5. Frances Shafto.

STATIONARY AND STATIONERY

Stationary means motionless. Stationery means writing-material.

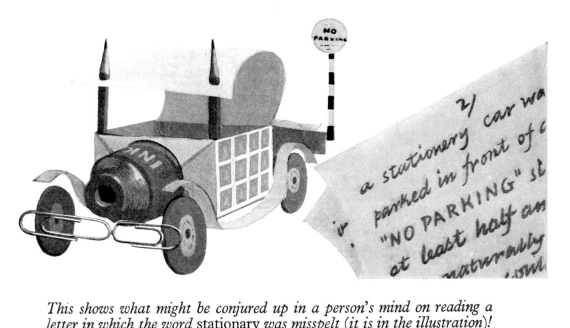

This shows what might be conjured up in a person's mind on reading a letter in which the word stationary *was misspelt (it is in the illustration)!*

COLLECTIVE NOUNS

Such as; herd, team, flock, committee.

> Do not say, "The team are good."
>> but, "The team is good."
> Do not say, "The flock have disappeared."
>> but, "The flock has disappeared."

for if the collective noun (team, flock) is to be regarded as a *single unit*   **153**
it is followed by a singular verb (has).

DON'T

means *do not*

> Do not say, "Why don't he come?" (Why do not he come)
>> but, "Why doesn't he come?" (Why does he not come).

IT DIDN'T USED TO BE *and* IT DIDN'T OUGHT TO BE
are both wrong. They should be:

> It used not to be
>
> It ought not to be

BEAUTIFUL AND BEAUTIFULLY

Beautiful is an adjective. Beautifully is an adverb.

> Do not say, "She sings beautiful."
>> but, "She sings beautifully."
>
> Do not say, "She was dressed beautiful."
>> but, "She was beautifully dressed."

SANG AND SUNG

> Do not say, "I sung last night."
>> but, "I sang last night."
>
> Do not say, "I have sang before."
>> but, "I have sung before."

WAS AND WERE

Was is used for the singular, and *were* for the plural. With *you*, always use *were*. Never say "we was" or "you was".

WHERE AND WERE

should not be confused. They are different in sound as well as in spelling:

> Where were you going?

BORROW AND LEND

You *lend* to someone, and *borrow* from someone:

> I lend you this book.
>
> You borrow this book from me.

WORDS USED TOO OFTEN

And and *so* and *then* are over-employed. A full stop can usually be used instead and a new sentence started. Discourage the frequent use of the following words unless they are absolutely necessary and correct:

terrible	terribly
get	got
awful	awfully
decent	lovely
nice	nasty
bad	pretty
said	wizard
thing	rotten
funny	really

Such words are often used because children (and adults!) are too lazy to find a more exact word. For instance, for *said* we could use one of the following words which would much more accurately express what we wished to say:

exclaimed	snarled	suggested
whispered	growled	replied
remarked	demanded	admitted
advised	announced	answered
asked	chattered	complained
confessed	cried	declared
drawled	enquired	explained
grumbled	informed	mentioned
mumbled	muttered	promised
laughed	reminded	shouted
snapped	stammered	warned

155

Have your child use each of the above words in a suitable sentence.

We sometimes find *nice* being used when: agreeable, delicious, fine, charming, polite, jolly or pleasant, would be more accurate.

Got is one of the world's most over-worked words. Encourage your child to use alternative and more suitable words. Here are some examples :

> *do not say* I got these apples in the market.
>> *but* I bought these apples in the market.
>
> *do not say* He got hold of a hammer.
>> *but* He seized a hammer.
>
> *do not say* I've got two shillings.
>> *but* I have two shillings.

See if your child can find words to replace *got* in these sentences :

> He got bacon for his breakfast — *was given*
> He got to school in good time — *arrived at*
> He got a bad mark yesterday — *received*
> His teacher got engaged last month — *became*
> He got a pencil with the sixpence he got from his father —
> *He bought a pencil with the sixpence he received from his father*

Get is also a word that is too often heard and seen.

Instead of *awfully*, use *very*. Never say "*awfully good*" when you mean "*very good*". Instead of *O.K.* use *yes, fine* or *certainly*.

The word *thing* is also over-used :

> *do not say* There is one thing I want to say.
>> *but* There is one statement I want to make.
>
> *do not say* I was talking about that thing.
>> *but* I was talking about that object.

Ask your child to use more suitable words in place of those in italic (keep the answers concealed):

It was a *nice* day.

(beautiful)

He was an *awful* boy.

(horrid)

She was *terribly decent*.

(very friendly)

It was an awfully funny smell.

(The smell was a peculiar one)

He *has really got to go.*

(He must go now)

It was *nice* to see you with that *nice* girl, at the *nice* party where we met those *nice* boys who sang so *nicely*.

(It was very pleasant to see you with that charming girl, at the enjoyable party, where we met those gay boys who sang so beautifully)

Some common pronunciation errors:

not *libery* but *library*

not *pitcher* but *picture*

not *hundrud* but *hundred*

not *jest* but *just*

157

UNNECESSARY WORDS

In each of the following sentences there is an unnecessary word. Cover the answers and see if your child can say which they are:

The two twins are here.	*two*
The shop should open up soon.	*up*
Are you coming later on?	*on*

Eat your food up.	*up*
Is everything all ready?	*all*
Which do you prefer better, sweets or chocolates?	*better*
He returned it back to me.	*back*
I hope to see more happier days.	*more*
He is much more taller than I am.	*more*
John is more heavier than Jim.	*more*

Does your child know the names for all the different parts of a bicycle?
(Answers are at the foot of page 160.)

Let your child correct these sentences:

He could neither read or write.	(nor write)
He speaks French very easy.	(easily)

He has wrote to her.	(written)
There son is their.	(Their son is there)
There was a lot of boys at the party.	(There were many)
You and me are going to the fair.	(You and I)
Teacher learnt us fractions today.	(taught)
He is as clever as her.	(as she [is])
I cannot see it nowhere.	(anywhere)
When you buy a bat and ball it is a pound.	(It costs a pound to buy a bat and ball)
That is for you and I.	(and me)
One of the sisters are early.	(is early)
She arrived later than him.	(than he [did])
The servants' are hurrying to carry parcel's to all the guest's rooms.	(The servants are hurrying to carry parcels to all the guests' rooms)
The two first songs were delightful.	(The first two songs [there cannot be *two* firsts!])
She and me are going for a walk.	(She and I)
Between you and I she is not coming.	(you and me)
Neither of the two boys were late.	(was)
Neither of us like eggs.	(likes)
He is the worst of the two.	(worse)
Which is the most sunny month, June or August?	(more)
Give him the larger of the 3 portions.	(largest)
Who do you see?	(Whom)
Who were you speaking to?	(To whom were you speaking?)

159

The envelope was addressed to Mr. John Brown Esq.	(either Mr. John Brown or John Brown Esq.)
I will try and do it.	(I will try to do it)
A large party of boys are expected today.	(is expected)
This room wants painting badly.	(This room very much needs to be painted)
None of the children were coming.	(was)
Can I lend your pen?	(May I borrow your pen?)
Try and be there.	(Try to be there)
If anyone comes, ask them to come in.	(him)
Have you those kind of sweets?	(that kind of sweet)
This bottle will be charged twopence.	(There will be a charge of twopence for the bottle. [The bottle is not going to pay twopence!])
He was riding a horse wearing flannel trousers.	(He was wearing flannel trousers and riding a horse. [The horse was not wearing flannel trousers!])

160

Answers to quiz on page 158: 1. saddle   2. handlebar grips   3. bell   4. handlebar stem   5. brake lever   6. brake cable   7. cross bar   8. gear lever   9. pennant or flag   10. front lamp   11. mudguard   12. front forks   13. tyre   14. hub   15. wing-nuts   16. mudflap   17. rim   18. pedal   19. chain   20. dynamo   21. pump   22. rear light   23. mudguard stays   24. reflector   25. carrier   26. saddlebag   27. seat pillar.

Which is correct:

> There coming tomorrow
>
> They're coming tomorrow
>
> Their coming tomorrow   (They're)

The following sentence is correct, answer it:

> A man left £20,000 to be divided equally between his sons, how much did each get and why?
>
> (£10,000 each, for *between* may only be used for two; it would be *among* if there were more than two.)

ENVELOPES

should be addressed in this way:

> Mrs. Brown,
>
>   7, Tudor Road,
>
>   London,
>
>   S.W.23.

begin the address half way down the envelope in the middle.

abbreviations

· ·

The following abbreviations are commonly used, and should be known by your child:

161

Mr.	*Mister*	S.O.S.	*Save our Souls*
O.H.M.S.	*On Her Majesty's Service*	H.M.S.	*Her Majesty's Ship*
		B.A.	*Bachelor of Arts*
R.A.F.	*Royal Air Force*	G.P.O.	*General Post Office*
P.O.	*Postal Order*	V.C.	*Victoria Cross*
M.A.	*Master of Arts*	P.T.O.	*please turn over*

11—H.T.

M.P.	*Member of Parliament*	J.P.	*Justice of the Peace*
Dr.	*Doctor*	B.B.C.	*British Broadcasting*
P.C.	*postcard, police constable*		*Corporation*
B.Sc.	*Bachelor of Science*	C.O.D.	*cash on delivery*
m.p.h.	*miles per hour*	m.p.g.	*miles per gallon*
No.	*number*	St.	*Saint or Street*
Rd.	*Road*	R.S.V.P.	*Please reply (from*
U.K.	*United Kingdom*		*French)*
l.b.w.	*leg before wicket*	Ltd.	*Limited*
Esq.	*Esquire*	B.C.	*Before Christ*
A.D.	*since Christ was born*	a.m.	*before noon (from*
	(from Latin)		*Latin)*
p.m.	*after noon (from*	o'clock	*of the clock*
	Latin)	Bart.	*Baronet*
viz.	*namely (from Latin)*	e.g.	*for example (from*
Rev.	*Reverend*		*Latin)*
Col.	*Colonel*	photo	*photograph*
phone	*telephone*	Co.	*Company*
etc.	*and so forth (from*	Mrs.	*Mistress, a married*
	Latin)		*woman*

Some abbreviations—although widely used in speech—should not be used in writing (unless one is quoting an actual conversation), but should be spelt out. Read out to your child the following abbreviations commonly used in conversation, and let him tell you how each one should be *written*:

162

I'm	*I am*	I haven't	*I have not*
I hadn't	*I had not*	I couldn't	*I could not*
I've	*I have*	We're	*We are*
You're	*You are*	They'll	*They will*

He doesn't	*He does not*	Don't	*Do not*
Shan't	*Shall not*	Wasn't	*Was not*
Aren't	*Are not*	Wouldn't	*Would not*
Isn't	*Is not*	Mustn't	*Must not*

Read out to your child the abbreviations below and let him write down the words in full:

exam.	*examination*	bike	*bicycle*
bus	*omnibus*	phone	*telephone*
photo.	*photograph*	pram.	*perambulator*
pub.	*public-house*	gym.	*gymnasium*
plane	*aeroplane*	Jan.	*January*
Feb.	*February*	Aug.	*August*
Sept.	*September*	Oct.	*October*
Nov.	*November*	Dec.	*December*

Ask your child what abbreviations are used for:

ounce	*oz.*	yard	*yd.*
feet	*ft.*	hundredweight	*cwt.*
pound	*lb.*		

Tell your child to write out in full the following abbreviations (be sure of the spelling):

Sq.	*Square*	Ave.	*Avenue*
Gdns.	*Gardens*	C. of E.	*Church of England*
S.W.	*South-West*	N.W.	*North-West*
N.E.	*North-East*	U.N.O.	*United Nations*
U.S.A.	*United States of America*		*Organisation*

163

VOCABULARY

. . . .

people

MOVEMENT

Words your child should be familiar with and know how to use (and spell). Have him use them in suitable sentences:

walk	march	stroll	saunter	trek	ramble
promenade	trot	tramp	stalk	roam	wander
prowl	step	tread	pace	stride	toddle
plod	shuffle	dance	limp	race	strut
hobble	swagger	stagger	stumble	loiter	

Ask your child to choose the most suitable words from among those in the brackets, to "go" with the following people:

a soldier (swaggers, marches, tramps, strides) *swaggers, marches*

a lady (steps, dances, treks) *dances*

a tired tramp (shuffles, plods, staggers, loiters, roves, strolls) *plods, staggers, loiters*

a fairy (saunters, dances) *dances*

PARTS OF THE BODY. *Ask your child to write down the names for all the parts shown opposite (answers at foot of page 166).*

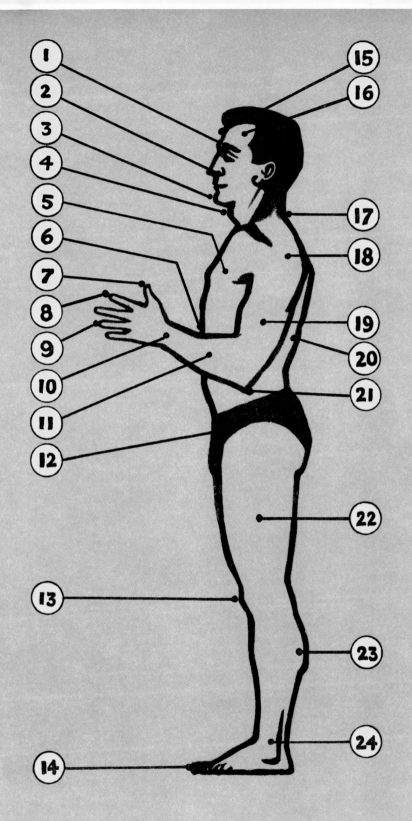

Read out to your child the following words that describe movements, and let him tell you the parts of the body with which they are usually associated (these are in italic):

clenching	*fists*	shrugging	*shoulders*
wringing	*hands*	twisting	*neck*
nodding	*head*	twiddling	*thumbs*
snapping	*fingers*	gnashing	*teeth*

APPEARANCE AND EMOTIONS

Now ask your child to put the following words into short and suitable sentences:

surprised	excited	amazed	sad	astonished
shocked	cheerful	depressed	dejected	elated
wretched	optimistic	horrified	astounded	pessimistic
melancholy	mournful	miserable	blink	laugh
giggle	titter	smirk	sing	chuckle
croon	hum	yodel	grin	sneer
guffaw	look	gaze	glance	stare

THE HUMAN VOICE

We speak of:

a sigh — *of relief*

a cry — *of delight, pain*

a groan— *of anguish*

a shriek — *of laughter, terror, anger, pain*

a bellow — *of pain, rage*

a gasp — *of relief, amazement*

166

Answers to quiz on previous page: 1. eyebrow 2. nostril 3. chin 4. Adam's apple 5. chest 6. stomach 7. thumb 8. index finger 9. ring finger 10. wrist 11. forearm 12. groin 13. knee 14. toe 15. forehead 16. temple 17. nape of neck 18. shoulder 19. upper arm 20. loin 21. elbow 22. thigh 23. calf 24. ankle.

This picture illustrates six words describing appearance or emotion. Can you decide which word fits which face: dejected, laughing, elated, pessimistic, shocked, wretched (answers at foot of page 168).

CLOTHING

Read out to your child the following descriptions of articles of clothing and ask him to name them. The answers he should give are in italic (check that he knows how to spell the answers):

167

    fireside or indoor shoes — *slippers*

    rubber shoes worn over ordinary shoes — *galoshes*

    large rubber boots worn in bad weather by children and gardeners — *Wellingtons*

    wooden shoes worn by peasants on the Continent — *clogs* (in which country generally? — *Holland*) shoes worn by the Romans and now worn in summer by children mainly — *sandals*

shoes worn by Red Indians — *moccasins*

a policeman's hat — *helmet*

a Bishop's hat — *mitre*

a motor cyclist's hat — *crash-helmet*

a hat sometimes worn by an undertaker — *top-hat*

hats worn at Easter by some women — *Easter bonnets*

a hat sometimes worn by a teacher — *mortar-board*

a peaked soft hat worn by men and boys — *cap*

a soft hat worn by men — *trilby*

sometimes worn by a bald man — *wig*

a bride's outfit — *trousseau*

Who wears the following?

Racing colours — *a jockey*

A wig and gown — *a judge*

A chain-of-office — *a mayor*

The following articles of clothing should be known and understood by your child. Make him put each into a suitable sentence:

beret	jacket	coat	waistcoat	overcoat
trousers	suit	collar	cardigan	overalls
apron	uniform	blazer	hood	pullover
sweater	busby	crown	fez	sombrero

168

GAMES AND SPORTS

Go through these with your child and make sure that he knows (and

Answers to quiz on page 167: from left to right, top row: shocked, dejected, pessimistic; bottom row: elated, wretched, laughing.

can spell) the words which are in italic:

An *archer* shoots with *bows* and *arrows*.

Boxing is done in a *ring* using *boxing gloves*. *Rounds* are boxed and a *count* may be taken.

Bowls is played on a *bowling green*.

Cricket is played on a *pitch* in a field using a *bat* and *pads*, and you may be *l.b.w.* (leg before wicket). Some people *bat*, some *field* and some *bowl*.

Football is played on a *pitch* using *shin-guards*, *goals* may be scored when *forwards* beat the *half-backs* and *backs* who are defending.

Golf is played on a *course* using *clubs*, a *driver* and *tees*. A *caddie* sometimes carries the clubs.

Running takes place on a *track* using *spiked shoes*. The order of finishing is *first, second, third . . . tenth* and so on. The race is begun by *firing* a *starting pistol* (by *pulling* the *trigger*).

Skating is done on a *rink*.

Swimming is done in a *swimming-pool* or *swimming-bath*.

Shooting is done on a *rifle-range*.

Tennis is played on a *court* using a *racket*.

An *athlete* is one *trained* in a sport.

JOBS AND TOOLS

Go through this list with your child, ask him what the person does and make sure that he knows and can spell the words in italic.

An *accountant* or *auditor* is one who *examines accounts*.

An *acrobat* is one who performs *gymnastic feats* on the *stage* or at a *circus*.

An *angler* is one who fishes with a rod.

An *architect* plans buildings.

169

An *artist* draws and paints pictures. He uses a *palette* and works in a *studio*.

An *astronomer* is one who studies the stars.

An *auctioneer* sells articles at *sales* to the highest *bidder*.

An *author* is one who writes a *book*. He may keep a *diary*, write an *auto-biography* (life story of himself) or a *biography* (life story of someone else).

An *aviator* flies—uses a *joystick* and *propeller*. He may have to use a *parachute* and a *jet-propelled* machine. A *barometer measures* the *pressure* of the air and helps others to *foretell* the weather for him.

A *baker* bakes bread in a *bakery* (*biscuit, icing, yeast, dough*).

These are the stages in making bread:

> *Ploughing* (the field)
> *Planting* or *sowing* (the seed—i.e. *planting corn to grow wheat*)
> *Hoeing* (digging up the *weeds*)
> *Reaping* (to cut the *harvest*)
> *Thrashing* (beating out the *grain* [which is kept in a *granary*] from the *straw*)
> *Grinding* (forming *flour*, from the *crop*. The man who does this is called a *miller*)
> *Kneading* (the *dough*)
> *Baking* (distinguish a *loaf* of bread from a *roll* of bread. What is *toast*? What do we mean by the "*bread-winner*"?)

A *barber* cuts hair and *shaves* men and uses a *razor*.

A *blackmailer demands* money by using *threats*.

A *blonde* is a woman with light-coloured hair.

JOBS AND TOOLS. *The picture opposite shows people who do different things; make sure that your child understands each term used.*

acrobats

aviator

bricklayer

glutton

orator

referee

A *bricklayer* lays bricks and uses *mortar,* a *trowel, plumb-line, spirit-level, hod.*

A *brunette* is a woman with dark-coloured hair.

A *butcher* is a man who cuts meat and uses a *cleaver* and also *scales, ounces, joint, weight, sausages, suet, poultry, fowl, veal, turkey.*

A *blacksmith* shoes a horse in a *smithy.*

A *cabinet-maker* makes *furniture,* a *carpenter* works with wood. In the building trade a *joiner* is a skilled carpenter (all use *pliers,* a *saw, plane, chisel, hammer*).

A *cashier* is in charge of money in a *business* or *bank.*

A *charwoman* is *employed* to clean *offices* and *houses.*

A *chauffeur* drives a car for a living.

A *chef* is the chief cook. He uses a *grill* or *oven* and works in a *kitchen.* (What is a *menu* ?)

A *chemist* is a person who makes and sells *chemicals* and *drugs* (*druggist, pharmacist, dispense, dose, scent, tonic, iron*).

A *chiropodist* looks after people's feet.

A *clergyman* or a *priest* is a man who guides us in religious matters (*spire, altar, organ, font, angel, Bible, prayer, pulpit, steeple, preach, service, halo*).

A *clerk* works in an *office* using a *desk* and writing *materials.*

A *cobbler* mends shoes and uses an *awl* and *last.* What is leather made from ? (the *hides* of animals).

172

A *collier* is a coal miner. The term is also used for a coal-carrying ship.

A *comedian* is an actor who is funny. People *clap* their hands to *applaud* him. People may have to *queue* to get into a theatre.

A *commercial traveller* is a man who travels from place to place selling *goods.*

A *competitor* is one who *competes* (i.e. takes part in something).

A *conductor* leads a *band* of musicians and uses a *baton*.

A *confectioner* sells sweets.

A *bus conductor* collects *fares* and gives you a *bus ticket*.

A *cutler* makes *cutlery* (knives and forks, etc.).

A *cyclist* rides a *bicycle* (*spokes, hub, valve, inflate* and *tandem*).

Does your child know the name for:

    The seat he sits on — *saddle*

    The things he applies to stop the cycle — *brakes*

    What are cogs — *the teeth on a gear wheel*

A *debtor* is one who cannot pay his debts to his *creditor* (*bankrupt*), (*valuable, treasure, salary, wealth, income, expense, cheque*).

A *dentist* attends to people's teeth and uses *forceps*.

A *detective tracks* down *criminals*. He *investigates* a *crime*.

A *docker* loads and unloads ships.

A *doctor* has *consultations* with *patients* in a *surgery*. The patients may be *delicate invalids* (some of whom may be *bed-ridden*), and may complain of a *fever* or *ache* and may be *infectious*. They are *examined* with a *stethoscope* and their temperature is taken with a *thermometer*. The name of their *illness* or *disease* may be written on a *certificate* and they may be given a *prescription* to take to the *chemist* in order to get *medicine* (*bruise, complaint, cough, cure, faint, germ, trouble, pulse, examine*). They may need an *operation* which is *performed* by a *surgeon*.

173

An *electrician installs* and repairs electrical articles which give heat, light or power.

A *draper* deals with cloth and uses a *yardstick* (*collars, scarf*).

A *draughtsman* draws *plans*.

A *drover* drives cattle.

An *exile* is one who is banished from his country.

An *explorer* searches for something new.

A *farmer* lives in a *farm-house*. He keeps his horses in the *stable* and his *hay* in the *barn* (*meadow, wheat*).

A *fishmonger* cuts and sells fish. He may *fillet* the fish for you (*bloater, eel, kipper, haddock, roe, sole, plaice, herring*).

A *fisherman* catches fish by *net* or *line*. *Bait* may be used in catching the fish. In shallow water the fisherman sometimes has to *wade*. In *arctic* waters *icicles* may form on the deck (*trawler, drifter*).

A *florist* sells flowers (*tulip, daffodil, bouquet, wreath, shears and scissors*).

A *furrier* deals with *furs*.

A *fugitive* is one who runs away from the law.

A *gardener* uses a *spade, fork, brush, rake, hoe, trowel, watering-can, wheel-barrow* (*soil, lawn, hedge, bean, cabbage, hoes* [compare with hose] *onion*). Use *trimming, digging* and *mowing* in sentences. Distinguish between a *farm* and an *allotment*.

A *glazier* sets glass into frames and uses a *glass cutter*.

A *glutton* is one who eats too much (*hunger, thirst*).

A *governor* is one who *governs*, or a part of a machine which *regulates* speed.

A *grocer* sells *groceries* (*tea, sugar, biscuits, cheese, coffee, cocoa, margarine, pepper, treacle, mustard, soup, porridge, beans, custard, errand, retail, sauce*).

A *greengrocer* sells *vegetables* and *fruit* (*tomato, onion, banana, cabbages, raspberries, lettuce, radish*).

To what items in a shop would you usually find attached the following notices:

new laid — *eggs*   good cookers — *apples*

freshly ground — *coffee*   sweet juicy — *oranges*

good fresh — *fish*

A *guard* is in charge of a train. A *fireman* feeds *fuel* (coal) to the *engine* or *locomotive*.

A *guest* is one who is entertained by someone else (*amuse, birthday. companion, entertain, feast, friend, invite, visitor, presents*).

A *hairdresser* attends to a lady's *hair-style* (*fashion, mirror*).

An *heir* will *inherit* someone's *wealth*.

A *hosier* sells socks and stockings.

A *host* is one who *entertains* others.

A *hypocrite* is one who pretends to be what he is not.

An *impostor* is one who is a *fraud* (*cheat*).

An *inventor* finds out something new.

A *jockey* rides a racehorse, using *stirrups, bridle, bit, saddle*, and *colours*. What does the following mean? :

to put the cart before the horse.

A *journalist* writes for a *journal* or *newspaper*.

A *labourer* is one who does work requiring little skill.

A *landlord* owns *land* or *property* and receives *rent* from a *tenant* (*owner, mansion, residence, view, pane, furniture, basin, curtain, cushion, mirror, pillow, wardrobe*).

A *lawyer* is a person who helps others deal with the law (*arrest, bail, confess, convict, disgrace, distress, guilty, jail, judge, justice, murder, oath, prison, trial*).

175

An *inquest* is an *inquiry* into the sudden death of a person. The person in charge of an inquest is known as the *coroner*.

What is meant by *bigamy*?

What do we call the *jury's decision*? (*verdict*).

A *librarian* looks after a library.

How many different kinds of books can you name?; here are some :

Bible	*dictionary*	*encyclopaedia*	*guide*
text	*travel*	*poetry*	*verse*
novel (fiction)	*romance*	*essays*	*fairy-tales*

Of course a book can be on any subject (e.g. history; such a book is known as a *history-book*, and is a *non-fiction book*).

A *locksmith* makes or mends locks (*hinge, slot*).

A *manicurist* attends to people's hands, particularly their nails.

A *mason* builds with stone and may use *cement*.

A *masseur* massages (*muscles, fat*).

A *matron* can mean either a married, elderly woman or the head of the nursing staff of a hospital, where are also to be found *sisters* in charge of *wards*, and *nurses* who use *thermometers* for measuring *temperature*.

A *mechanic* works with *machines* in a *factory* and uses a *spanner* as well as other *tools*.

Do you know and can you spell the name of the tool used by :

    a gardener to cut long grass — *scythe*

    a gardener to *trim* a *hedge* — *shears*

    a gardener to cut grass evenly — *mowing-machine*

    a barber for shaving — *razor*

    a tailor for cutting cloth — *scissors*

    a lumberjack to fell a tree — *axe*

176

A *merchant deals* or *trades* with *goods*, which he may keep in a *warehouse*.

A *milliner* makes headdresses for women (*sewing* [a seam], compare with *sowing* [seeds]. What do we call the border made by turning the edge of a piece of cloth and sewing it ? — *hem*. Also know and use : *stitch, thimble, pattern, machine, gown, tweed, thread, measure, blouse, fashion, knickers, embroider.* What does to talk through one's hat mean ? — *to talk nonsense*).

A *miner* digs in a *mine* and uses a *safety-lamp.*

A *miser hoards* money.

A *navvy* works on roads or *railways* and uses a *pick* and *shovel.*

A *newsagent* sells *newspapers* and *periodicals.*

Do you know what paper is made from ? — *wood, or certain grass or old rags.*

A *novelist* writes *novels* (or *fiction*).

An *optician* makes or sells *spectacles.*

An *optimist* sees the bright side of things (a *pessimist* sees the sad side).

An *orator* makes public *speeches.*

A *patriot* loves his country.

A *pauper* is a poor person who depends on other people's *charity.*

A *pedestrian walks, trudges, strolls, plods, marches, strides, paces, struts, limps, staggers, swaggers*; use all these words in interesting sentences.

12—H.T.

177

A *pedlar travels on foot* selling things which he carries in a *pack*. Sometimes he sells brushes. How many brushes do you know? — *tooth, paint, nail, scrubbing, boot, hair, distemper, clothes*. In what way is a broom different from a brush?

A *physician* heals people without *operating* surgically on them. This is done by a *surgeon* using a *lancet* or *forceps* in an *operating theatre*. They both write *prescriptions*. What is a *splint*?

Ripe and Juicy a	*Dairy Fresh* b
Contains Preservative c	*Freshly Roasted* d
Today's Catch e	*Local Grown* f
Home Killed g	*New Laid* h

178 *Here are some labels waiting to be attached to the foodstuffs on the right; write down which label should go with which foodstuff (answers at foot of page 180).*

A *pianist* plays the piano.

A *pilot* is one who steers a ship or a plane. He is helped by a *navigator* who advises him on the *course* being taken.

A *pilgrim* is a man who makes a long journey to a *sacred* place.

A *plumber* is an expert on the water system of a house and uses *solder*.

A *poacher trespasses* onto another's land in order to catch and steal *game*. What is meant by *game*?

A *porter* is an *attendant* or *doorkeeper* who often carries *luggage*.

A *postmaster* is in charge of a *post office* where *postage stamps* are bought (use in sentences: *telephone, licences, postal-orders, saving-certificates, parcels, packages, telegrams*).

A *potter* is one who makes *earthenware* articles.

A *poulterer* is one who sells *poultry*.

A *president* is one who *presides* (has control of, or is in charge of).

A *prospector explores* for *precious* metals, stones or *oil*.

A *railway guard* is in charge of a train and uses a *flag* and *whistle*. A flag may be waved when held (on a *mast-head* it is said to *flutter*). Use in sentences: *bridge, guard, engine, driver, platform, rail, signal, tunnel, wheel, whistle, arrival, journey*. What are *sleepers*?

A *recruit* is a *newly enlisted* sailor, soldier or airman.

A *reporter* takes notes in *shorthand* on behalf of a newspaper.

A *refugee* is a person who has taken refuge in another country.

A *referee* judges between two people or *sides*.

A *sculptor* carves or models figures (*statues*) in stone or wood.

A *seamstress* is a woman who *sews* a *seam*. She uses a *thimble*. She may work in a *laundry*.

A *servant* is one who *serves*.

179

A *shepherd* looks after sheep. He may carry a *crook*.

A *spendthrift* spends money *recklessly*.

A *star* is a very good player or performer.

A *stationer* sells writing material (*stationery*). What does *stationary* mean?

A *steeplejack* repairs tall buildings.

A *stevedore* is one who loads and unloads ships. Use in sentences: *aboard, admiral, afloat, anchor, cabin, crew, fleet, harbour, voyage, steamer, funnel, berth, cargo, saloon, compass, knot, leak, skipper, steward, yacht.*

A *stoker* attends to fires, feeding them with coal or oil.

A *stowaway* is one who hides in a ship and plans to get a free *passage*.

A *student* is one who spends his time studying (*pupil, prize, taught, learn, examine, absence, teacher, excellent, cheat, dunce, error, exercise, stupid, prove, discuss, question, answer, pencil, blackboard, easel, chalk, lesson, scholar*).

A *substitute* takes the place of another.

A *surveyor* measures land.

A *tailor* makes *suits*. Do not confuse with *suite* (of *furniture*).

A *teetotaller* is one who does not drink *alcoholic* drinks.

A *telephonist* works in a *telephone exchange* and uses *headphones* and a *switchboard.*

A *tinker* mends pans and kettles, etc.

A *tobacconist* sells tobacco (*cigar, cigarettes, lighter, packet, pouch*).

A *trapper* traps animals. If he uses a gun, he has to *load* it.

A *treasurer* looks after *money*. (A *manual worker* earns *wages*, whilst a *professional* man earns a *salary*. A *retired* man gets a *pension*. We pay *fares* when riding on trains, and pay *fines* if *guilty* of certain *minor* crimes. We give a *tip* to a waiter and may pay *rent* for our house. We would have to pay a *fee* to a *lawyer*. Use the following words correctly: *ransom, deposit, bribe, discount, interest.*)

A *tourist* makes *journeys*. He may see a *light-house*, use a *deck-chair*

180

Answers to quiz on page 178:   a — 2 or 4, b — 5, c — 7, d — 8, e — 3, f — 4 or 2, g — 6, h — 1.

and *bathe* (not *bath!*) in the sea, cross on a *ferry* and *bask* in the sunshine (*amusement, pier, restaurant, theatre, beach, breeze, ocean, luggage, parcel, pleasure, route, ticket*).

A *traitor betrays* his country or friends.

A *typist* writes letters using *shorthand*, a *typewriter* and sometimes a *duplicating machine*.

A *tyrant* is one who uses his *power unjustly*.

An *undertaker* is a man who takes charge of *funerals*. The body is *buried* in a *cemetery*.

A *valet* is a man who looks after clothes.

A *ventriloquist*, by not moving his lips, makes his voice appear to come from a "*dummy*".

A *vegetarian* is one who never eats meat or fish.

A *veteran* is one who has had much experience or practice.

A *violinist* plays the violin.

A *volunteer* offers his services of his own free will (*battle, general, cannon, victory, uniform, nation*).

A *waiter* or *waitress* is one who serves food.

A *warder* guards *convicts* in a *prison*.

A *witness* gives evidence in a *court-of-law*.

The names for some jobs end in or, er, ist, ian, ar.
Make sure your child knows when to use the correct word-ending.
It is easy to use the wrong one!

181

-OR

actor	auditor	author	aviator	competitor
conductor	decorator	doctor	editor	juror
major	orator	prospector	sculptor	surveyor
tailor	sailor			

-ER

adviser	barber	butcher	confectioner
cricketer	crooner	dispenser	docker
draper	drover	fighter	fruiterer
importer	jeweller	jester	miner
photographer	plumber	smuggler	stationer
stoker	tinker	writer	

-IST

pianist	florist	artist	dentist
cyclist	motorist	organist	tourist
journalist	novelist	ventriloquist	typist
specialist			

-IAN

librarian   mathematician   physician

-AR

pedlar   scholar   burglar

A man who *mines* is called a *miner*, what do we call:

A man who pursues?	*pursuer*
A man who acts?	*actor*
A man who presides?	*president*
A man who glazes?	*glazier*
A man who governs?	*governor*
A man who guards?	*guard*

182

A Captain is in charge of a ship. What do we call the person in charge of:

A household?	*master*
A school?	*headmaster*

A library ?	*librarian*
A shop ?	*shopkeeper*
A factory ?	*works manager*
A group of workers ?	*foreman*
A bank ?	*bank manager*
A hospital ?	*matron*
A train ?	*guard*
A railway station ?	*stationmaster*
A college ?	*dean*
A light-house ?	*keeper*
An army ?	*general*
A navy ?	*admiral*
All the armed forces ?	*war minister*
The Church ?	*archbishop*
A committee ?	*chairman*
A court-of-law ?	*judge*
A newspaper ?	*editor*
An orchestra ?	*conductor*
A government ?	*prime minister*

A man may be:

broad-shouldered
on foot (walking)
tongue-tied (speechless)
head-over-heels (falling over himself, i.e. very eager)
heavy-hearted (sad)
light-fingered (a thief)
weak-kneed (cowardly)

deep-chested
hard-hearted (cruel or stern)
half-hearted (not very keen)
heavy-handed (clumsy with his hands)
steel-, or iron-nerved (brave)
open-handed (generous)
on his toes (ready)

183

a queer fish (peculiar)   a road hog (a selfish car driver)

a low-brow (have a low taste   a skinflint (a miser)

in art)

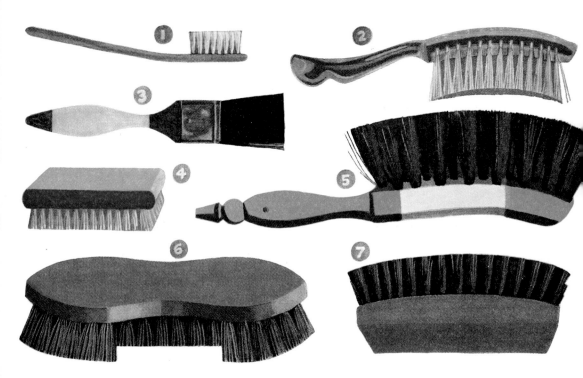

Here are a few of the many different kinds of brushes that are made. Write down on a slip of paper the name for each of them and then turn to the answers at the foot of page 186.

184

A woman may have:

     a woman's crowning glory (hair)   rosebud lips

     a peaches and cream complexion   teeth like pearls

     (what do we mean by a dusky   a sour look

     complexion?)   a sweet tooth (likes sweet

     a smooth tongue (a glib talker)   things to eat)

     twinkling eyes

Questions for your child. What do we call:

A child whose parents are dead?	*orphan*
The person who looks after an orphan?	*guardian*
A savage who eats human flesh?	*cannibal*
Somebody who pretends to be what he is not?	*impostor, hypocrite, pretender*
A person who lives entirely alone?	*hermit*
A person who cannot pay his debts?	*bankrupt*
A person who eats too much?	*glutton, hog*
A person who talks too much about other people's business?	*gossip*
A boy who runs errands in an hotel?	*page*
One who is cruel to those weaker than himself?	*bully*

houses

. . . .

Does your child know the names given to the following rooms:

Where food is stored?	*pantry or larder*
Where food is prepared?	*kitchen*
Where the dirty and rough work of the kitchen is done?	*scullery*
Where food is eaten?	*dining-room*
Where people have parties, entertain and relax?	*parlour, sitting room, drawing-room or lounge*
Where books are kept?	*library*
Where the car is kept?	*garage*
Sometimes found beneath the roof of the house?	*attic or garret*

185

Sometimes found below the ground in older houses ?   *cellar or basement (wine or coal may be stored here)*

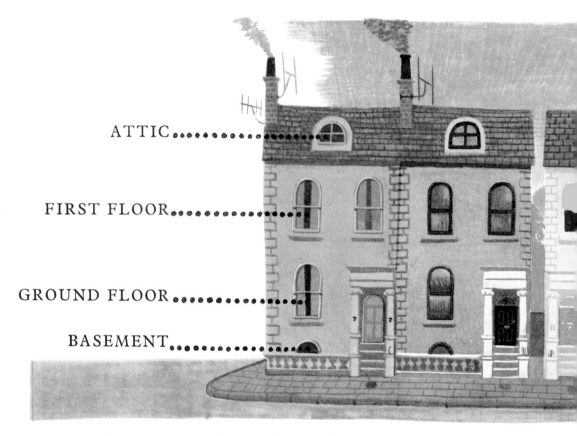

ATTIC.........................

FIRST FLOOR...................

GROUND FLOOR.................

BASEMENT....................

Make sure that your child understands the terms used here, and have him point out to you the chimney-stack, eaves, tiles, window-frame, porch, etc.

186

Where passengers sleep aboard ship ?   *cabin*

Which contains a large number of beds ?   *dormitory* (in a hospital a *ward*)

Answers to quiz on page 184: 1. toothbrush   2. lady's hairbrush   3. paint brush 4. nail brush   5. hand or carpet brush   6. scrubbing brush   7. shoe or clothes brush.

Where odds and ends and pieces of
furniture are kept ?   *lumber-room*

Can your child supply the correct names for these rooms :

A room reserved for children to play in ?   *nursery*

A room used for exercising ?   *gymnasium*

A room where clerks and typists work ?   *office*

A room where an artist works ?   *studio*

A room where patients sleep in hospital ?   *ward*

A room where a doctor sees his patients ?   *surgery*

A room where medicines are made ?   *dispensary*

A room where milk is kept and butter made ?   *dairy*

A room in the garden for growing young and
other plants ?   *greenhouse*

A few general questions relating to houses :

What is scaffolding ?   *the temporary framework used in con-
structing a house*

What do we call the cross pieces of a ladder ? *rungs*

What do we call the boards of wood running across a cupboard ? *shelves*

What is the difference between (a) a detached and a semi-
detached house, (b) a cottage and a flat ?   (a) *a detached house
stands alone, while a semi-detached house joins onto another house
that is built onto the side of it* (b) *a cottage is a small house, a flat
is a suite of rooms on one floor or storey forming a complete
residence*

What is a pre-fabricated house (pre-fab.) ?   *A house whose
parts were made separately and then brought together for quick
erection*

188   *Here are some familiar objects that might be found in any house. What are they and in which room would you find them? (answers at foot of page 190).*

Does your child know, and can he spell, these things found in a house (use each word in a sentence):

basin	bucket	cabinet	ceiling	chimney
couch	curtain	cushion	kitchen	mirror

grate	saucer	porch	shovel	piano
radio	sponge	blanket	tray	mattress
towel	quilt	picture	cupboard	ornament
vase	linen	cutlery	sheets	

Ask your child the difference between a rug and a carpet.

Ask your child to supply the missing words:

The people who live near you are your ——   *neighbours*

You live with other —— of your family   *members*

The people you know are your acquainta——   *acquaintances*

People who visit you are known as ——   *friends, visitors*

The people born in your family a long time
ago are known as your ancest——   *ancestors*

The people who live in a residence are
known as ——   *residents*

nations

. . . .

The boundary between two countries is known as a *frontier*.

In America live Americans who sell American goods.

In Belgium live Belgians who sell Belgian goods.

In China live Chinese who sell Chinese goods.

In Denmark live Danes who sell Danish goods.

In Finland live Finns who sell Finnish goods.

In France live Frenchmen who sell French goods.

In Germany live Germans who sell German goods.

In Greece live Greeks who sell Greek goods.

In Holland live Dutchmen who sell Dutch goods.

189

In Ireland live Irishmen who sell Irish goods.

In Italy live Italians who sell Italian goods.

In Japan live Japanese who sell Japanese goods.

In Malta live Maltese who sell Maltese goods.

In Norway live Norwegians who sell Norwegian goods.

In Peru live Peruvians who sell Peruvian goods.

In Portugal live Portuguese who sell Portuguese goods.

In Russia live Russians who sell Russian goods.

In Scotland live Scotsmen who sell Scottish goods.

In Spain live Spaniards who sell Spanish goods.

In Sweden live Swedes who sell Swedish goods.

In Switzerland live Swiss who sell Swiss goods.

In Turkey live Turks who sell Turkish goods.

In Wales live Welshmen who sell Welsh goods.

Where would you ride on:

a bob-sleigh	*Switzerland*
a rickshaw	*China*
a gondola	*Venice*
a camel	*Arabia or in any desert*
a donkey or jaunting car	*Ireland*

Which is:

The land of the Rising Sun?	*Japan*
The Holy Land?	*Israel and part of Jordan*
The Dark Continent?	*Africa*
The Emerald Isle?	*Ireland*

190

Answers to quiz on page 188: 1. tap, bathroom or kitchen 2. mattress, bedroom
3. vase, ornament in any room 4. light switch, any room 5. bowl, any room 6. door
knob, any room 7. kettle, kitchen 8. bulb, any room 9. poker, sitting-room
10. wardrobe, bedroom 11. cruet set, kitchen or dining-room 12. rafters, attic
13. toothbrushes, bathroom 14. television, sitting-room 15. toys, children's room
16. tools, father's workroom.

With what countries, people or parts of the world, are the following
connected:

chopsticks	*China*
tomahawk	*Red Indians*
boomerang	*Australia*
beret	*France*
kilt	*Scotland*
turban	*Many Eastern Nations*
fez	*Egypt*
hammer-and-sickle	*Russia*
stars-and-stripes	*U.S.A.*

Does your child know the difference between an Indian and a Red Indian?
Have him point out to you the different things here, e.g. mosque, turban,
wigwam, cobra, tomahawk, etc.

skyscrapers	*U.S.A.*
pagodas	*Burma, Siam*

macaroni   *Italy*
mummies   *Egypt*
watches   *Switzerland*

What are they and with which countries do you connect them? Write your answers on a slip of paper and compare them with those at the foot of page 194.

clogs   *Holland*
vodka   *Russia*
harem   *The Middle East and India*
rajah   *India*

192

laird	*Scotland*
sultan	*The Middle East*
mikado	*Japan*
mandarin	*China*
windmills	*Holland*
pyramids	*Egypt*
The Vatican	*Italy*
sombrero	*Mexico and U.S.A.*
tulips	*Holland*

animals

. . . .

A *cub* may be:

a young bear	a young fox	a young lion
a young tiger	a young wolf	

A *calf* may be:

a young elephant	a young seal	a young whale ✓
a young porpoise	the young of cattle	

We speak of:

a *litter* of pups, kittens, cubs or pigs	a *clutch* of eggs
a *brood* of chicks	a *swarm* of bees

See if your child knows the correct word to use when he writes about the young of the following animals:

goat	*kid*	pig	*piglet, pigling*
swan	*cygnet*	dog	*pup, puppy*
duck	*duckling*	goose	*gosling*
sheep	*lamb*	horse	*foal, colt* or *filly*

193

13—H.T.

cat	*kitten*	eagle	*eaglet*
hen	*chicken, chick*	owl	*owlet*
deer	*fawn*	bird	*fledgeling*

Frogs' spawn changes into tadpoles, and they then change into frogs.

-ling at the end of a word means little:

duckling   gosling

sapling (a young tree)   seedling (a young plant)

Ask your child what is meant by these sayings about animals:

busy as a bee	bats in the belfry
raining cats and dogs	like a cat on hot bricks
as the crow flies	a fine kettle of fish
a queer fish	run like a hare
lion-hearted	the lion's share
horse play	crocodile tears
like a tortoise	a leopard never changes his
an elephant never forgets	spots
help a lame dog over a style	keep the wolf from the door
like a bear with a sore head	to act like a dog in a manger
snake in the grass	set a sprat to catch a mackerel
run with the hare and hunt	ride the high horse
with the hounds	chewing the cud
a book-worm	let sleeping dogs lie
give a dog a bad name and hang him	

Answers to quiz on page 192: 1. kiwi, New Zealand 2. maple leaf, Canada 3. shamrock, Ireland 4. daffodil, Wales 5. thistle, Scotland 6. rose, England 7. kangaroo, Australia 8. dachshund, Germany 9. bulldog, Great Britain 10. Uncle Sam, U.S.A. 11. rising sun, Japan 12. poodle, France.

This picture shows countryside in which many different animals make their homes. On a slip of paper write down the names of all the animals you can think of who might live in the different parts of the countryside shown here, and state whereabouts they would make their homes. Suggested answers are to be found at the foot of page 196.

Does your child know which animals have:

tusks	*elephant*	claws	*tiger, cat and others*
a mane	*lion, horse*	a beak	*bird*
a hump	*camel*	gills	*fish*
paws	*cat, dog*	scales	*fish, reptile*
a snout	*pig*	fins	*fish*
webbed feet	*duck*	stripes	*zebra*
spots	*leopard*	hoofs	*horse, cow, deer and others*

Some general questions about animals for your child:

What is a zebra crossing? — *part of the road, painted with black and white stripes, where pedestrians may cross*

Which animal is used by Father Christmas? — *a reindeer*

Which animal gobbles until Christmas and is then itself gobbled? — *a turkey*

Which animal carries a pouch? — *a kangaroo*

Which insect is said to be industrious? — *a bee, beaver or ant*

Here are some brief descriptions of *birds*; can your child recognise them and spell their names:

a yellow pet — *canary*

a cheeky bird — *sparrow*

a big-beaked talker — *parrot*

a wise old bird — *owl*

a bird with a spotted chest — *thrush*

one with a red breast — *robin*

Suggested answers to quiz on page 195: in the pond: fish, frogs, newts, insects, etc., in the holes in the bank: otters, water-rats; in the tree: birds (in nests), squirrels (in dreys), tree-lizards, insects; in the sea: fish; in the grass: field-mice, voles also rabbits and moles in burrows; in the cliff: sea-gulls and other sea-birds. This is not a complete list by any means, and perhaps your child can think of many more.

a white bird of peace — *dove*

one that sings in the night — *nightingale*

one that is used for sending messages — *pigeon*

the King of the air — big and powerful — *eagle*

she lays her eggs in another bird's nest — *cuckoo*

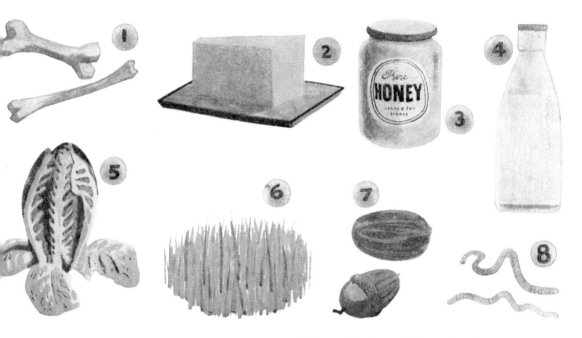

Write down on a slip of paper the names of these objects and the animals that like to eat them. (Answers at foot of page 199.)

Animals' homes. Does your child know them? :

> a bee lives in a — *hive*
>
> a bird (mouse, or wasp) lives in a — *nest*
>
> birds are kept in an — *aviary, or a cage*
>
> a dog lives in a — *kennel*
>
> fish are kept in an — *aquarium*
>
> a fowl lives in a — *coop*

197

a fox, and other wild animals—tiger and wolf—live in a — *lair*

a horse lives in a — *stable*

a lion lives in a — *den*

a mouse lives in a — *hole*

an owl lives in a — *barn, or tree*

a pig lives in a — *sty*

a pigeon or dove lives in a — *cot, or cote*

a tame rabbit lives in a — *hutch*, a wild rabbit in a — *burrow, or warren*

a sheep lives in a — *fold, or pen*

a snail lives in a — *shell*

a squirrel lives in a — *drey*

Does your child know:

the dead body of an animal is called a — *carcase*

the dead body of a human being is called a — *corpse*

the meat of deer is known as — *venison*

the meat of sheep is known as — *mutton*

the meat of cow is known as — *beef*

the meat of calf is known as — *veal*

the meat of pig is known as — *pork, or ham*

Familiar names for animals:

Bruno or Bruin the bear	Fido the dog
Leo the lion	Reynard the fox
Polly the parrot	Jumbo the elephant
Jacko the monkey	Neddy the donkey
Dobbin the horse	Bunny the rabbit
Pussy the cat	Nanny the goat
Chanticleer the cock	

SOUNDS MADE BY ANIMALS

Pay special attention to the words in italic:

An ass *brays* (he *jogs* along and is *stupid*).

A bee *hums* (he *flits* and *gathers* and is *busy*—he also *buzzes* and *drones*).

A bird *chirps* ("tweet-tweet"), *chatters* or *whistles, hovers* or *soars, swoops, hops* or *flits* and *sings* or *twitters*—a hawk is said to *swoop* down onto its *prey*—a lark *soars* up into the clouds ("blind as a bat"—what does this mean?).

A bull *bellows, charges* and may be *wild* (what does getting a "bull" or "bull's eye" in darts or shooting mean?).

A cat *purrs* (mee-ow) or *mews, steals, pounces* on mice, and is *sleek* ("playful as a kitten"—explain this).

A cock *crows* (cock-a-doodle-doo), it *struts* and is *proud* (to "*crow*" means to *boast*).

A cow *lows* (moo).

A crow *caws, flaps* his wings and is *black*.

A dog *barks* (bow-wow), *howls, growls, yelps, snarls, whines* or *whimpers, scampers* and is *faithful*—he has *paws* and a *muzzle* (*muzzle* has more than one meaning—look it up in the dictionary).

A donkey *brays* (hee-haw) *trots* and is *obstinate*.

A duck *quacks* and *waddles*.

An elephant *trumpets* and *wallows* in the mud, he has a *trunk* and *tusks* and is said *never to forget*.

A frog *croaks, leaps* and is *clammy* (or slimy).

A goat *bleats*.

199

Answers to quiz on page 197: 1. bones — dogs 2. cheese — mice 3. honey — bears (note that honey is made by bees but eaten by bears) 4. milk — cats 5. lettuce — rabbits 6. grass — cows, sheep, etc. 7. acorns — pigs 8. worms — birds, fish.

A goose *hisses* and *cackles*.

A hen *cackles*, *struts* and *pecks* corn—she may *brood* on eggs to *hatch* them ("as motherly as a hen" what does that mean?).

A horse *neighs*, *snorts*, *whinnies*, *gallops* (a pony *trots*), it sometimes *bolts* and is *noble* (a horse has fore-legs in front and two legs behind —has he 6 legs?) his hoofs *thunder* or *clatter* (children's feet are said to *patter*, perhaps *clatter* would be more accurate sometimes!).

What is the name of this bird and what sort of noise does he make?
(The answer is to be found somewhere on these two pages.)

200

A hound *bays* when near to the animal it is hunting.

A hyena *screams*.

Insects *drone*, *buzz* or *hum*.

A lion *roars* and *prowls* and has a *mane*, it is the King of *beasts* and is *brave*.

A monkey *chatters* and is *mischievous*.

A mouse *squeaks, scampers* back to its hole and is *timid*.

A nightingale *sings*.

An owl *hoots* and is *wise*.

A parrot *screeches* or *chatters*.

A pig *grunts*, and when frightened *squeals or squeaks*, he *trots* and is *fat*—a piglet *squeals* (what is a pig's *snout*?).

A rabbit *squeals*, is *timid* and *gnaws* young plants and trees.

A rook *caws*.

A seagull *screams*, and *glides* and is *tireless* (why do we find so many in fishing-ports and harbours?).

A sheep *bleats* (baa).

A snake *hisses* and *glides* (its teeth are called *fangs*)—it is often said to be *horrid* or *loathsome*.

A turkey *gobbles, struts* and is *plump*.

Wolves *howl*—we speak of a *lean* wolf (what does "a wolf in sheep's clothing" mean?).

Which animals make the following sounds?:

bellow	*bulls*	grunt	*pigs*
boo	*human beings*	neigh	*horses*
chirp	*birds*	sigh	*human beings*
coo	*doves*	scream	*seagulls*
croon	*human beings*	twitter	*birds*
groan	*human beings*	yelp	*dogs*
growl	*dogs*	buzz	*bees*

201

Which group of animals prowl? — *the cat family*. Name some members of the cat family — *tiger, lion, leopard*.

Words especially connected with animals :

a beetle *crawls* and is *horrid*

a deer has *antlers*

an eagle is *proud* and *swoops* on its *prey*

an eel *wriggles* ("slippery as an eel")

a fox has a *brush* (what does this mean ?) and is *cunning*

a hedgehog is *prickly*

a peacock *struts*

a kangaroo *leaps*

a mule is *obstinate,*
or *stubborn*

a pony *trots*

a swallow is *swift*

a butterfly *flits*

a camel has a *hump*

a worm *wriggles*

a *pack* of hounds

a *bitch* may have a
litter of *puppies*
(what is a mongrel?)

What is the name of this bird ? He is sometimes called the "king of the air".
(Answer at foot of page 204.)

Canine means "like a dog". What do the following mean? :

lucky dog	a dog's chance
a dog's life	to dog someone's footsteps
dog tired	to go to the dogs
to help a lame dog over a stile	every dog has his day
you can't teach an old dog new tricks	

Name the following:

England's national dog	*bulldog*
the dog used for racing in England	*greyhound*
a story, which is meant to teach us a lesson, in which the characters are talking animals	*fable (Aesop's fables)*

What sort of noise do the hoofs of galloping horses make? You learnt this in the section on "sounds made by animals". Note the spelling of hoofs; hooves *is seldom used. Now write down on a slip of paper all the things you can see in this picture that begin with the letter S. (Answers at foot of page 204.)*

vocabulary exercises

• •

SAYINGS INVOLVING COLOUR

Ask your child what we mean by:

blue-blooded — *to be of noble birth*

to have green fingers — *to be a good gardener*

to be green with envy — *to be very jealous*

to show the white feather — *to show cowardice*

a red-letter day — *a very happy day—a day to be remembered*

to be silver-tongued — *to be persuasive*

a golden rule — *the best rule*

a bolt from the blue — *something which happens unexpectedly*

a greybeard — *an old man*

a greenhorn — *someone inexperienced—a novice*

to be blue with cold — *to be very cold*

to go red with blushing — *to blush very much*

What would be the best adjective to use in describing this donkey? (You will find the correct answer somewhere on page 199.)

What colour would you use:

204

to indicate that you wished to surrender? — *white*

to indicate that you are in mourning? — *black*

to indicate that there is danger? — *red*

to indicate that the way is clear? — *green*

Answer to picture quiz: p. 202, eagle.

Answers to quiz on page 203: Saddle, scarf, sheriff, shoe, sidewhiskers, sleeve, smoke, sombrero, spur, stirrup, strap, "sweater".

What do we call this animal and what is the correct name for his horns?
(Answer at foot of page 206.)

Ask your child to complete these sentences:

In autumn we like to pick black—— — *berries*

A bully is a black—— — *guard*

Teacher writes on a black—— — *board*

When the electricity fails we have a black—— — *out*

A man who works when his mates are on strike is known as a
black—— — *leg*

——lights were used for spotting planes in the last war — *search*

In a baby's bedroom we use a ——light — *night*

To illuminate a building we use a ——light — *flood*

An actor on the stage likes the ——light — *spot*

Someone in the news is said to be in the ——light — *lime*

205

A light may be:

sparkling	shining	flaring
gleaming	glistening	blinding

flashing	flickering	glaring
twinkling	dazzling	

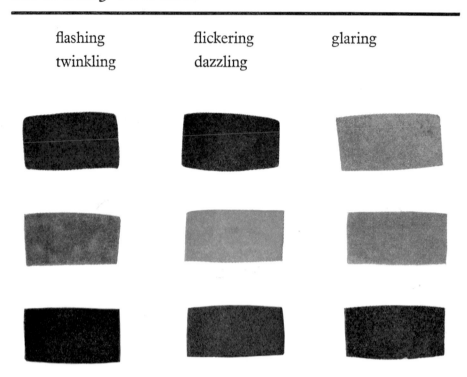

Sometimes we use the name of a colour and put a describing word in front of it, for instance navy-blue. The names of the colours here have been jumbled and attached to the wrong colours. Sort them out and write down the correct descriptions for each colour (e.g. top row, left to right: blood-red, etc.) Here are the jumbled colours: bottle-black, sky-green, nut-grey, rose-blue, charcoal-red, blood-brown, brick-green, coal-pink, pea-red. (Answers at foot of page 208.)

Which of the above words would you most typically apply to:

the sun	*dazzling or shining*
diamonds	*sparkling or flashing*
headlights	*dazzling*
eyes	*twinkling or sparkling*
the stars	*twinkling*

use *ignite* and *kindle* in sentences.

206

Answer to picture-question on page 205: deer — antlers

Read to your child the following list of fastenings one by one. Ask him to tell you with what object he would normally associate each, and make sure that he can spell them (suggested answers in italics):

bolt	*door*	braces	*trousers*
putty	*glass*	brooch	*blouse*
pin	*paper, cloth*	button	*shirt, clothing*
rivet	*steel*	belt	*trousers*
rope or string	*packages*	cable	*ship*
cement	*bricks*	solder	*metal*
chain	*machinery*	staple	*papers*
clip	*tie, paper*	suspenders	*socks, stockings*
cord	*parcels*	thread	*cloth*
glue	*wood*	twine	*leather*
gum	*paper*	zip	*material*
hook and eye	*dresses*	handcuffs	*hands*
lock	*door*	latch	*door*
padlock	*cupboard*	nail	*wood*
paste	*paper*		

SHIPS

What do we call a ship used for:

Carrying oil? — *tanker*

Pulling other ships? — *tug*

Travelling under water? — *submarine*

Carrying passengers? — *liner*

Rescue work? — *lifeboat*

Carrying goods on canals? — *barge* (which is pulled by a *tug*)

Carrying people or cars across a river? — *ferry*

207

SNOW

Falling pieces of snow are called snow—— — *flakes*

Children play throwing snow—— at each other — *balls*

Snow piled up by the wind is called a snow—— — *drift*

A small white flower blooming early in spring is known as a snow—— — *drop*

A mountain-top covered with snow is said to be snow—— — *capped*

A snow—— is used for clearing a path through the snow — *plough*

VERBS DENOTING SIZE

Use the following words correctly in sentences (check with your dictionary):

enlarge	expand	exaggerate	increase
magnify	multiply	contract	decrease
dwindle	reduce	shrink	wane

wax (with *wane* usually refers to the moon)

SOME GENERAL EXERCISES

What is meant by the words in italic?:

it is all *cut and dried*

while phoning he was *cut off*

he had to *cut down* on his spending

he is *cut out* to be a doctor

he was very *cut up* at the news

he *cut up* the cloth

he *cuts a fine figure*

Answers to quiz on page 206: left to right, top row: blood-red, brick-red, rose-pink; middle row: bottle-green, pea-green, sky-blue; bottom row: coal-black, charcoal-grey, nut-brown.

Use one word for the group of words underlined:

> That is a <u>building where a car is kept</u>. — *garage*
> Some socks <u>become smaller</u> after washing. — *shrink*
> The <u>people watching the play</u> were very amused. — *audience*
> Most of the goods are to be <u>sent abroad</u>. — *exported*
> He tried to <u>do exactly</u> what the teacher was doing. — *imitate*
> <u>Masses of people</u> were leaving the ground. — *crowds*
> He said the same thing <u>over and over again</u>. — *repeatedly*
> She <u>put off</u> her visit for two or three days. — *postponed*
> In Manchester it rains <u>very often</u>. — *frequently*
> He <u>reduced the strength of</u> the tea by adding water. — *diluted,*
> *or weakened*

How many different pins does your child know?:

> hat   safety   tie   hair   nine   drawing   ordinary

How many different hooks does your child know?:

> picture   crochet   fish   hook and eye   coat

What supports the blackboard on the easel? — *pegs*
What supports a man's trousers? — *braces or belt*

Read out these sentences to your child and get him to choose the right word from those in italics:

> He was very hungry.
> (*He was: impatient, ready, ravenous*)   (*ravenous*)
> He keeps on trying.
> (*He is a: champion, expert, plodder*)   (*plodder*)
> He will not spend if he can help it.
> (*He is a: spendthrift, miser, charitable*)   (*miser*)
> He is good at games.
> (*He is: strong, eager, athletic, hardworking*)   (*athletic*)

209

He tried to ascertain the cause of the trouble.
(Which of these words could be used in place
of *ascertain?: calculate, tell, discover, recognise*) (*discover*)
He took part in the discussion.
(Which of these words could be used in place
of *discussion?: talk, quarrel, argument, gossip*) (*talk*)
He was very grateful.
(Which of these words could be used in place
of *grateful?: friendly, generous, happy, thankful*) (*thankful*)
To *repent* is to: *forgive, be sorry for, rejoice,
weep*.   (*be sorry for*)
To be *modest* is to be: *shy, timid, backward,
moderate, humble*.   (*humble*)
The Captain dropped : *passengers, cargo, anchor.* (*anchor*)
Cereals are : *stories, magazines, grain.*   (*grain*)
The chemist : *bottled, diagnosed, dispensed* the
prescription.   (*dispensed*)
Someone who fights on your side in war is
called an : *alloy, ally, alley.*   (*ally*)
The shopkeeper : *rapped, settled, wrapped,* the
goods.   (*wrapped*)

210 What do we call :
   every 24 hours — *daily*
   every night — *nightly*
   every 7 days — *weekly*
   every 14 days — *fortnightly*
   every 4 weeks — *monthly*
   every 3 months — *quarterly*

every 12 months — *yearly*

a period of 10 years — *a decade*

a period of 100 years — *a century*

a period over which a King rules — *a reign*

a period of about 30 years — *a generation* (the time between the birth of one generation and the next)

METHODS OF TELLING THE TIME. *The clock is not the only one, and here are four other methods of measuring it accurately. From left to right you can see: a candle which has the hours marked on its side; a glass jar, also with the hours marked on it, which slowly empties itself by allowing the water to escape in drips from a pipe at the bottom; an hour-glass which can be "rewound" by turning it upside down (these are often used in the kitchen for boiling eggs); a sundial which casts a shadow on to a plate which is engraved as a clock-face.*

211

How many sticks does your child know (e.g. candle-stick)? :

walking-stick	yard-stick	broom-stick
hockey-stick	match-stick	drum-stick
a stick of rock	shooting-stick	joystick

WORDS USED TOGETHER

Here is a list of words that are very often used together. Let your child incorporate them in sentences, using them as they are here, and not splitting them up.

knife-and-fork	David-and-Jonathan
bread-and-butter	deaf-and-dumb
in-and-out	give-and-take
one-and-all	here-and-there
then-and-there	touch-and-go
beck-and-call	one-and-only
fits-and-starts	fast-and-loose
free-and-easy	rack-and-ruin
meek-and-mild	flesh-and-blood
fire-and-water	down-and-out
tooth-and-nail	hammer-and-chisel
hammer-and-tongs	pen-and-ink
life-and-death	lock-and-key
body-and-soul	heart-and-soul
wear-and-tear	long-and-short
safe-and-sound	ups-and-downs
once-and-for-all	bow-and-arrow
odds-and-ends	needle-and-thread
heaven-and-earth	cup-and-saucer
rough-and-tumble	rough-and-ready
this-and-that	tit-for-tat
zig-zag	fair-and-square
by-hook-or-by-crook	might-and-main
high-and-dry	to-and-fro
high-and-low	again-and-again

over-and-over   so-and-so

by-and-by   such-and-such

all-in-all   thick-and-thin

(Egg goes with bacon, what goes with pepper? — *salt*)

WHERE PEOPLE AND "THINGS" ARE TO BE FOUND

Aeroplanes are to be found in a hangar. ✓

A wild animal may be found in a zoo.

An art gallery contains paintings.

An atlas is a collection of maps.

An audience is to be found in a theatre.

A barn is a building for storing hay or grain.

A bin is a container for refuse.

Books are to be found in a library.

A school book may be found in a satchel.

A brewery is a place where beer is made.

A bungalow is a house with no upper storey.

A caddy is a small box for holding tea (a caddie carries golf clubs on a golf course).

A camp is a collection of tents or huts.

A car is to be found in a garage. ✓

An attaché-case, or brief-case is for carrying papers, a satchel for books, and a suit-case for clothes.

A leather case for a knife is a sheath.

A cellar is a room below ground level where coal or wine may be stored.

A choir is a collection of singers.

A churn is a metal container for milk.

Clerks work in an office.

213

Clothes are to be found in a wardrobe, or suitcase.

A crate is a case for crockery, glass, or fruit.

A cruet is a container for table salt, pepper, mustard and vinegar.

A depot is a place where foods or general goods are stored.

A directory contains addresses and telephone numbers.

A doctor is to be found in a surgery.

An eskimo lives in an igloo.

A filing-cabinet contains papers.

A fire burns in a grate.

Fruit trees grow in an orchard.

Food is to be found in a hamper or larder.

Gas is to be found in a gasometer.

A greenhouse is a glasshouse where young and delicate plants are reared.

A gypsy lives in a caravan.

Grapes grow in a vineyard.

A hotel is a place where travellers sleep and eat.

A hostel is a place where students sleep and eat.

Ice skating takes place at an ice-rink.

A Red Indian lives in a wigwam.

A Jew worships in a synagogue (who worships in a church, chapel or a temple?).

214

A junction is a place where railway lines or roads meet.

A keg is a small barrel.

A laboratory is a place where experiments are conducted.

FACING-PAGE QUIZ. *On a slip of paper write down the names of these objects and what you would expect to find inside them. (Answers at foot of page 216.)*

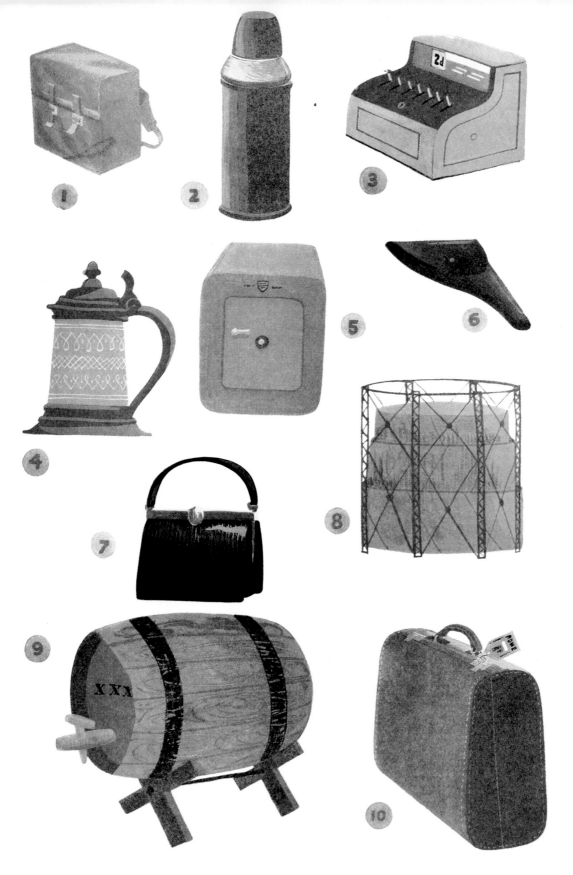

A monk lives in a monastery.

A museum is a building where objects of interest are kept.

A nun lives in a convent.

An observatory contains a telescope.

Orphans are to be found in an orphanage.

A peasant lives in a cottage.

Wealthy people may live in a mansion.

A prisoner is to be found in a cell.

A purse contains money (what is a wallet? — *a leather container for holding notes*).

A pistol is kept in a holster.

A reservoir is a place where water is stored.

A restaurant is a place where people may buy and eat a meal.

Royalty live in a palace (a Bishop also lives in a palace).

A safe contains valuables.

A scuttle is a container for coal.

A soldier lives in barracks.

A collection of stamps is to be found in an album.

A sword is kept in a scabbard.

A till is a box for holding money in a shop.

Tobacco is kept in a pouch.

A train is a collection of carriages or wagons pulled by an engine (or locomotive). The coal and water are contained in a tender. A guard's van contains the guard and the luggage.

Railway wagons are kept in sidings (what is a goods train?).

A vicar lives in a vicarage.

Answers to quiz on page 215:   1. haversack or pack — soldier's kit 2. thermos — tea or any hot drink 3. till — money 4. tankard — beer 5. safe — money or valuables 6. holster — pistol 7. handkerchief — purse, cosmetics, etc. 8. gasometer — gas 9. barrel — beer 10. suit-case — clothes.

SOUNDS

an anvil *clangs*

a baby *cries* or *bawls*

a bell *rings, peals, tolls, chimes, or clangs*

a bow *twangs* — the bow of a violin *scrapes*

brakes *grind* or *screech*

a brook *babbles*

a bugle *calls* or *sounds*

a car (also an aeroplane, or gear) *crashes* — it *swerves* to avoid

a *collision*, it sometimes *rattles*

chains *clank* or *jangle*

a clock *ticks* and *chimes*

a coin *clinks, jingles, tinkles*

a cork *pops*

dishes *rattle*

a door *bangs, slams* or *creaks*

a dove *coos*

a drum *beats*

217

an engine *chugs, purrs* or *throbs* or *puffs*

feet *patter, shuffle* or *tramp*

a fire *crackles* (so does wood and dry leaves)

frying food *sizzles*

glasses *tinkle*

a gun *fires, booms*

a horn *toots*

a kettle *sings*

a kitten *mews*

a lamb *bleats, frisks* or *gambols*, and is *gentle* or *meek*

leaves *rustle*

paper *rustles* and *crinkles*

rain *patters* and *plops*

reeds *rustle*

a river *gurgles*

a rocket *whizzes*

silk *rustles*

218

a siren *wails*

a skirt *swishes*

steam *hisses* (do you know that *steam* is a *vapour*, *water* is a *liquid* and *ice* is *solid?*)

a storm *rages*

a tap *drips*

a telephone *buzzes* or *rings*

thunder *claps*, *roars* or *rumbles*, and lightning *flashes*

a top *hums*

traffic *roars*

a train *chugs* or *puffs*

a trumpet *blares*

a twig *crackles* underfoot

water *laps*, *drips*, *bubbles*, *splashes*

a stream *babbles*, *gurgles* or *murmurs*

a whip *cracks* or *lashes* (the mark it leaves on the skin is known as a *weal*—how do you spell the other wheel?)

a whistle *shrieks* or *hoots*

wind *howls*, *sighs*, *moans*—a tree *sways* in the wind

window-panes *rattle*

a stone falling into water *plops*

BOXES

How many does your child know?:

match	pillar	letter	sentry	signal
jewel	money	pencil	tool	hat
shoe	sewing	deed	cigarette	cigar
stage	chocolate			

What does "a Christmas box" mean?

What is a:

box-office	boxing-match	Jack-in-the-box
box-room	window-box	

What does "To box someone's ears" mean?

Some more "sounds" to learn: what noise does a kitten make?

THE RIGHT WORD TO USE

a *breath* of air	a *bevy* of beauty
a *bunch* of grapes	a *ball* of string
a *blade* of grass	a *chip* of wood
a *chunk* of bread or wood	a *crumb* of bread, also a *crust*
a *drop* of rain, blood or water	or *morsel*
a *flake* of snow	a *glimmer* of light or hope
a *grain* of sand	a *gust* of wind
a *load* of trouble or worries	a *lock* of hair
a *pat* of butter	a *posy* of flowers
a *puff* of smoke	a *pinch* of salt or snuff
a *ray* of sunshine	a *rope* of pearls
a *scrap* of paper or food	a *sip* of water
a *skein* of silk or wool	a *smut* of soot

220

a *speck* of dirt or dust

a *splinter* of wood or glass

a *string* of onions or race-horses

a *tint* of colour

a *twinge* of pain

a *spot* of ink or rain

a *squeeze* of lemon or tooth-paste

a *stroke* of luck

a *truss* of hay

a *wisp* of straw, smoke, or hay

What sound does a kettle make when it is boiling?

Questions for your child:

the outside of a nut — *shell*

the outside of an egg — *shell*

the outside of an orange — *peel*

the outside of a banana — *skin*

the outside of a lemon — *peel or rind*

the outside of an apple — *skin*

the outside of a pear — *skin*

the outside of a peach — *skin*

the centre of an apple — *core*

the centre of a nut — *kernel*

the centre of a dartboard — *bull's eye*

221

the centre of a wheel — *hub*

the centre of a bone — *marrow*

the centre of a stalk — *pith*

the centre of a ship — *midships*

Labrador, poodle, bulldog, mongrel, spaniel: which do you think this is and what sort of noise does he make? (*Answer at foot of page 223.*)

Parts of things:

a chain has — *links*	a rope has — *strands*
a ladder has — *rungs*	a clock has — *hands*
a saw has — *teeth*	knitting has — *stitches*
a net has a — *mesh*	a wheel has a — *hub and spokes*

We also speak of:

the *head* of a match	an *ear* of corn
the *hands* of a clock	the *eye* of a needle
the *face* of a clock	the *mouth* of a river
the *brow* of a hill	the *eyes* in a potato
the *teeth* of a saw	a *chest* of drawers
the *tongue* of a shoe	the *lip* of a cup
the *leg* of a chair	an *arm*chair
a ship's crew may be called *hands*	a wooden box may be called a *chest*

Note: A chair has legs, back, seat, and may also have arms.

Distinguish between:

    on no account

    money on account

    to turn to good account

Also:

  Different sorts of roads:

      an avenue (a road, lined with trees)

      an alley (a narrow roadway or footpath)

      a crescent (a roadway shaped like a new moon)

      a cul-de-sac (a roadway open only at one end)

      a drive (a private roadway to a house)

      a road (a public way for travelling)

      a square (a four-sided area with houses on each side)

      a street (a road lined with houses)

A general question: can your child name six different kinds of bag — *cricket-bag, hand-bag, money-bag, paper-bag, shopping-bag, sugar-bag, travelling-bag, sand-bag.*

Answer to picture question on p. 222: mongrel, bark   **223**

IDIOMS

. . . .

An idiom is an expression the meaning of which is different from the meaning of the words of which it is composed. Read the following idioms to your child, and see if he can give you brief explanations which come near to the words set in italic :

Build castles in the air — *to daydream* or *aim at the unattainable*.

Take up arms — *to get ready to fight*.

Make allowance for — *to excuse*.

With open arms — *eagerly*.

Put on airs — *to show off* or *swank*.

Cut someone dead — *to ignore someone well known to you*.

Hit below the belt — *to attack unfairly*.

Put someone's back up — *to upset someone*.

Put one's back into a thing — *to try hard*.

Make a clean breast of — *to confess*.

Behind someone's back — *without someone's knowledge*.

In the background — *not in view*.

Make no bones about a thing — *to be direct*.

Knit one's brow — *to concentrate*.

Blue-blooded — *having aristocratic ancestors*.

Cold-blooded — *cruel*.

Hot-blooded — *quick tempered*.

Have no backbone — *to be a coward.*

Make one's blood boil — *to make one angry.*

Turn one's back on — *to refuse to help.*

A bolt from the blue — *an unexpected happening.*

Burn one's boats — *to commit oneself without the possibility of retreat.*

Beat about the bush — *to go about something in an indirect way.*

A wet blanket — *a spoil-sport.*

Which idiom on these two pages does this picture best illustrate? (Answers to this and the following pictures are on page 240.)

In someone's good books — *to be well thought of by someone (the reverse of being in someone's bad books).*

Keep the ball rolling — *to keep things going.*

Kill two birds with one stone — *to do two things with one action.*

Call one's bluff — *to challenge someone's threat.*

Nipped in the bud — *stopped before it could grow into anything large* or *stopped in the early stages.*

In the same boat — *to be in the same circumstances.*

Get out of bed on the wrong side — *to be difficult and moody.*

15—H T.

225

Make bricks without straw — *to do something without the essential materials.*

Know which side your bread is buttered — *to know what is best for you.*

Which idiom on these pages do you think this picture fits best?

Give someone a wide berth — *to avoid someone.*

Have a bone to pick — *to have something to argue over.*

Make-believe — *to pretend.*

Cock and bull story — *a ridiculous, unbelievable story.*

Let the cat out of the bag — *to expose something (a secret perhaps).*

A feather in one's cap — *something to be proud of.*

Sail under false colours — *to pretend to be different than one is.*

Put your cards on the table — *to be frank and to explain everything.*

Come what may — *whatever happens.*

In clover — *to be well off* or *in good circumstances.*

226

Under a cloud — *to be in disfavour.*

Paddle your own canoe — *to attend to your own business.*

Come a cropper — *to fail.*

Put on your thinking cap — *to think.*

Wait till the clouds roll by — *to wait until trouble passes.*

Take the cake — *to carry off the prize.*

Burn the candle at both ends — *to be so occupied with work and play that one's health is bound to suffer.*

Checkmate someone — *to outsmart someone.*

Cut your coat according to your cloth — *to live according to your means (compare with "don't bite off more than you can chew").*

Keep your chin up, or keep a stiff upper lip — *be brave.*

First class — *the very best.*

Going to the dogs — *getting worse or losing one's good character.*

Help a lame dog over a stile — *to help someone who is in trouble.*

Call it a day — *to stop.*

Eat dirt, or humble-pie — *to humble oneself.*

Between the devil and the deep blue sea — *between two equally unpleasant alternatives.*

A rough diamond — *a good man with a rough appearance.*

To have seen better days — *to have been better-off formerly.*

High and dry — *not wanted.*

A white elephant — *something expensive that you do not really want.*

A bad egg or a bad penny — *a worthless person.*

227

An eye for an eye — *to give or receive similar payment or treatment.*

Eye to the main chance — *to keep the main point in mind for one's own advantage.*

Lend me your ears — *listen to me.*

Lend a deaf ear — *not to listen.*

All ears — *to listen closely.*

Up to your ears — *to be very busy.*

The apple of someone's eye — *the most dearly beloved of someone.*

Have (or keep) an eye on — *to watch.*

Take it easy — *to relax.*

To keep one's eyes open — *to be alert.*

Throw dust in someone's eyes, or pull the wool over someone's eyes — *to mislead.*

Turn a blind eye — *to ignore (Nelson is said to have put his telescope to his blind eye when he wanted to ignore a signal).*

Bird's-eye view — *to get a view of the whole thing (as a bird gets from a height).*

Without batting an eyelid — *showing no concern.*

In the twinkling of an eye — *quickly.*

See eye to eye — *to agree with.*

Unable to believe one's eyes — *to find something almost unbelievable.*

Play with fire — *to do something dangerous.*

Have at one's finger-tips — *to have readily available.*

Twist round your little finger — *to be able to do as you wish with.*

A thorn in the flesh — *a disadvantage, an annoyance.*

Put a good face on it — *to make the best of.*

Putting the fat in the fire — *causing trouble.*

Put one's foot down — *to be firm.*

Having too many irons in the fire — *attempting too much.*

A pretty kettle of fish — *trouble.*

Put one's foot in it — *to make a stupid mistake.*

A fish out of water — *a person who is ill-at-ease.*

Go the way of all flesh — *to die.*

Make one's flesh creep — *to make one afraid.*

Sit on the fence — *to wait for more information before deciding in a quarrel,* or *try to please both sides.*

Show the white feather — *to show signs of cowardice.*

Through fire and water — *through any hardship.*

Standing-up for a friend — *supporting a friend.*

Playing second fiddle — *letting someone else take the more important position.*

Look forward to — *to anticipate something eagerly (with pleasure).*

Make good — *to succeed.*

A lukewarm greeting, or a cold reception — *to be unwelcome.*

Play the game — *to be fair and just.*

Pick out the idiom on these two pages that this picture represents.

Fit like a glove — *to be a perfect fit.*

Lead up the garden path — *to deceive.*

Have a go — *to try.*

Throw down the gauntlet — *to challenge someone.*

Sour grapes — *belittling what you want yet cannot have.*

Play to the gallery — *to show off.*

Get away with — *to escape punishment for doing something wrong.*

229

Which idiom do you think best describes this picture?

Have one foot in the grave — *to be almost dead.*

A wild goose chase, or a wild-cat scheme — *a foolish undertaking.*

Cook one's goose — *to ruin one's chances.*

Make things hum — *to cause things to become very active.*

Have one's head in the clouds — *to be a dreamer.*

Take heart — *to take courage.*

Have a heart — *be generous.*

Have a heart of gold — *be kind hearted.*

Have one's heart in one's mouth, or one's boots — *to be frightened.*

Take to heart — *to be deeply moved.*

230

Eat one's heart out — *to grieve.*

Cool one's heels — *to be kept waiting.*

Put heads together — *to consult.*

Not to turn a hair — *to be unmoved.*

Have a swollen head — *be conceited.*

At loggerheads — *to disagree strongly.*

Take it into one's head — *to get an idea (perhaps unwise).*

The upper hand — *the advantage.*

Give someone enough rope to hang himself — *to allow a mischievous person to go on making trouble until he himself gets into trouble.*

To split hairs — *to make small, silly alterations, or to be too particular.*

A hand to mouth existence — *only just making a living; to live from day to day.*

Wash your hands of something, or throw in one's hand — *to give up.*

Give someone a hand, or lend a hand — *to help.*

Keep one's hand in — *to keep in practice.*

Have one's hands full — *to be very occupied.*

Have someone eating out of your hand — *to have someone doing exactly what you want him to do.*

Eat one's head off — *to eat too much.*

Not to make head or tail of — *to be unable to understand.*

Talk one's head off — *to talk too much.*

Talk through one's hat — *to talk nonsense.*

Hard of hearing — *to be deaf.*

Have it out — *to settle by fighting, or talking.*

Caught red-handed — *caught in the act.*

Make haste — *to hurry.*

Put the cart before the horse — *to do things in the wrong order.*

At the eleventh hour — *just in time.*

Hale and hearty — *healthy.*

Have a hand in — *to be concerned with.*

To put one's hands on — *to find.*

Hand over — *to give up.*

With heavy hand — *severely.*

Run with the hare and hunt with the hounds — *to be on both sides.*

To bury the hatchet — *to make peace.*

Take the bull by the horns — *to start overcoming a difficulty.*

Ride the high horse — *to show off* or *to be haughty and arrogant.*

Hit the nail on the head — *to be absolutely right.*

By hook or by crook — *by fair means or foul.*

Take to one's heels — *run away.*

Break the ice — *to make a determined beginning.*

Jack of all trades and master of none — *to try too many things and be proficient in none.*

Take a joke — *to laugh at a joke which is at your own expense.*

The pot calling the kettle black — *someone who is just as guilty accusing someone else.*

Turn over a new leaf — *to make a fresh start.*

Pull someone's leg — *to mislead jokingly, or to tease someone.*

Show a leg — *to get up.*

Red-letter day — *an important day in one's life.*

A white lie — *a lie told for a good purpose.*

Throw light on — *to make something clear.*

To see the light — *to understand the truth.*

Make light of — *to treat as if it does not matter.*

Make little of — *to belittle something thought highly of by someone else.*

The lion's share — *the larger part.*

Look after — *to take care of.*

Look down on — *not to respect.*

Look down one's nose — *to look with disrespect and scorn.*

To look into — *to investigate.*

Look up to — *to respect.*

Dog in the manger — *someone who refuses to allow another to have something that is of no use to himself.*

Pick out the idiom that best fits this picture.

233

Tell it to the Marines — *I do not believe it.*

Steal a march — *to get ahead of.*

Make ends meet — *to manage on the money one has.*

Make much of — *to make a fuss of.*

Take one's own medicine — *to receive one's own punishment.*

Put someone through the mill — *to give someone a severe training.*

Be in two minds — *to be undecided.*

Have something on one's mind — *to be worried.*

Bear in mind — *to remember.*

Find the idiom that best suits this illustration.

234

To give someone a piece of your mind — *to scold someone.*

Absent-minded — *forgetful.*

Made of money, or rolling in wealth — *to be very wealthy.*

Make a mountain out of a molehill — *to treat a little thing as if it were a very big one.*

Down in the mouth — *to be depressed.*

Make one's mouth water — *to arouse one's appetite.*

On the spur of the moment — *without thinking.*

To face the music — *to take one's punishment.*

He gives me a pain in the neck — *he irritates me.*

Neck and neck — *to be level (a term often used to describe runners in a race).*

Look for a needle in a haystack — *to look for something almost impossible to find.*

Feather one's own nest — *to do something for oneself at the expense of others.*

Carry coal to Newcastle — *to do something that is unnecessary.*

Put your nose into other people's business — *to interfere in what does not concern you.*

Six of one and half a dozen of the other — *there is much to be said for both sides.*

Mind one's p's and q's — *to be careful.*

Put someone through his paces — *to get someone to show his abilities.*

The straight and narrow path — *to be honest.*

Hold your peace — *keep silent.*

Cut off without a penny — *to be left nothing in a will.*

Put someone in his place, or to take someone down a peg or two — *to show up someone who is perhaps trying to "show off".*

Play about — *waste time.*

Child's play — *very easy.*

Play someone up — *to annoy someone.*

Take all the plums — *to keep the best for oneself.*

Be on the point of — *to be almost ready.*

Make a practice — *to make a habit of doing.*

Pull oneself together — *to compose oneself.*

At close quarters — *very near.*

235

See red — *to be angry.*

Run rings around — *to show great superiority to.*

Know the ropes, or know what's what — *to know how things work.*

Run across — *to meet by chance.*

Touched by a sad sight — *being affected by a sad sight.*

Plain sailing — *easy.*

Take something with a pinch of salt — *to hesitate to believe.*

Take a back seat — *to make oneself inconspicuous.*

A black sheep — *one who brings disgrace on the family.*

On the shelf — *not wanted.*

To give someone the cold shoulder — *to snub someone (to give a guest a cold shoulder of mutton is not very flattering).*

Straight from the shoulder, or to talk plain English — *to be blunt and frank.*

At sixes and sevens — *to be in trouble.*

Spoiling the ship for a ha'p'orth of tar — *making a bad job by neglecting a little extra effort or expense.*

To have a soft spot for — *to be fond of.*

To see through someone — *to understand what kind of a person someone else really is.*

Be out of sorts, or off colour — *to be unwell.*

In the soup — *in trouble.*

A snake in the grass — *a hidden enemy.*

Call a spade a spade — *to speak plainly.*

Spick and span — *very neat.*

Throw up the sponge — *to give in.*

Born with a silver spoon in one's mouth — *to be born with rich parents.*

Watch your step — *take care.*

A blue-stocking — *a learned woman.*

Here is a very easy idiom for you to find.

Leave no stone unturned — *to take every possible step.*

Pull strings, or pull wires — *to use one's influence.*

Stumped — *not to know.*

Make hay while the sun shines, or strike while the iron is hot — *to do things while conditions are favourable.*

Cross swords with — *to argue with* or *to oppose.*

Take someone in — *to deceive someone.*

Take to task — *to reprimand.*

Turn tail — *to run away, or to shirk a fight.*

Shed crocodile tears — *to show false sympathy (the crocodile is said to cry as it devours its victim).*

Armed to the teeth — *to have many weapons to fight with.*

Set one's teeth — *to be determined.*

237

By the skin of one's teeth — *only just, or by the smallest margin.*

On tenterhooks — *to be anxiously uncertain.*

Set the Thames on fire — *to cause a sensation.*

Lay it on thick — *to exaggerate.*

Can you find this idiom on these two pages ? The climber looks as if he is only just holding on by his finger-tips.

238

Through thick and thin — *faithful in all circumstances.*

Twiddle one's thumbs — *to be idle.*

Tit for tat — *to get your own back.*

Be behind the times — *old-fashioned.*

Toe the mark, or to toe the line — *to be ready,* or *to be on tiptoe.*

Hold your tongue — *be silent.*

Not see the wood for the trees — *to miss the main point looking at the less important details.*

Blow one's own trumpet — *to sing one's own praises, to be boastful.*

Put two and two together — *to reason correctly.*

To be up against it — *having a difficult time.*

Be quick on the uptake — *to be very intelligent.*

Throw cold water on something — *to discourage.*

To be in deep water — *to be in trouble.*

Getting into hot water — *getting into trouble.*

Pour oil on troubled water — *to make peace.*

Rub someone up the wrong way — *to displease someone.*

Mend one's ways — *to reform.*

Pull one's weight — *to do one's share.*

A warm welcome — *an affectionate greeting.*

Be at one's wits end — *not to know what to do next.*

Wolf in sheep's clothing — *someone who is dangerous, but does not appear to be so.*

Cry wolf — *to give a false alarm.*

In a word — *briefly.*

A man of his word — *a man you can trust.*

Take one at his word — *to believe someone.*

Eat one's words — *to go back on what one has said.*

Have words with someone — *to quarrel with.*

Knock off work — *to stop work.*

On top of the world — *to be most successful, or to feel very well.*

239

Questions for your child about idioms. What do these mean:

| To ape someone? | *to imitate* |
| To badger someone? | *to worry* |

To crow over someone?	*to gloat*
To dog someone?	*to worry*
To duck someone?	*to immerse in water*
To ferret someone or something out?	*to find out*
To fox someone?	*to mislead*
To hound someone?	*to worry*
To ram something?	*to drive hard onto*
To wolf something?	*to gobble up*
A piece of cake?	*something very easy*
My cup of tea?	*to my liking*
A peppery colonel?	*a bad tempered colonel*
A saucy child?	*a rude child*
An old salt?	*an old sailor*
A queer fish?	*a peculiar person*
A road hog?	*a selfish and inconsiderate car driver*
Hard words?	*harsh criticism*
A close shave?	*a near disaster*
A windfall?	*an unexpected benefit*

Suitable answers to the picture-questions in this chapter: page 225: cut someone dead, or put on airs   page 226: come a cropper   page 229: show the white feather   page 230: caught red-handed   page 233: put someone through the mill   page 234: made of money   page 237: armed to the teeth   page 238: by the skin of one's teeth.

SIMILES

· ·

These are comparisons put in an entertaining and more illustrative way, introduced by *like* or *as*.

The similes that follow are commonly used and frequently set in examinations with the vital words left out—for your child to write in. Go through this list as a game by reading out the simile to your child, but omitting to give the words in italic.

When you get the correct reply, see if your child can spell the word too. Explain to him any simile of which he is not quite sure.

Agile as a *monkey* or *cat*.

Angry as a *bear with a sore head.*

Awkward as a *bull in a china shop.*

Bald as a *billiard ball.*

Black as *pitch* or *coal* or *soot.*

Blind as a *bat.*

Bold as *brass.*

Bright as *day* or a *lark.*

Brown as a *berry.*

Busy as a *bee.*

Caught like a *rat in a trap.*

Clean as a *whistle* or *new pin.*

Clear as a *bell* or *crystal.*

Cold as *ice* or *the grave.*

Cool as a *cucumber.*

Crafty or cunning as a *fox.*

Crooked as a *corkscrew.*

Dark as *night.*

Dead as a *doornail.*

Deaf as a *post.*

Deep as the *sea* or *ocean.*

Docile as a *lamb.*

Drink like a *fish.*

Dry as *dust* or a *bone.*

16—H.T.

241

Dull as *ditchwater*.

Easy as *winking* or *pie* or *falling off a log*.

Fat as a *pig*.

Fast as a *deer* or *hare*.

Firm as a *rock*.

Fit as a *fiddle*.

Fits like a *glove*.

Fight like a *demon*.

Flat as a *pancake*.

Fresh as a *daisy*.

Friendly as a *puppy*.

Frisky as a *lamb*.

Gentle as a *lamb* or *dove*.

Good as *gold* or *new*.

Graceful as a *swan*.

Greedy as a *pig*.

Green as *grass*.

Happy as a *king* or *lark* or *sand-boy* or *the day is long* or *dog with two tails*.

Hard as a *rock* or *iron* or *nails* or *steel*.

Heavy as an *elephant* or *lead*.

Helpless as a *babe*.

Hungry as a *horse* or *hunter* or *wolf* or *church mouse*.

Innocent as a *new born babe* or *lamb*.

This farmer is as fat as a — ?

Jump like a *cat on hot bricks*.

Keen as *mustard* (to be *mustard* at something means to be good at it).

Large as *life*.

Lazy as *the day is long*.

Like as *two peas in a pod*.

Light as a *feather*.

Lively as a *cricket*.

Loathsome as a *toad*.

Mad as a *March hare* or *hatter*.

Numerous as the *sands on the seashore*.

Obstinate as a *mule* or *pig*.

Old as *Methuselah* or *the hills* or *time*.

Pale as a *sheet*.

242

Playful as a *kitten* or *puppy*.

Pleased as *Punch*.

Plain as *the nose on your face* or *a pike-staff*.

Poor as a *church mouse*.

Pretty as a *picture*.

Proud as a *peacock* or *queen*.

Quick as *lightning* or *a wink* or *a flash*.

Safe as *houses* or *The Bank of England*.

Sharp as a *needle* or *razor*.

Shake like a *jelly* or *leaf*.

Sick as a *dog*.

Silent as a *tomb*.

Simple as *ABC*.

Slippery as an *eel*.

Slow as a *snail* or *tortoise*.

The prisoner's food is as hard as — ?

243

Quiet as *the grave*.

Red as a *beetroot* or *rose*.

Regular as *clockwork* or *sunrise*.

Restless as a *compass needle*.

Right as *rain*.

Sleep like a *top* or *log*.

Sly as a *fox*.

Soft as *butter*.

Snug as a *bug in a rug*.

Sober as a *judge*.

Sticky as *treacle*.

Stiff as a *poker* or *ramrod*.

Straight as *a die* or *an arrow*.

Strong as *a horse* or *an ox*.

Stubborn as a *mule*.

Sure as *fate* or *I am standing here*.

Sweet as *honey* or *sugar*.

Swift as *a deer* or *a hawk* or *an arrow* or *a hare* or *lightning*.

Timid as a *mouse*.

Tremble like a *leaf* or *jelly*.

True as *steel*.

Turn up like a *bad penny*.

Ugly as *sin*.

Warm as *toast*.

Watch like a *hawk*.

Welcome as *flowers in May*.

White as *a ghost* or *a sheet* or *snow* or *a lily*.

Wise as *an owl* or *Solomon*.

Work like a *horse* or *beaver* or *galley slave*.

It works like a *charm*.

PROVERBS

A proverb is a short saying which neatly stresses a well-known truth. The following proverbs should be understood (explanations are in italic).

A bird in the hand is worth two in the bush, or half a loaf is better than no bread — *it is better to be certain of a little than to have the possibility of more.*

The early bird catches the worm — *the first in the field has a big advantage.*

A burnt child dreads the fire, or once bitten twice shy — *if you make a painful mistake once you are less likely to do it again.*

Birds of a feather flock together — *similar people get together.*

Blood is thicker than water — *relations do more for one another than strangers.*

New brooms sweep clean — *people newly appointed to a job give satisfaction at first but perhaps not for long.*

Don't count your chickens before they are hatched — *don't be too sure that your plans will work out exactly as you anticipate.*

Every cloud has a silver lining — *in every miserable situation there is something hopeful.*

Too many cooks spoil the broth — *too many helpers are often a handicap.*

Let sleeping dogs lie — *let well alone.*

Don't put all your eggs in one basket — *don't bet all you have on one thing.*

Like father, like son — *the son "takes after" (resembles) the father.*

Don't look a gift horse in the mouth — *do not refuse a good offer without due consideration.*

All that glitters is not gold — *appearances may be deceptive.*

What is sauce for the goose is sauce for the gander — *what is good enough for one, is good enough for the other.*

People who live in glass houses should not throw stones — *don't attack others if you are in a position to be attacked similarly yourself.*

You can't put an old head on young shoulders — *a young person cannot be expected to have the wisdom of older people.*

More haste less speed — *trying to go too quickly may in the long run slow you down.*

246 It's a long lane that has no turning — *all troubles must come to an end sometime.*

Live and let live — *look after yourself but don't harm other people in the process.*

Look before you leap — *consider carefully before you make an important decision.*

*Here is a hungry sailor shipwrecked on a raft. He is overjoyed when he sees
a box floating towards him with a stale crust of bread in it. It will not
provide him with a very big meal but it is better than nothing. That is
what is meant by the proverb "half a loaf is better than no bread" — one
must be thankful for small mercies.*

A miss is as good as a mile — *the result of just failing or missing something is often just as bad as if it had been badly failed or missed.*

Never say die — *never give in, keep on trying.*

It's no good crying over spilt milk — *it's no use crying over what can't
be put right.*

One man's meat is another man's poison — *what suits one person may
not suit another.*

In for a penny, in for a pound, or one may as well be hanged for a
sheep as for a lamb — *once you commit yourself, you might as well
carry on to the finish.*

Penny-wise and pound-foolish — *being careful over details, but being
careless over important things.*

It never rains but it pours — *troubles always come together.*

Rome was not built in a day — *it takes time to do something worthwhile.*

When in Rome do as the Romans do — *keep to the customs of the people with whom you are living or working.*

Set a thief to catch a thief — *one rogue recognises another.*

There is no smoke without a fire — *there is usually some cause for rumour.*

Any port in a storm — *in time of desperate trouble any help is welcome.*

Speech is silver, silence is golden — *most people talk too much.*

A stitch in time saves nine — *quick action may save much trouble later.*

A rolling stone gathers no moss — *if you do not persevere you will not be a success* (The saying is often applied to a person who is frequently changing his job).

Time and tide wait for no man — *don't delay or you may miss the opportunity.*

Well begun is half done — *a good beginning is a great help.*

Beggars cannot be choosers — *if one is in a very inferior position, one's choice of action may be very limited.*

Necessity knows no law — *desperate needs require desperate remedies.*

Have your child tell you the words to complete these proverbs:

    First come — *first served.*
    Better late — *than never.*
    A friend in need — *is a friend indeed.*
    A penny saved — *is a penny gained.*
    Fine feathers — *make fine birds.*
    Penny wise — *pound foolish.*
    Once bitten — *twice shy.*

Have your child answer :

    Where does charity begin ? — *at home.*

    What gathers no moss ? — *a rolling stone.*

    What sweeps clean ? — *a new broom.*

    What will a drowning man clutch at ? — *a straw.* ✓

    What is the mother of invention ? — *necessity.*

    What was not built in a day ? — *Rome.*

    What makes the heart grow fonder ? — *absence.*

    Who catches the worm ? — *the early bird.*

    What keeps the doctor away ? — *an apple a day.*

ESSAYS

· ·

Many examinations include the writing of an essay. The ability to plan and write a good essay is not easily acquired. Muddled thinking means muddled writing. One of the great values in essay-writing as an exercise is that the writer learns to set his thoughts clearly on to paper with as few wasted words as possible.

It is important to *think* before writing, for a person examining a written passage is far more likely to notice mistakes of grammar than when he is listening to the spoken word. We should also think before speaking—but of the *sense* of what we are about to say, rather than the grammar. In everyday speech small grammatical errors go un-recognised (e.g. "it is me") but a higher standard is expected in our writing.

When we write anything in adult life we are free to revise and rewrite extensively, but your child's teacher will discourage him from altering what he has already written and thereby producing untidy pages. An examiner will usually consider an untidy page to indicate an untidy mind.

An examiner is only human and may easily award a very different mark to an essay on reading it for the second time under different conditions. Impress upon your child the importance of neatness and tidiness in his essays.

251

Parents and teachers must distinguish between second thoughts and reflections, which will (or should) appear in a child's attempts at expressing himself in writing, and untidiness which is the result of slovenliness. The former spring from a desire to be as accurate as possible and are commendable—the latter requires frowning upon, and is just another bad habit to be conquered. In drawing, a child will use a rubber fairly frequently until he has his form and shape as perfect as his efforts can make it—so with the writing of English (and words are far more difficult to use correctly than lines and colour). To fashion words correctly and into lovely rhythms is a very great asset.

In spite of all the objections to the essay, the University of Bristol Institute of Education in their *Studies in Selection Techniques for admission to Grammar Schools* conclude that it is after all a crucial test of literacy and of vocabulary. "The essay, although it cannot be assessed on a numerical scale with satisfactory reliability, nevertheless has an important function in the written examination, representing an essential element, making for grammar school success or failure."

Should your child be asked to write an essay or to describe a picture, he must remember his main purpose—*to satisfy the examiner.*

The examiner will assess your child's essay on the following:

Handwriting; your child should develop a good clear easily legible style. If his handwriting is not easy to read, then it must be improved, every letter should be clear and well-formed.

Neatness; divide work into paragraphs.

Spelling.

Punctuation; thought by some to be at this stage more important than spelling.

Vocabulary.

Grammar.

Sense and knowledge of what is being described and signs of original thought in the composition.

PLANNING THE ESSAY

Tell your child to choose the subject about which he knows most and about which he can write most. Good sense—as well as the way in which the essay is written—is most important. Thinking must come before writing.

2. He should very briefly write down on a piece of paper his thoughts and ideas on the subject. The items in this list need not be complete sentences. The examiner will be more impressed by signs of originality than by a series of trivial and obvious remarks.

3. He must group the headings in a logical order as topics for the paragraphs. (In each paragraph there must be a collection of sentences with a common theme.)

4. He must ensure that none of the items are in the wrong group.

5. Each paragraph must begin with a good opening sentence. It should tell the reader what the paragraph is about, and the rest of the paragraph should elaborate the point that is to be made.

6. Only when he has worked out the complete plan of the essay, its opening paragraph and the theme of each succeeding paragraph, should he start writing.

7. The paragraphs should be short—quality rather than quantity matters. Three or four sentences in each paragraph will usually be ample. He should think out each sentence before he begins to write it.

8. Each paragraph should be indented (i.e. begun about one inch from the left-hand margin of the paper).

An essay should have:

    (a) *a beginning*—an introduction, short and confident. It should hold the reader's attention and make him want to continue.

(b) *a middle*—the main part that tells the story.

(c) *an end*—the finishing off of the narrative—the conclusion.
This means that we must have at least three paragraphs.

Explain to your child that he should display his knowledge in order to impress the examiner. He should use some of the well-known similes, idioms and other figures of speech that he has been learning from our book.

The end of the essay should be felt to be an ending. This often proves to be difficult and many children's essays seem to finish in mid-air. Very often it is a good thing to end the essay with a sentence which reminds the reader of the beginning. A witty summing-up could be the perfect ending.

Let us imagine that we are to write an essay on "A day in the Country". Our rough notes might be something like this:

Beginning (*introduction*)   The peace and quiet of the country, noise and bustle of town life. Country life is natural—not artificial like town life, healthier and more satisfying. Although towns are getting larger modern transport makes it easier to get to the country.

Middle (*story*)   Dawn—cock crowing. Noon—hot sun. Use the words landscape, horizon, hills, valleys etc. The Seasons. Sights, smells, noises.   Absence of crowds. Work in phrases that we have been learning—hungry as a hunter, busy as a bee, babbling brooks, turkeys gobbling, twigs crackling underfoot. Farmer's life —crops, haymaking, tractors. Windmills. Wild life—rabbits, squirrels, hedgehogs, and all the farm animals. Trees—different kinds, also wild flowers (if you know them). The beauty of a sunset. You can in fact work in anything about the country that you know well.

End (*summing-up*)   The journey home. We feel refreshed for the day in the open air. Town life too has its advantages. More and more people are leaving the country for the town, but it does us good to see the country occasionally—we should do so more often.

You can see that there is more than enough to write about. Impress upon your child that when he has to write an essay and is given a choice of subjects, he must choose the one in which he is most interested and about which he knows the most.

Special points to remember

Sentences and people's names begin with capital letters.

A sentence must end with a full stop, an exclamation mark or a question mark.

What people *say* is put into quotation marks.

Where short words will convey the meaning do not use long ones; there is no special virtue in a long word.

Never write down a word that you cannot spell correctly.

Keep sentences short and simple; this saves punctuation worries and will make a better impression on the examiner than long involved sentences.

Write as if you were talking to an intelligent friend, *but never use slang*.

The essay must be revised. Such things as correcting spelling errors, and inserting punctuation marks and capital letters will improve considerably the finished article. It helps to read the essay aloud. If it is necessary to pause for breath in the middle of a sentence, insert a comma.

255

Arithmetic

· ·

We must recognise that arithmetic is to most children (particularly younger girls), not as interesting as English and intelligence testing. But children must of course learn arithmetic, and *learn it well*.

Nothing will help your child more in his arithmetic than if *he* has to teach *you*. It will enable him to realise whether or not he has really understood the method or principle; it will give him confidence in thinking out problems for himself and will make the whole process more one of co-operation than compulsion. Some occasional pretences of ignorance by the parent (if adopted with discretion) could be most fruitful.

Do not tackle too many of the child's difficulties in any one session —one difficult subject a session is quite enough. In any case it is essential that each stage in arithmetic should be mastered thoroughly before subsequent steps are built upon it. Once a child loses a little ground in this subject (whether it be due to boredom, change of school, absence from school or to emotional stresses) a snowball effect is obtained. Progress in arithmetic is like going upstairs—you have to go up one step at a time, and if too many steps are missing, further progress becomes impossible. One thing is certain—the only solid foundation for learning arithmetic is an automatic knowledge of number combinations.

Your child must know automatically (without the use of "crutches", like counting on fingers or the writing down of numbers to be carried over) what $7+4$, $9+6$, $13-4$, $17-9$, etc., make. His responses must become automatic, quick and accurate. Get him to add and then to subtract 9 from a long list of mixed numbers, and the same for 8, and 7 and so on. Children find 7, 8, and 9 combinations more difficult to work with than 2, 3, and 4 combinations. A little extra practice on the difficult numbers is to be advised.

Running through the multiplication tables during school holidays at the ages of 7, 8, 9 and 10 years is time very well spent. By the age of 8 or 9 years, all the tables to twelve should be known. Length, weight, time and capacity tables must also be known.

After discovering your child's weaknesses in arithmetic, you should try to make up your own examples to illustrate the points you wish to enlarge upon. If you are unable to do this, use the exercises in your child's school arithmetic book.

If you cannot get hold of your child's school text-book (and only then) we recommend:

> "The New Realistic Arithmetic" Teachers' Book IV by
> H. G. Wood. Published by James Nisbet & Co. Ltd.

This can be obtained from your bookseller or newsagent.

The methods your child uses in his school for multiplying and dividing may be different from those you learnt yourself. They are almost certainly better than the methods you were taught at school! Keep to the teaching of his school. Do not try to teach him *your* method, for that will only confuse him. Learn the new methods yourself, if necessary.

Some text-books contain exercises with no explanation of how they should be done. You will probably be able to give the necessary

257

17—H.T.

explanation; if not, you should mention the difficulty to your child's schoolteacher, who will, almost certainly, himself help to clarify the matter for your child.

Finally, never get ahead of your child's schooling. Do not teach him a new subject. Some schools do not get to decimal points before the grammar school examination. If such is the case in your child's school, it would do more harm than good for you to try to teach him decimals.

THE ARITHMETIC QUESTIONS IN THIS BOOK

The questions given in this book are searching and yet can be done rapidly (many of them come in the mental arithmetic category). They will soon show you where your efforts are most needed. Each one of them is completely comparable to the type of arithmetic question which is set in an examination.

Once your child fully understands a process, do not waste time doing all the examples. Go on to some other work, but do not forget the importance of revision of newly-mastered material. Revise this new knowledge for a number of consecutive sessions, so that the correct working becomes a habit. Let your child have enough easy problems to give him a feeling of confidence; go on to more difficult work very slowly.

With complicated sums, your child may be able to get to the core of the problem and understand more easily what is wanted by substituting smaller numbers.

Make full use of diagrams, and in explaining fractions use squared paper if necessary and fold and tear it to show halves and quarters.

Insist on your child keeping his work neat and his columns vertical. This will save him from making many unnecessary errors.

You must inculcate good habits until the correct methods of work are automatic. Apart from any entrance examination reason, the right help given in the early stages of learning arithmetic is most important.

Make your child show as much of the working of a sum as he can on his paper. If, during an examination, he does not show his working and makes a silly blunder in writing his answers (like writing 748, for an answer which should be 758), he will get *no* marks; whereas, if all his working is shown and some is right, he will definitely be given a few marks, even if his final answer is wrong.

The early correction of work as soon as possible after completion is very important. This is an instance where the parent has a great advantage over the class teacher who cannot, although he would very much like to, correct all his pupils' exercises immediately.

In this connection, remember also, that there is no correction like self-correction. Encourage your child to find the mistake for himself.

Furthermore, you must keep your child happy in his work—as happy as you can anyway!

Remember your fundamental purpose in going through these exercises—to find your child's weaknesses, which you and he must then correct.

terms used in arithmetic

· **259**

A FACTOR

is a number which goes into another number an exact number of times:

> 4 is a factor of 12 (it goes into it 3 times), 3 is of course, therefore, also a factor of 12 as are also 2 and 6.

DIGITS

are the figures used to make a number:

57 has 2 digits, 5 and 7.

A MULTIPLE

is a number that contains another number an exact number of times:

12 is a multiple of 4 (and of 3 and 2 and 6).

A PRIME NUMBER

is one that has no factors, e.g. 1, 2, 3, 5, 7, 11, 13, 17, 19. 2 is the only prime *even* number—for 2 is of course a factor of all other even numbers. A number will divide by 2 if it is even, i.e. if it ends in 2, 4, 6, 8, or 0.

To find the prime factors we need to try each prime number in turn—your child need not try the prime numbers after 11 for this examination.

All numbers ending in 0 will divide by 10.

All numbers ending in 5 or 0 will divide by 5.

A FRACTION

is a piece of something—$\frac{3}{4}$ means 3 parts of something divided into 4 parts. The upper figure (3) is known as the *numerator* (number of parts), and the lower figure (4) as the *denominator* (the name of the parts). A fraction such as the one above is sometimes called a *vulgar, common* or *ordinary fraction* to distinguish it from an improper fraction.

260

AN IMPROPER FRACTION

has a numerator greater than the denominator (e.g. $\frac{7}{2}$ which $= 3\frac{1}{2}$).

A MIXED NUMBER

means a whole number $+$ a fraction (e.g. $2\frac{1}{8}$).

A DIVISOR

is a number or quantity by which another number is divided:
e.g. $144 \div 12$, 12 is the divisor.

HIGHEST COMMON FACTOR (H.C.F.)

The highest common factor is the largest number which will divide
exactly into two or more numbers. To find the H.C.F. of two numbers
—for example 28 and 70—work in the following way:

  (a) *Find the factors of each number.*

    28; the factors of this number are 2 and 7 and 2

    70; the factors of this number are 7 and 5 and 2

  (b) *Find the factors which are common to all numbers.*

    2 and 7 are common to both numbers

  (c) *Multiply the common factors together.*

    $2 \times 7 = 14$

    14 is therefore the H.C.F. of 28 and 70

The H.C.F. is useful in cancelling fractions:

  $\frac{28}{70}$; since the H.C.F. is 14, both top and bottom can be divided
  by 14 and so reduce the fraction to $\frac{2}{5}$ (remember; fractions are
  left unaltered in value if both the numerator and the denominator are multiplied or divided by the same figure).

LOWEST COMMON MULTIPLE (L.C.M.)

The Lowest Common Multiple is the lowest number into which two
or more numbers will divide exactly. To find the L.C.M. of three
numbers—for example 6, 9 and 12—work in the following way:

  (a) *Find a factor which occurs in all three numbers, or, failing
    that, in at least two.*

    3 is a factor which occurs in all three numbers.

(b) *Divide the three numbers by this factor.*

$$3 \,)\, 6 \quad 9 \quad 12$$
$$ 2 \quad 3 \quad 4$$

(c) *If it is possible, repeat this process with the remaining numbers.*
2 is a factor which occurs in two of the remaining numbers.

$$2 \,)\, 2 \quad 3 \quad 4$$
$$ 1 \quad 3 \quad 2$$

notice that where it is impossible to divide a number (3) the entire number is carried down.

(d) *When it is no longer possible to find any further common factors, multiply the remaining numbers (1, 3, 2) and the divisors (3, 2) together.*

$1 \times 3 \times 2 = 6$

$6 \times 3 \times 2 = 36$

36 is therefore the L.C.M. of 6, 9 and 12.

As an exercise, find the L.C.M. of these three numbers:

14   12   20   (answer: 420)

A TABLE OF MEASUREMENT

To be learned by your child.

12 inches = 1 foot	1 dozen = 12
3 feet = 1 yard	1 score = 20
1760 yards = 1 mile	1 gross = 144
16 ounces = 1 pound	2 pints = 1 quart
14 pounds = 1 stone	4 quarts = 1 gallon (8 pints)
28 pounds = 1 quarter	
4 quarters = 1 hundredweight	
20 hundredweights = 1 ton (2240 pounds)	

262

numbers

. . . .

Numbers are recognised in groups of three—*hundreds, tens* and *units*.

232 (two hundred and thirty-two) equals:

two hundreds	100
	100
three lots of ten	10
	10
	10
and two single units	1
	1
	232

Beyond 999 we come to a thousand. When thousands are added together they are also counted in *hundreds, tens* and *units*.

123,000 (one hundred and twenty-three thousand) equals:

one hundred-thousand	100,000
two lots of ten-thousand	10,000
	10,000
and three single thousands	1,000
	1,000
	1,000
	123,000

When we get above 999,999 we come to a million, and millions too, are counted in *hundreds, tens* and *units*.

341,000,000 (three hundred and forty-one million) equals:

three hundred-millions	100,000,000
	100,000,000
	100,000,000
four ten-millions	10,000,000
	10,000,000
	10,000,000
	10,000,000
and one single million	1,000,000
	341,000,000

263

After thousands, there must be a comma and three figures :

    2,567   4,532   45,632   57,400   563,908

After millions, there must be a comma and two groups of three figures separated by commas :

    1,435,928   74,074,302   984,072,847

Ask your child to write in figures :

1. One hundred and one
2. One hundred and ten
3. One half of ten thousand
4. Ten thousand and ten
5. One hundred and one thousand and ten
6. Thirteen thousand and thirteen
7. Three hundred and twenty thousand and five
8. Three quarters of one million
9. Ten thousand and ninety nine

Answers : **I** 101 **2** 110 **3** 5,000 **4** 10,010 **5** 101,010 **6** 13,013 **7** 320,005 **8** 750,000 **9** 10,099

What is the largest number that can be made from the four figures 1379 ? (9,731)

Ask your child to write in words :

    1. 3,504   2. 11,101,001

264

Answers : **I** *three thousand, five hundred and four* **2** *eleven million, one hundred and one thousand, and one*

What is the value of the 9 in the following numbers ?

    1. 290
    2. 905

3. 69,551

4. 981,206

Answers: **1** *ninety* **2** *nine hundred* **3** *nine thousand* **4** *nine hundred-thousand*

We write first as 1st, also 21st, 31st, etc. Second as 2nd, third as 3rd, and after all others we put th, e.g. 4th, 5th, 26th, 70th.

addition

Do the following addition:

```
763
546
739
879
——   Answer: 2,927
```

Method of addition: Add from the top of each column downwards, starting with the right-hand column. In the above sum the addition should have been done in this way:

$3+6=\ 9$

$9+9=18$

$18+9=27$

write down 7 and carry 2 to the top of the next column

$2+6=\ 8$

$8+4=12$

$12+3=15$

$15+7=22$

write down 2 and carry 2 to the top of the next column and complete the sum.

Your child must be taught to make a habit of checking his answers, and this should be done by reversing the above method and checking his columns *from the bottom upwards*. If he can get the same answer both ways, he can be sure his addition is correct.

Now get him to add these numbers in this way:

(a)	27		(b)	287
	798			408
	456			790
	789			67

Answers: (a) 2,070 (b) 1,552

Has your child done the sums both upwards and downwards?

A few general sums:

1. Add £27 8s. 7½d. and £9 14s. 8d.
2. How many inches in 2 yards?
3. Multiply 1 foot 10 inches by 3.
4. Divide 3 yards 1 foot by 5.
5. What is left after dividing 111 by 12?

Answers: **1** £37. 3s. 3½d **2** 72 **3** *1 yard 2 feet 6 inches* **4** *2 feet* **5** 3

subtraction

· ·

266   To check subtraction add the answer to the number taken away. This total (if the answer is correct) will be the number "taken away from".

example:

$$11,340 \text{ (number taken away from)}$$
$$-\underline{8,974} \text{ (number taken away)}$$
$$2,366 \text{ (answer)}$$

to check this:

add the answer 2,366 to the number taken away—
           8,974
           ―――――
          11,340

The subtraction is therefore correct.

Now let your child do this sum:

       9,786
     − 5,998   Answer = 3,788

and make him check his answer in the way described above.

Point out to your child the different ways a problem of subtraction may be put:

1. "Take away ..."
2. "Subtract ..."
3. "What is the difference between ... ?"
4. "How much more is ... ?"
5. "How much less is ... ?"
6. "How much greater is ... ?"

multiplication

• •

Multiplication tables must be known THOROUGHLY and parrot-wise, by habit and not be conscious recall. Your child must also be able to dodge about quickly, i.e. from 3×7 to 9×6 to 4×8 etc. Children should also recognise that 4×3 is the same as 3×4, that 9×5 is the same as 5×9. This helps them enormously when they are doing division sums. Thus:

$1 \times 5 = 5$ $2 \times 5 = 10$ $3 \times 5 = 15$
$5 \times 1 = 5$ $5 \times 2 = 10$ $5 \times 3 = 15$

A normal tone of voice should be used during Table memorising periods—no chanting or singing. So that it will be as natural to recognise that $4 \times 7 = 28$ as that c-a-t spells cat. Some of the practice period should be spent seeing the Tables, some saying the Tables, some writing and some hearing the Tables, so that all faculties are involved in the learning process.

Practical work with books and stamps—showing that so many rows of so many units equals a certain product, should be used at every opportunity.

A few memory aids:

10 times a number always ends in 0.

5 times a number always ends in 5 or 0.

11 times any number up to 10 has the same number in the tens and units (e.g. $11 \times 7 = 77$ $11 \times 8 = 88$).

9 times Table = 9 18 27 36 45 54 63 72 81 90 99, etc.

8 times Table = 8 16 24 32 40 48 56 64 72 80 88 96 104, etc.

(i.e. 9 times Table goes down by 1, and the 8 times Table by 2 in units).

In fractions, the numerator and denominator may *both* be multiplied or divided by the same number without altering the value of the fraction.

268

division

· ·

In checking division sums if you multiply the answer by the divisor you should get the original number.

example: 496 divided by 17.

```
     29 (and 3 over)
17)496
     34
     156
     153
       3
```

to check this:

multiply the answer 29 by the divisor—

```
                       17
                      203
                       29
                      493
```

then add 3 (the remainder) to 493 and you get the original number of 496. The sum is therefore correct.

Now, divide 3,799 by 79 and check the answer similarly.

(answer: 48, *remainder* 7)

It is worth while to remember that a number (however large) is always exactly divisible by 4 if the last two digits are divisible by 4:

```
4)573416      4)45384      4)392912
  143354        11346        98228
```

money

. . . .

Money and shopping sums are the most frequently used sums in the grammar school examinations. Such sums will be much easier for your child if he learns the following facts about money:

$2 \times 1\frac{1}{2}d = 3d$	$5 \times 1\frac{1}{2}d = 7\frac{1}{2}d$	$7 \times 1\frac{1}{2}d = 10\frac{1}{2}d$
$3 \times 1\frac{1}{2}d = 4\frac{1}{2}d$	$6 \times 1\frac{1}{2}d = 9d$	$8 \times 1\frac{1}{2}d = 1/-$
$4 \times 1\frac{1}{2}d = 6d$		

269

$1/- = 2 \times 6d$	$1/- = 6 \times 2d$	$1/- = 24 \times \frac{1}{2}d$
$1/- = 3 \times 4d$	$1/- = 12 \times 1d$	$1/- = 4 \times 3d$
$18d = 1/6d$	$42d = 3/6d$	$84d = 7/-$
$20d = 1/8d$	$48d = 4/-$	$96d = 8/-$
$24d = 2/-$	$54d = 4/6d$	$100d = 8/4d$
$30d = 2/6d$	$60d = 5/-$	$120d = 10/-$
$36d = 3/-$	$72d = 6/-$	$144d = 12/-$
$40d = 3/4d$	$80d = 6/8d$	$240d = £1$

5 shillings = 1 crown   2 shillings = 1 florin

$2\frac{1}{2}$ shillings = $\frac{1}{2}$ crown   21 shillings = 1 guinea

$3 \times 3/4d = 10/-$ $3 \times 6/8d = £1$

$£1 = 8$ half-crowns $£1 = 160 \times 1\frac{1}{2}d$

$£1 = 20$ shillings $£1 = 240d$

$£1 = 40 \times 6d$ $£1 = 480 \times \frac{1}{2}d$

$£1 = 80 \times 3d$

Ask your child to change the following to shillings and pence (a child of 10 to 11 years of age should be able to do these correctly without resorting to pencil and paper):

19d (1/7d)	47d (3/11d)	77d (6/5d)
half-a-crown (2/6d)	55d (4/7d)	87d (7/3d)
27d (2/3d)	61d (5/1d)	100d (8/4d)
35d (2/11d)		

Change to pence:

1/5d (17d)	5/11d (71d)	8/7d (103d)
2/9d (33d)	6/7d (79d)	9/5d (113d)
3/7d (43d)	7/9d (93d)	half-a-guinea
4/3d (51d)		(126d)

270

Change to sixpences:

3/6d	(7)	11/6d	(23)
4/6d	(9)	13/6d	(27)
5/6d	(11)	17/6d	(35)
6/6d	(13)	18/6d	(37)
8/6d	(17)	£1. 0. 6	(41)

Change these sixpences to £.s.d.:

3	(1/6d)	15	(7/6d)
7	(3/6d)	21	(10/6d)
8	(4/–)	33	(16/6d)
9	(4/6d)	37	(18/6d)
11	(5/6d)	42	(£1. 1. 0)

Change to shillings:

£1. 7. 0	(27)	£4. 3. 0	(83)
£1. 15. 0	(35)	£4. 9. 0	(89)
£2. 6. 0	(46)	£4. 16. 0	(96)
£2. 13. 0	(53)	£5. 19. 0	(119)
£3. 4. 0	(64)	£6. 6. 0	(126)
£3. 11. 0	(71)	£10. 0. 0	(200)

How many half-crowns in:

5/–	(2)	15/–	(6)	£2. 10. 0	(20)
7/6d	(3)	17/6d	(7)	5 guineas	(42)

Change to pounds and shillings:

29/–	(£1. 9. 0)	57/–	(£2. 17. 0)
31/–	(£1. 11. 0)	64/–	(£3. 4. 0)
37/–	(£1. 17. 0)	78/–	(£3. 18. 0)
39/–	(£1. 19. 0)	83/–	(£4. 3. 0)

45/–	(£2. 5. 0)	96/–	(£4. 16. 0)
51/–	(£2. 11. 0)	103/–	(£5. 3. 0)

Add:

$2\frac{1}{2}$d + $9\frac{1}{2}$d	(1/–)	$3\frac{1}{2}$d + $7\frac{1}{2}$d	(11d)
$3\frac{1}{2}$d + 8d	($11\frac{1}{2}$d)	$2\frac{1}{2}$d + $9\frac{1}{2}$d	(1/–)
$3\frac{1}{2}$d + 9d	(1/$0\frac{1}{2}$d)	$5\frac{1}{2}$d + $6\frac{1}{2}$d	(1/–)
$4\frac{1}{2}$d + 7d	($11\frac{1}{2}$d)	7d + $6\frac{1}{2}$d	(1/$1\frac{1}{2}$d)
1/4d + 1/8d	(3/–)	$7\frac{1}{2}$d + 8d	(1/$3\frac{1}{2}$d)
1/5d + 1/7d	(3/–)	$6\frac{1}{2}$d + 10d	(1/$4\frac{1}{2}$d)
1/5d + 1/$6\frac{1}{2}$d	(2/$11\frac{1}{2}$d)	$8\frac{1}{2}$d + $9\frac{1}{2}$d	(1/6d)
1/7d + 3/6d	(5/1d)	$10\frac{1}{2}$d + 11d	(1/$9\frac{1}{2}$d)
1/8d + 2/$7\frac{1}{2}$d	(4/$3\frac{1}{2}$d)	$9\frac{1}{2}$d + 10d	(1/$7\frac{1}{2}$d)
3/$9\frac{1}{2}$d + 5/7d	(9/$4\frac{1}{2}$d)	1/1d + $11\frac{1}{2}$d	(2/$0\frac{1}{2}$d)
2/$3\frac{1}{2}$d + 4/$9\frac{1}{2}$d	(7/1d)	1/2d + $10\frac{1}{2}$d	(2/$0\frac{1}{2}$d)
5/$9\frac{1}{2}$d + 6/$7\frac{1}{2}$d	(12/5d)	1/3d + 1/9d	(3/–)

Subtract:

$9\frac{1}{2}$d – 4d	($5\frac{1}{2}$d)	2/6d – $9\frac{1}{2}$d	(1/$8\frac{1}{2}$d)
$8\frac{1}{2}$d – $3\frac{1}{2}$d	(5d)	2/6d – 1/$7\frac{1}{2}$d	($10\frac{1}{2}$d)
1/– – $1\frac{1}{2}$d	($10\frac{1}{2}$d)	2/6d – 1/$0\frac{1}{2}$d	(1/$5\frac{1}{2}$d)
1/– – $2\frac{1}{2}$d	($9\frac{1}{2}$d)	10/– – 3/$6\frac{1}{2}$d	(6/$5\frac{1}{2}$d)
1/– – $6\frac{1}{2}$d	($5\frac{1}{2}$d)	10/– – 5/$7\frac{1}{2}$d	(4/$4\frac{1}{2}$d)
1/– – $8\frac{1}{2}$d	($3\frac{1}{2}$d)	10/– – 7/$3\frac{1}{2}$d	(2/$8\frac{1}{2}$d)
1/3d – 6d	(9d)	10/– – 8/$1\frac{1}{2}$d	(1/$10\frac{1}{2}$d)
1/6d – 1/1d	(5d)	10/– – 9/$2\frac{1}{2}$d	($9\frac{1}{2}$d)
2/– – $7\frac{1}{2}$d	(1/$4\frac{1}{2}$d)	£1 – 3/$6\frac{1}{2}$d	(16/$5\frac{1}{2}$d)
2/– – $9\frac{1}{2}$d	(1/$2\frac{1}{2}$d)	£1 – 6/8d	(13/4d)
2/– – $11\frac{1}{2}$d	(1/$0\frac{1}{2}$d)	£1 – 7/$9\frac{1}{2}$d	(12/$2\frac{1}{2}$d)
2/– – 1/5d	(7d)	£1 – 11/$3\frac{1}{2}$d	(8/$8\frac{1}{2}$d)

272

Multiply (answers to be given in £.s.d):

$2d \times 4$	(8d)	$9d \times 7$	(5/3d)
$3d \times 7$	(1/9d)	$8d \times 10$	(6/8d)
$4d \times 8$	(2/8d)	$9d \times 11$	(8/3d)
$5d \times 9$	(3/9d)	$8d \times 12$	(8/–)
$6d \times 7$	(3/6d)	$7\frac{1}{2}d \times 11$	(6/10$\frac{1}{2}$d)
$7d \times 8$	(4/8d)	$8\frac{1}{2}d \times 10$	(7/1d)
$8d \times 9$	(6/–)	$10d \times 11$	(9/2d)
$9d \times 6$	(4/6d)	$3/– \times 9$	(£1. 7. 0)
$8d \times 11$	(7/4d)	$7/– \times 8$	(£2. 16. 0)
$10d \times 11$	(9/2d)	$1/3d \times 5$	(6/3d)
$11d \times 11$	(10/1d)	$1/4d \times 7$	(9/4d)
$11d \times 12$	(11/–)	$1/9d \times 11$	(19/3d)
$\frac{1}{2}d \times 5$	(2$\frac{1}{2}$d)	$1/10\frac{1}{2}d \times 3$	(5/7$\frac{1}{2}$d)
$\frac{1}{2}d \times 9$	(4$\frac{1}{2}$d)	$3/8\frac{1}{2}d \times 12$	(£2. 4. 6)
$1\frac{1}{2}d \times 7$	(10$\frac{1}{2}$d)	$4/9\frac{1}{2}d \times 12$	(£2. 17. 6)
$10d \times 5$	(4/2d)	$2\frac{1}{2}d \times 9$	(1/10$\frac{1}{2}$d)
$11d \times 7$	(6/5d)	$3d \times 8$	(2/0d)
$8d \times 6$	(4/–)	$4d \times 7$	(2/4d)
$10d \times 8$	(6/8d)	$6\frac{1}{2}d \times 7$	(3/9$\frac{1}{2}$d)

Divide:

$6d \div 4$	(1$\frac{1}{2}$d)	$5\frac{1}{2}d \div 11$	($\frac{1}{2}$d)
$9d \div 6$	(1$\frac{1}{2}$d)	$4d \div 8$	($\frac{1}{2}$d)
$1/8d \div 4$	(5d)	$1/0d \div 6$	(2d)
$2/1d \div 5$	(5d)	$1/0\frac{1}{2}d \div 5$	(2$\frac{1}{2}$d)
$1/10\frac{1}{2}d \div 9$	(2$\frac{1}{2}$d)	$2/4d \div 7$	(4d)
$4\frac{1}{2}d \div 3$	(1$\frac{1}{2}$d)	$4/7d \div 11$	(5d)
$3d \div 2$	(1$\frac{1}{2}$d)	$£1. 4. 0 \div 4$	(6/–)

273

18—H.T.

$6d \div 4$	$(1\frac{1}{2}d)$	3 guineas $\div 9$	$(7/-)$
$3\frac{1}{2}d \div 7$	$(\frac{1}{2}d)$	£5. 8. 0 $\div 12$	$(9/-)$

SHORT CUTS IN MONEY PROBLEMS

Be careful not to confuse your child with short cuts. They must be simple. Applied to 12 and 20, 12 things at $1d = 1/-$ and 20 things at $1/- = £1$, are by far the most important. He should learn that by changing the pence to shillings, he can rapidly calculate that:

> 12 things at 1d cost 1/-
>   at 3d cost 3/-
>   at 11d cost 11/-
>   at 1/2d cost 14/- (for 1/2d. = 14d.)
>   at 1/6d cost 18/-

Also by considering the $\frac{1}{2}d$ as a *fraction*, he can rapidly calculate that:

> 6 things at $\frac{1}{2}d$ cost 3d
> 8 ,,   at $\frac{1}{2}d$ cost 4d
> 15 ,,   at $\frac{1}{2}d$ cost $7\frac{1}{2}d$

Since $20 \times 1/- = £1$, to find the cost of 20 articles at 2/- each, you need only change the shillings to pounds:

> 20 at 2/- = £2
> 20 at 3/6d = £3$\frac{1}{2}$ (6d is $\frac{1}{2}$ of a shilling)
> 20 at 4/3d = £4$\frac{1}{4}$ (3d is $\frac{1}{4}$ of a shilling)
> 20 at 5/9d = £5$\frac{3}{4}$ (9d is $\frac{3}{4}$ of a shilling)

274

If you need to multiply by 240—change the pence to pounds.

> Since 240d = £1, 240 articles at 2d cost £2
>   240 articles at 1$\frac{1}{4}$d cost £1$\frac{1}{4}$

Questions in which short cuts can be used:
1. What will 4 dozen pencils at $1\frac{1}{2}$d each cost?
2. What is the cost of 60 articles at $2\frac{1}{2}$d each?
3. What will 20 articles at $11\frac{1}{2}$d each cost?
4. What will 2 articles cost at 7/6d a dozen? What will 9 articles cost?
5. What will 8 dozen oranges cost at 8 a 1/-?
6. What will 12 hats cost at 19/11d each?
7. If 3 gross articles cost 36/-, what do 3 dozen cost?
8. Divide 21 dozen by 7.
9. What is the cost of 240 pencils at $1\frac{1}{2}$d each?
10. What is the cost of 480 pencils at $\frac{1}{2}$d each?
11. What is the cost of 250 books at 1d each?
12. Take £4 from 1000 pence.
13. How many pounds are there in $\frac{1}{112}$ of 7 hundredweights?
14. 56 articles cost £4. 17. 4. How much would 7 cost?
15. Multiply $19/11\frac{1}{2}$d by 10.
16. From £2. 10. 0×15 take £5 × 7.
17. From $3\frac{1}{2}$ score take $3\frac{1}{2}$ dozen.
18. Take 6 dozen from $2\frac{1}{2}$ gross.
19. How much greater are 20 half guineas than 20 half crowns?
20. How much greater are 15 half sovereigns than 15 florins?
21. From 18 × 57 take 57 × 9.
22. Divide 65 × 70 by 13 × 35.
23. How many times is 7 × 9 contained in 56 × 81?
24. From 9 times $7/9\frac{1}{2}$d take 5 times $7/9\frac{1}{2}$d.
25. A man buys 12 articles at $11\frac{1}{2}$d each and sells them at $1/2\frac{1}{2}$d each. What is the total profit made?

answers on next page

275

Answers : **1** 6/– (4 × 1/6d) **2** 12/6d (5 × 2/6d) **3** 19/2d (20/–, *minus* 20 × $\frac{1}{2}$d) **4** 1/3d, 5/7$\frac{1}{2}$d **5** 12/– **6** £11. 19. 0 (£12 – 1/–) **7** 3/– (36/– ÷ 12) **8** 3 *dozen* **9** £1. 10. 0 **10** £1. 0. 0 **11** £1. 0. 10 **12** 40 *pence* **13** 7 *pounds* **14** 12/2d (£4. 17. 4 ÷ 8) **15** £9. 19. 7 (£10 – 10 × $\frac{1}{2}$d) **16** £2. 10. 0 (£2. 10. 0 × 1 *for* £5 × 7 = £2. 10. 0 × 14) **17** 28 (3$\frac{1}{2}$ × 8) **18** 2 *gross* **19** £8 (20 × 8/–) **20** £6 (15 × 8/–) **21** 513 (57 × 9) **22** 10 (*cancel*: 13 *divides into* 65 *five times — and* 35 *into* 70, *twice*: *so the answer is* 5 × 2) **23** 72 (*cancel*: *as in previous answer, until sum comes to* 8 × 9) **24** £1. 11. 2 (4 × 7/9$\frac{1}{2}$d) **25** 3/0d (12 × 3d)

fractions

• •

ADDING, SUBTRACTING AND COMPARING

In order to add, subtract or compare fractions, they must first be reduced to a common denominator (the figure below the line). The common denominator should be the *Lowest Common Multiple* (explanation of L.C.M. on page 261) of all the denominators.

example (a) $\frac{3}{4} + \frac{2}{3} + \frac{7}{8}$

The L.C.M. of 4, 3 and 8 is 24 and the fractions become

$\frac{18}{24} + \frac{16}{24} + \frac{21}{24} = \frac{55}{24}$ $(2\frac{7}{24})$

example (b) Which is the largest and which is the smallest of these

fractions, $\frac{5}{8}$ $\frac{2}{3}$ $\frac{7}{9}$

The L.C.M. of 8, 3 and 9 is 72 and the fractions become

$\frac{45}{72}$ $\frac{48}{72}$ $\frac{56}{72}$

276

They can now be accurately compared, and it will be seen that $\frac{7}{9}$ $(\frac{56}{72})$ is the largest and $\frac{5}{8}$ $(\frac{45}{72})$ the smallest fraction.

example (c) $\frac{2}{3} - \frac{3}{8}$

The L.C.M. of 3 and 8 is 24 and the fractions become

$\frac{16}{24} - \frac{9}{24} = \frac{7}{24}$

Therefore $\frac{2}{3} - \frac{3}{8} = \frac{7}{24}$

MULTIPLICATION OF FRACTIONS

Multiply the numerators together to form the numerator for the answer, and multiply the denominators together to form the denominator for the answer:

$$\frac{2}{3} \times \frac{4}{5} = \frac{8}{15}$$

CANCELLING

It is often possible to save much work by cancelling. Take for example, the following sums:

example (a)

$$\frac{5}{36} \times \frac{24}{25} = \frac{120}{900}$$

example (b)

$$\frac{1}{3} \times \frac{3}{8} \times \frac{4}{5} = \frac{12}{120}$$

In both these cases much work could have been saved if (before multiplication) the following cancelling had been done:

example (a)

$$\frac{\overset{1}{\cancel{5}}}{\underset{3}{\cancel{36}}} \times \frac{\overset{2}{\cancel{24}}}{\underset{5}{\cancel{25}}} = \frac{2}{15}$$

example (b)

$$\frac{1}{\underset{1}{\cancel{3}}} \times \frac{\overset{1}{\cancel{3}}}{\underset{2}{\cancel{8}}} \times \frac{\overset{1}{\cancel{4}}}{5} = \frac{1}{10}$$

277

In cancelling, one must find a factor (for explanation of factors see page 259) which is common to both a numerator and a denominator, and divide them each by it. For instance, in (a) the numerator 24 and the denominator 36, have a common factor of 12; by dividing them both by 12 it is possible to reduce them to 2 and 3. In the same way,

5 and 25 have been reduced to 1 and 5, by dividing them by their common factor of 5. What were the common factors used in the cancellings in example (b)?   (3 and 4)

DIVISION OF FRACTIONS

Turn the divisor (the second fraction) upside down and proceed as in multiplication:

$$\frac{2}{3} \div \frac{2}{9} \text{ becomes } \frac{2}{3} \times \frac{9}{2} \text{ and now by cancelling, } \frac{\overset{1}{\cancel{2}}}{\underset{1}{\cancel{3}}} \times \frac{\overset{3}{\cancel{9}}}{\underset{1}{\cancel{2}}} = 3$$

MONEY FRACTIONS

Your child must learn the following:

$£\frac{1}{2}=10/-$	$£\frac{1}{4}=5/-$	$£\frac{1}{8}=2/6d$	$£\frac{1}{10}=2/-$
$£\frac{1}{6}=3/4d$	$£\frac{1}{3}=6/8d$	$£\frac{1}{20}=1/-$	$£\frac{1}{40}=6d$
$\frac{1}{2}/-=6d$	$\frac{1}{4}/-=3d$	$\frac{1}{3}/-=4d$	$\frac{1}{6}/-=2d$
$\frac{1}{8}/-=1\frac{1}{2}d$	$\frac{1}{12}/-=1d$	$\frac{1}{24}/-=\frac{1}{2}d$	$\frac{1}{48}/-=\frac{1}{4}d$

Exercises in using fractions:

1. How many pence are there in $\frac{1}{2}, \frac{1}{3}, \frac{1}{4}, \frac{1}{6}, \frac{1}{12}$ of a shilling?
2. How many ounces are there in $\frac{1}{2}, \frac{1}{4}, \frac{1}{8}, \frac{1}{16}$ of a pound?
3. How many pints are there in $\frac{1}{2}, \frac{1}{4}, \frac{1}{8}$ of a gallon?
4. How many hours are there in $\frac{1}{2}, \frac{3}{4}, \frac{1}{3}, \frac{1}{6}, \frac{1}{8}, \frac{1}{12}, \frac{1}{24}$ of a day?
5. How many inches are there in $\frac{1}{2}, \frac{1}{4}, \frac{1}{3}, \frac{1}{6}, \frac{1}{9}, \frac{1}{12}, \frac{1}{18}$ of a yard?
6. How many shillings are there in $\frac{1}{2}, \frac{1}{4}, \frac{1}{5}, \frac{1}{10}, \frac{1}{20}$ of a pound?
7. Add together the smallest and greatest of $\frac{1}{4}, \frac{1}{8}, \frac{1}{7}, \frac{1}{5}$.
8. Which is smaller, $\frac{3}{4}$ or $\frac{5}{7}$?
9. What fraction comes half way between $\frac{1}{2}$ and $\frac{1}{4}$?
10. What fraction comes half way between $5\frac{1}{4}$ and $3\frac{3}{4}$?
11. How many times can $\frac{1}{4}$ be taken from $2\frac{3}{4}$?
12. How many times can $\frac{1}{3}$ be taken from 9?

13. How many eighths in $3\frac{1}{4}$?

14. What weight will $\frac{1}{2}$ of $\frac{1}{2}$ of $\frac{1}{2}$ of 1 pound have?

15. What is $\frac{1}{2}$ of $\frac{2}{3}$ of $\frac{3}{4}$ of £1?

16. What is 7 times $\frac{1}{14}$ of 10/–?

17. What is 15 times $\frac{1}{5}$ of 10/–?

18. What fraction of £1 is 4/–?

19. What is 4 times a quarter of 2/7?

20. What is $\frac{1}{5}$ of 25×5?

21. $\frac{2}{7}$ of a number $= 8$. What is the number?

22. $\frac{2}{5}$ of a number is 18. What is the number?

23. What fraction of 1 cwt. is 1 stone?

24. Divide 8 by $\frac{1}{2}$.

25. What is the difference between $\frac{3}{4} \times \frac{1}{2}$ and $\frac{1}{2}$ of $\frac{3}{4}$?

26. $\frac{1}{3}$ of a number $= 12$. What is $\frac{1}{4}$ of the number?

27. $\frac{1}{4}$ of my age $= \frac{1}{5}$ of my brother's. If I am 24 years old, how old is my brother?

28. $\frac{3}{4}$ of my money is 12/–. How much have I?

29. I spent $\frac{4}{7}$ of my money and had 6/– left. How much had I at first?

30. $\frac{1}{3}$ of my money $= \frac{1}{2}$ of my sister's. If I have 30/– how much has she?

31. I spent $\frac{3}{4}$ of my money, then $\frac{1}{2}$ of what I had left. If I now have 5/–, how much had I at first?

279

32. Divide 6 by $\frac{3}{4}$.

33. How many 3d's in 17/9d?

34. $3\frac{1}{2}$ times a number is 70. What is the number?

35. How many $2\frac{1}{2}$ yard lengths can you get in 40 yards?

36. A car does 36 miles on $1\frac{1}{2}$ gallons of petrol. How far will it go on 4 gallons?

37. If $\frac{1}{7}$ of a number $= 479$, what is $\frac{1}{479}$ of that number?

38. $\frac{1}{2}$ of a number is 3 more than $\frac{1}{3}$ of the number. What is the number?

39. A brick weighs 4 pounds plus $\frac{1}{2}$ its own weight. What is its weight?

40. There are 360 pupils going to school. $\frac{1}{6}$ go by tram, $\frac{1}{4}$ by bus, $\frac{1}{9}$ by cycle. How many walk?

41. Of 222 pupils, there are twice as many girls as there are boys. How many are there of each?

42. James had 3 times as many sweets as Bob, and Bill had as many as James and Bob together. If there were 32 sweets in all how many did each have?

Answers: **1** 6, 4, 3, 2, 1 **2** 8, 4, 2, 1 **3** 4, 2, 1 **4** 12, 18, 8, 4, 3, 2, 1 **5** 18, 9, 12, 6, 4, 3, 2 **6** 10, 5, 4, 2, 1 **7** $\frac{1}{8}+\frac{1}{4}=\frac{3}{8}$ **8** $\frac{5}{7}$ $(\frac{5}{7}=\frac{20}{28}$ and $\frac{3}{4}=\frac{21}{28})$ **9** $\frac{3}{8}$ **10** $4\frac{1}{2}$ $(5\frac{1}{4}=\frac{21}{4}$ and $3\frac{3}{4}=\frac{15}{4}.$ $\frac{18}{4}$ [$4\frac{1}{2}$] *lies between the two* **11** 11 $(2\frac{3}{4}\div\frac{1}{4}=\frac{11}{4}\times\frac{4}{1})$ **12** 27 $(9\div\frac{1}{3}=\frac{9}{1}\times\frac{3}{1})$ **13** 26 $(3\frac{1}{4}\div\frac{1}{8}=\frac{13}{4}\times\frac{8}{1})$ **14** 2 *ounces* **15** 5/- *(for:* $\frac{1}{2}$ *of* $\frac{2}{3}=\frac{1}{3}$ *and* $\frac{1}{3}$ *of* $\frac{3}{4}=\frac{1}{4})$ **16** 5/- **17** 30/- **18** $\frac{1}{5}$ **19** 2/7 *(4 times* $\frac{1}{4}=$ *1whole)* **20** 25 **21** 28 *(since* $\frac{2}{7}=8$, $\frac{1}{7}=4$ *so the number is* $7\times4)$ **22** 45 **23** $\frac{1}{8}$ **24** 16 $(8\div\frac{1}{2}=\frac{8}{1}\times\frac{2}{1}=16)$ **25** *they are the same* **26** 9 **27** 30 **28** 16/- **29** 14/- $(6/-=\frac{3}{7})$ **30** £1 **31** £2 **32** 8 $(6\div\frac{3}{4}=\frac{6}{1}\times\frac{4}{3}=8)$ **33** 71 **34** 20 $(70\div3\frac{1}{2})$ **35** 16 **36** 96 **37** 7 **38** 18 $(\frac{1}{2}-\frac{1}{3}=\frac{1}{6}$ *and this we are told is* 3) **39** 8 *pounds (4 pounds must therefore be half its own weight)* **40** 170 **41** *74 boys and 148 girls (for of every 3 pupils, 1 is a boy and 2 are girls)* **42** *16 Bill, 12 James and 4 Bob (for if Bob has 1, James must have 3 and Bill 4 and since that makes a unit of 8, we must first divide 32 by 8 to get Bob's share)*

time

280

A.M. AND P.M.

A.M. means ante meridiem and P.M. means post meridiem. These are Latin phrases meaning before noon and after noon.

What is the briefest way of writing:

A quarter past two in the morning?   (2.15 a.m.)

SUBTRACTION OF TIME

How many minutes between 1.42 a.m. and 3.15 a.m. ?   (93)
If (as in the above example) both times are a.m. or p.m. the problem
is a simple one of straightforward subtraction. On the other hand, if
the two items contain *both a.m. and p.m.* it is a little more complicated
and your child should work in this way:

How many minutes between 11.15 a.m. and 12.17 p.m. ?

(a) *First work out the difference to noon or midnight.*
   11.15 a.m. to 12 noon equals 45 minutes.
(b) *Then add the further interval of time.*
   12 noon to 12.17 p.m. equals 17 minutes, 45 minutes plus
   17 minutes equals 62 minutes.

The answer is therefore 62 minutes.

Exercises in subtracting Time:

1. How many minutes between 1.15 p.m. and 3.8 p.m. ?

2. How many minutes between 11.29 p.m. and 1.15 a.m. ?

3. What time is it 85 minutes before noon? What time is it 66
minutes before midnight?

4. The sun rose at 6.5 a.m. and shone for 11 hours 25 minutes.
When did it set?

5. A man took 17 minutes to walk from home to the station and
had 5 minutes to wait for the 9.16. When did he leave home?

6. How many times as fast as the hour hand does the minute hand
of a clock go?

7. How many times in 12 hours are the hands of a clock opposite
each other?

8. A clock gains 4 minutes a day. What time will it show 8 p.m.
Thursday, if it was put right at 8 a.m. on Tuesday?

Answers: **1** 113 **2** 106 **3** 10.35 a.m., 10.54 p.m. **4** 5.30 p.m. **5** 8.54 **6** 12 **7** 12 **8** 8.10

281

Questions on Time and Distance:

1. A walker takes 10 minutes to walk $\frac{1}{2}$ mile. How many miles per hour is this?

2. If a train goes 15 miles in 20 minutes, how far will it go in 30 minutes?

3. How long will it take to go $7\frac{1}{2}$ miles, going at 20 miles per hour?

4. Travelling at 15 miles in 15 minutes—how many m.p.h.?

5. Travelling at 1 mile in $1\frac{1}{2}$ minutes—how many m.p.h.?

6. It takes 3 hours to do a journey going at 50 m.p.h. How long would it take going at 25 m.p.h.?

7. A man took 5 hours to do a journey walking at 3 m.p.h. How long would it have taken cycling at 10 m.p.h.?

8. 30 m.p.h.—how many yards per minute?

9. Whilst travelling in a number 6 bus, I noticed that number 6 buses coming towards me, passed at 2.15; 2.20; 2.25 p.m. How often do these buses run?

Answers: **1** 3 **2** $22\frac{1}{2}$ *miles* **3** $22\frac{1}{2}$ *minutes* **4** 60 *miles per hour* **5** 40 *m.p.h.* ($\frac{2}{3}$ *mile a minute*)
6 6 *hours (for the journey is 150 miles long)* **7** $1\frac{1}{2}$ *hours (for the journey is 15 miles long)*
8 880 **9** *every* 10 *minutes (for I am travelling towards each bus at the same speed as it is travelling towards me)*

averages

282 ·

An *average number* means a number which is intermediate to a series of numbers. It is found by adding all the numbers together, and then dividing the total by the number of numbers. A cricketer in four innings makes four different scores. To find his average score for each innings we find the total number of runs scored and then divide by 4.

example:

What is the average of 1, 3, 5, 7?

$1+3+5+7=16$

There are four numbers and so

$16 \div 4 = 4$

4, is therefore, the average.

Questions on averages:

1. What is the average of 7, 9, 11, 13?

2. What is the average of 1/4, 2/2, 2/6?

3. What sum of money lies halfway between 5/7d and 9/5d?

4. The average of four numbers is 10, three of them are 9, 11, and 12. What is the fourth?

5. The average of 6 numbers is 7; the average of 5 of them is 6. What is the sixth number?

6. A cricketer's average for four innings is 20. How many must he make in his next innings to make his average 22?

7. John has 47 marbles, Harry has 29. How many must John give to Harry to make the numbers equal?

8. Jack has twice as many marbles as Tom. If Tom has 24, how many marbles must Jack give Tom to make the numbers equal?

9. If a father's and son's total age is 40 and the father is 7 times as old as his son, how old is the son?

10. A man is four times as old as his son. Their total age is 30— how old is the son?

283

Answers: **1** 10 **2** 2/- **3** 7/6d (5/7d+9/5d÷2) **4** 8 (*the average of four numbers is 10, the total must be 40. Three of the numbers are 9, 11 and 12—add these together to make 32. The fourth number must be 40−32=8*) **5** 12 **6** 30 [*he has already scored 80, take this from 5×22 (which is to be his next grand total)=30*] **7** 9 (*47+29=76. Divide this by 2 equals 38*) **8** 12 (*similar to previous question*) **9** 5 (*for each 8 years in the total, the father would have 7 and the son 1, therefore divide 40 by 8*) **10** 6

areas

. . . .

Distinguish between the area, and the distance round a square or rectangle (the perimeter). The area is found by multiplying the length by the breadth, and is given as *square* inches, *square* feet or *square* yards. Thus a room 3 yards by 4 yards has an area of 12 *square* yards. Its perimeter is 14 yards (3 yards + 4 yards + 3 yards + 4 yards). In finding the area of the path round a garden, or of a surround to a carpet in a room, the easiest way is to subtract the area of the inner rectangle from the area of the outer (for instance—the area of a carpet from the area of a room).

Here, as in fractions, make use if necessary of a squared paper and of paper folding and paper tearing to clarify the subject.

Questions on areas:

1. How many square inches in:
   - (a) 1 square foot
   - (b) $\frac{1}{2}$ a square foot
   - (c) $1\frac{1}{2}$ square feet
   - (d) $\frac{1}{2}$ a foot squared?

2. The area of a room is 30 square yards. One side is five yards. What is the other?

3. What is the area of a door 6 feet 6 inches × 3 feet 6 inches?

4. How much larger is a carpet 16 feet square than one measuring 17 feet × 13 feet?

5. How many times is the area of a square increased:
   - (a) if each side is doubled?
   - (b) if each side is trebled?

6. What is the difference in area between a square of 8 inch side and that of a square of 4 inch side?

7. The area of a square is 144 square inches. What is the distance round the square?

8. Find the distance round a square of 121 square inches.

9. The distance round a square is 1 yard. What is its area?

10. How many times is a 1 inch square contained in a 4 inch square?

11. How many tiles 3 inches square are needed to cover an area 2 feet × 3 feet?

12. A piece of paper 4 inches long and 3 inches wide is ruled in squares of ½ inch size. How many small squares are there?

13. A square sheet of paper has an area of 4 square inches. What would be the length of the side of a piece of paper in the shape of a square four times the area of the first piece?

14. Round a square of 2 inch sides is a border 2 inches wide. What is the area of the larger square?

15. A room is twice as long as it is wide and covers 200 square feet. What is its length and breadth?

16. The distance around a room is 50 feet. If one side is 12 feet what is the size of the other?

17. If the distance round a room is 54 feet and the length is 17 feet what is the width?

18. If the area of a wall is 72 square feet and its height is 4 yards, what is its length in yards?

19. Two oblongs put end to end have an area of 36 square inches. One of them measures 3 inches by 4 inches, what is the length of the other?

285

Answers: **1** (a) 144 (b) 72 (c) 216 (d) 36 **2** 6 *yards* **3** 22¾ *square feet* (6½ *feet* × 3½ *feet*) **4** 35 *square feet* **5** (a) 4 (b) 9 **6** 48 *square inches* **7** 48 *inches* **8** 44 *inches* **9** 81 *square inches* **10** 16 **11** 96 (3 *inches square* = 1/16 *square foot. Therefore we must divide 6 square feet by* 1/16 *square feet*) **12** 48 **13** 4 *inches* **14** 36 *square inches (the sides of the big square are 6 inches)* **15** 20 *feet* 10 *feet* **16** 13 *feet (draw a diagram if necessary)* **17** 10 *feet* **18** 2 *yards* **19** 8 *inches*

problems

· ·

Problems test intelligence and ability to understand what one is reading:

example:

> $5\frac{1}{2}$ years ago John was half as old as he is today. How old will he be in 4 years' time? (Half John's present age is $5\frac{1}{2}$, therefore he is 11 now, and will be 15 in four years' time.)

General problems:

1. A man now 30 was 24 when his son was born. How old will his son be in 7 years' time?

2. A man at 30 is 6 times as old as his son. How many times as old as his son will he be in 20 years' time?

3. In 24 years' time a boy will be 3 times his present age. How old is he now?

4. How many poles 10 yards apart are needed to support 60 yards of wire?

5. How many posts 20 yards apart are needed to support 200 yards of wire?

6. 18 boys stood in a straight line each 3 yards from the next. How long was the line?

286

Answers: **1** 13 **2** *twice* **3** 12 *years* (24 *is twice his present age*) **4** 7 (*two poles are needed for the first* 10 *yard stretch*) **5** 11 **6** 51 *yards* (*the first* 2 *boys form one space of* 3 *yards*)

Problems involving taps, etc.

1. 2 similar taps filled a bath in 5 minutes. How long would 1 tap alone take?

2. A can was $\frac{1}{2}$ full of oil, after adding 5 pints it was $\frac{3}{4}$ full. How

much would the full can hold?

3. One tap fills a tank in 4 minutes, another in 2 minutes. How long would it take to fill the tank if they were both turned on together?

4. One tap fills a tank in 4 minutes, and another in 6 minutes. The drain empties it in 3 minutes. If they are all in use how long will it take to fill the tank?

Answers: **1** 10 *minutes* **2** 20 *pints* **3** 1 *minute* 20 *seconds* (*in* 1 *minute, one tap fills* $\frac{1}{4}$ *of the tank and the other tap* $\frac{1}{2}$ *of the tank, so together in* 1 *minute they would fill* $\frac{3}{4}$ *of the tank. The other* $\frac{1}{4}$ *tankful would therefore take* 20 *seconds*) **4** 12 *minutes* (*in one minute the first tap will fill* $\frac{1}{4}$ *and the second* $\frac{1}{6}$*, and the drain will empty* $\frac{1}{3}$*, therefore in* 1 *minute it will be* $\frac{1}{4}+\frac{1}{6}-\frac{1}{3}=\frac{1}{12}$ *full*)

Problems involving unequal division:

example :

> There are 424 pupils in a school and there are 18 more girls than boys. How many are there of each?
>
> (a) *Eliminate by subtraction the unequal factor.*
>
> $424 - 18 = 406$
>
> (b) *Then do the division.*
>
> $406 \div 2 = 203$
>
> the number of boys will equal 203
>
> the number of girls will equal $203 + 18$

Answer $= 221$ girls and 203 boys

287

1. The sum of two numbers is 97, one is 79 more than the other. What is the smaller number?

2. A carving knife 12 inches long, has a blade 3 inches longer than the handle. How long is each?

3. A father is 24 years older than his son. Their total years are 40. How old is the son?

4. In a gathering, there were 5 men to every 4 women. There were 81 altogether. How many of each?

5. Divide 6/– so that Tom gets 6d more than Dick.

6. Divide 2/6d between two boys so that one gets 2d for every 1d the other gets.

7. Divide 1/– between 2 boys so that one has 1d more than the other.

8. Divide 5/– between 2 boys giving one 2d to every 3d of the other boy.

9. (a) Divide 9/– so that Tom gets 1/– more than Harry, who gets 1/– more than Dick. (b) Divide £1. 1. 0 in the same way.

10. Mr. A owns $\frac{5}{8}$ of a business and Mr. B is the other partner. Mr. A's share is worth £1,500 more than Mr. B's. What is the value of:

(a) The business   (b) Mr. B's share?

Answers: **1** 9 **2** $4\frac{1}{2}$ *inches and* $7\frac{1}{2}$ *inches* **3** 8 **4** 45 *men* 36 *women (for of every* 9, 5 *are men and* 4 *are women)* **5** 3/3 *and* 2/9 **6** 1/8 *and* 10d (*as in question* **4**, *but divide the* 2/6d *into groups of threepence*) **7** $6\frac{1}{2}$d *and* $5\frac{1}{2}$d **8** 2/– *and* 3/– **9** (a) 4/– 3/– 2/– (b) 8/– 7/– 6/– **10** (a) £6,000 ($\frac{5}{8}-\frac{3}{8}=\frac{1}{4}$ *so* £1,500=$\frac{1}{4}$) (b) £2,250 ($\frac{3}{8}$ *of* £6,000)

Problems involving proportion:

example:

    If 9 books cost 27/–, what will 5 cost?

    Work in this way:

    9 books cost 27/–

    1 book will cost 27/– divided by 9, which is 3/– and so 5 books will cost 3/– × 5

Answer = 15/–

1. If 7 oranges cost 3/6d, what will 11 cost?

2. If a car travels 240 miles on 8 gallons of petrol, how far will it go on 5 gallons?

Answers: **1** 5/6d **2** 150 *miles*

More problems involving proportion:

In doing proportion sums common-sense must be used.

example:

> If 10 men do a job in 5 days how long will it take 20 men?
>
> Work in this way:
>
> 10 men do job in 5 days, so
>
> 1 man would do job in 5×10 days (not $5 \div 10$ for obviously it must take 1 man more time than 10 men!) so 20 men take
>
> $$\frac{5 \times 10}{20}$$

Answer $= 2\frac{1}{2}$ *days*

1. 12 handkerchiefs cost 21/–. What will 7 cost?

2. We have 360 pupils in 12 classes. How many classes would we need for 480 pupils?

3. If 5 men take 10 days to do a job, how long will it take 50 men?

4. 2 men took 5 days to do a job. How long would it take 1 man working at the same rate?

5. One man did some work in 8 hours. How long would it have taken 8 men?

6. 3 boys weed a garden in 2 hours. How many are needed to do it in half an hour?

7. 4 men do a piece of work in 10 days. How long would it take 8 men? How many men are needed to do it in 1 day?

289

19—H.T.

8. 3 men dig a hole in 4 days. How long would it take 6 men? How many men are needed to do it in 1 day?

9. A man can dig his garden in 3 days—his son in 6 days. How long will they take digging together?

10. 3 girls earned £3 in 3 days. How much did 1 girl earn in 1 day?

11. 6 men can build a shed in 3 days. When it is half-built 3 of the men leave. How many more days will the rest take to finish the shed?

Answers: **1** 12/3d **2** 16 **3** 1 *day* **4** 10 *days* **5** 1 *hour* **6** 12 **7** 5 *days* 40 *men* **8** 2 *days* 12 *men* **9** 2 *days* (*in* 1 *day they will do* $\frac{1}{3}+\frac{1}{6}=\frac{1}{2}$) **10** 6/8d **11** 3 *days*

Compass problems:

1. A man walks 1 mile north, 2 miles west, and then 1 mile south. How far is he from where he started?

2. "A" town is 3 miles south of "B" town. "B" town is 3 miles west of "C" town. In what direction would you travel going from "A" town to "C" town?

Answers: **1** 2 *miles* **2** *N.E.*

decimals

• •

Do the decimals only if your child has done decimals in school. Many schools do not get to decimals until after the grammar school examinations.

ADDING

Place the items under each other accurately, i.e. tenths under tenths and hundredths under hundredths, etc. and then add the columns in the same way as shown on page 265.

example:

$$23\cdot45 + 6\cdot7 + 8\cdot91 + \cdot07$$

$$
\begin{array}{r}
23\cdot45 \\
6\cdot7 \\
8\cdot91 \\
\cdot07 \\
\hline
39\cdot13
\end{array}
$$

SUBTRACTING

Here, as in addition, place the items in their correct columns.

example:

$$9\cdot87 - 5\cdot658$$

$$
\begin{array}{r}
9\cdot87 \\
5\cdot658 \\
\hline
4\cdot212
\end{array}
$$

MULTIPLYING

To multiply a decimal by 10, move the decimal point one place to the right.

example:

$$1\cdot2 \times 10 = 12.$$

To multiply by 100 move it one extra place:

$$1\cdot2 \times 100 = 120 \ (\textit{two places to the right})$$

To multiply decimals by other numbers, proceed exactly as in ordinary multiplication. But—there must be as many decimal places in the answer as there are decimal places in both the factors:

$$\cdot03 \times 5 = \cdot15 \ (\textit{two decimal places})$$
$$\cdot03 \times \cdot5 = \cdot015 \ (\textit{three decimal places})$$

DIVIDING

To divide decimals change the divisor into a whole number and then divide as in simple arithmetic.

example (a) $7\cdot89 \div \cdot3$

> To change the divisor ($\cdot3$) into a whole number we have to move the decimal point one place to the right ($3\cdot$), and the number to be divided must also have its decimal point moved *in the same way*. The sum therefore becomes:
>
> $78\cdot9 \div 3$
>
> $3\overline{)78\cdot9}$
>
> $26\cdot3$ Answer $= 26\cdot3$

example (b) $\cdot352 \div \cdot22$

> Change the divisor ($\cdot22$) into a whole number by moving the decimal point two places to the right ($22\cdot$), also moving the decimal point in the number to be divided, in the same way. The sum therefore becomes:
>
> $35\cdot2 \div 22$
>
> $22\overline{)35\cdot2}$
>
> $1\cdot6$ Answer $= 1\cdot6$

CHANGING VULGAR FRACTIONS TO DECIMALS

Method 1:

292

> This method can only be used where the denominator (the lower figure) is 2, 4 or 8. Bring the denominator to 10, 100 or 1000 by multiplying top and bottom by the same number—5, 25 or 125, e.g.

$\frac{1}{2}$, multiply top and bottom by $5 = \frac{5}{10} = \cdot5$

$\frac{3}{4}$, multiply top and bottom by $25 = \frac{75}{100} = \cdot75$

$\frac{5}{8}$, multiply top and bottom by $125 = \frac{625}{1000} = \cdot625$

Method 2:

This method is by short division and can be used with any fraction. For example: to convert $\frac{3}{8}$ into a decimal, divide 3 by 8:

$\frac{8)3\cdot000.}{0\cdot375}$ 8 into 3 will not go, so 0 and carry over 3, and then 8 into

30 goes 3 and 6 over, carry over 6; 8 into 60 goes 7 and 4 over, carry over 4. 8 into 40 goes 5. ·375 is therefore the decimal of $\frac{3}{8}$.

DECIMAL FRACTIONS

Decimal fractions are fractions with the denominator of 10, 100, 1000 or further multiples of ten, and are written in this way:

·1 $\left(\frac{1}{10}\right)$

·32 $\left(\frac{32}{100}\right)$

·479 $\left(\frac{479}{1000}\right)$

·071 $\left(\frac{71}{1000}\right)$

Exercises in using decimals:

1. Write as decimals $\frac{7}{10}$ $\frac{13}{100}$.

2. In 9·8 express the 8 as a vulgar fraction.

3. Put in correct order of greatness ·6 $\frac{65}{100}$ ·68, starting with the largest.

4. What is 8·5 − 4·05?

5. In ·44 what is the difference in value between the two 4's?

6. Write down 17 tenths as a decimal.

7. Write down 17 twentieths as a decimal.

8. What decimal number lies halfway between ·25 and ·45?

9. Write down as vulgar fractions ·625 ·375 ·875.

10. How many tens in ten thousand and ten?

293

11. (a) $89 \cdot 07 \times 100$ (e) $5 \cdot 7 \times 1000$ (h) $\cdot 08 \times \cdot 11$

    (b) $1 \cdot 1 \times \cdot 09$ (f) $1 \cdot 1 \times 1 \cdot 1$ (i) $\cdot 1 \times \cdot 1 \times \cdot 1$

    (c) $\cdot 4 \times \cdot 4 \times \cdot 4$ (g) $1 \cdot 8 \div \cdot 09$ (j) $6 \cdot 4 - \cdot 08$

    (d) $9 \cdot 6 \div 1 \cdot 2$

12. How many times can $\cdot 4$ be taken from 8 ?

13. What decimal of £1 is 5/–, of 1/– is $10\frac{1}{2}$d ?

Answers : **1** $\cdot 7$ $\cdot 13$ **2** $\frac{4}{5}$ (*i.e.* $\frac{8}{10}$) **3** $\cdot 68 \frac{65}{100}$ $\cdot 6$ **4** $4 \cdot 45$ **5** $\cdot 36$ ($\cdot 4 - \cdot 04$) **6** $1 \cdot 7$ **7** $\cdot 85$ ($\frac{1}{2}$ *of* $1 \cdot 7$) **8** $\cdot 35$ **9** $\frac{625}{1000}$ $\frac{375}{1000}$ $\frac{875}{1000}$ *cancel each one and you get* $\frac{5}{8}$ $\frac{3}{8}$ $\frac{7}{8}$ **10** $1,001$ (*i.e.* $10,010 \div 10$) **11** (a) 8907 (b) $\cdot 099$ (c) $\cdot 064$ (d) 8 (e) 5700 (f) $1 \cdot 21$ (g) 20 (h) $\cdot 0088$ (i) $\cdot 001$ (j) 80 **12** 20 **13** $\cdot 25$ $\cdot 875$

Make your child learn these :

$\frac{1}{10} = \cdot 1$	$\frac{1}{8} = \cdot 125$	$\frac{1}{5} = \cdot 2$	$\frac{1}{4} = \cdot 25$
$\frac{3}{8} = \cdot 375$	$\frac{2}{5} = \cdot 4$	$\frac{1}{2} = \cdot 5$	$\frac{3}{5} = \cdot 6$
$\frac{5}{8} = \cdot 625$	$\frac{3}{4} = \cdot 75$	$\frac{4}{5} = \cdot 8$	$\frac{7}{8} = \cdot 875$

$£\frac{1}{20} = £\cdot 05 = 1/–$

$£\frac{1}{10} = £\cdot 1 = 2/–$

$£\frac{1}{8} = £\cdot 125 = 2/6d$

$£\frac{1}{4} = £\cdot 25 = 5/–$

$£\frac{3}{8} = £\cdot 375 = 7/6d$

$£\frac{1}{2} = £\cdot 5 = 10/–$

$£\frac{5}{8} = £\cdot 625 = 12/6d$

$£\frac{3}{4} = £\cdot 75 = 15/–$

$£\frac{7}{8} = £\cdot 875 = 17/6d$

Intelligence Tests

. . . .

The purpose of intelligence tests is to determine the natural inborn ability of the child and not the knowledge that he has acquired. Ill-health, broken or bad schooling, or an unhappy home environment will affect his English and arithmetic, but not so obviously his Intelligence Quotient (I.Q.). He is born with intelligence, not with knowledge, and intelligence tests aim to discover this degree of intelligence. In this respect, intelligence tests differ from all other examinations, for other examinations are concerned in finding out what has already been learned of the subjects that have been studied.

Intelligence does of course grow with age (a boy of 11 years is more intelligent than he was at 10 years). There is, however, a limit to this. Just as one stops growing in height at a certain age, so one's intelligence is thought to be fully developed before the age of 20 years. Therefore, one is not more intelligent at 40 years than one is at 19 years. One does, however, acquire more knowledge and more experience. It is not greater intelligence, but greater knowledge and experience, that enables older business executives and statesmen to keep their "hands on the helm".

295

Parents should remember that the I.Q. is not the end of the story. No task in life depends on I.Q. alone. Confidence and "guts" are needed for success in life, and are even *more important than I.Q.*

Being a good orator, conversationalist or after-dinner speaker has carried many people with low I.Q.s (and perhaps not overmuch knowledge) to the peaks of success.

In doing intelligence tests at home you must beware of unconsciously helping your child. Do not help him because you think that *he could have done the question, had he understood it.* Understanding the question is often the main part of the test.

Going through our questions will help him to feel at home with the closely similar ones that he will get in school tests and examinations, and he will not become nervous or flustered and will give of his best under test conditions. These tests will be found enjoyable by both parent and child, but do not spend too much time on them. Time spent on English and arithmetic will be much more beneficial to your child's education than too much practice with intelligence tests. Fill up odd moments with them. Use them when your child is tired of something you have been doing and needs a break, or use them to finish a session on a carefree note. Use them as an instructive game, rather than work. They can (as can also some of the English work) be used as a game when travelling in a car. One of the authors of this book got through much successful studying with his child, taking him to school each morning on his way to work!

Cultivate quick thinking. Speed in these intelligence tests is important. These papers are frequently so long that even the most brilliant child can hardly finish them in the time allowed.

296

UNDERSTANDING AND FOLLOWING INSTRUCTIONS

In these tests your child must do *exactly* as he is told. The instructions may be unusual and complicated. He must read the instructions very carefully, and if necessary do a little at a time. Here are two example questions:

1. Underline the middle figure 1 2 3 4 3 2 1　　　　　　　　(4)

2. Underline the fourth consonant in this sentence.

(in *Underline*, *l* is the fourth consonant, therefore, we underline that l)

Now have your child do this test:

1. Underline the words in this sentence which contain three different vowels.

2. If November is the last month of the year, write Yes, if it is the one before the last, write No.

3. Draw a circle, place a square inside it and put an X in the bottom right-hand corner of the square.

4. If 6 goes into 30 exactly write No, unless 17 is less than 30 in which case write Yes, but if $60-40=20$ just ignore the first two and write Well.

5. Count the letters in the words Great Britain. If you can form the words GET TRAIN from them, using each letter once only, write down the number, but if you can form RAIN AGAIN write No, instead.

Answers: **I** underline, contain **2** *No* **3**  **4** *Well* **5** 12

common opposites

. . . .

This is a very widely used and worthwhile test, even though it does depend to a large degree on the child's background. Read aloud the first word to your child and have him give you the opposite. (There are many other acceptable answers as well as those given below.) Do not attempt to go straight through this test from A to Z at one session. It is best to do a section at a time and then to pass on to another exercise, coming back to this list at a later time.

absence	*presence*	artificial	*natural*
accept	*refuse*	arrival	*departure*
accurate	*inaccurate*	attack	*defence*
alive	*dead*	attractive	*repulsive*
always	*never*	attention	*inattention*
ancient	*modern*	asleep	*awake*

REVISION OF SIMILES. *Can you think of a suitable simile to describe this old man? If you turn back to page 241 you should find the correct answer somewhere on the page.*

answer	*question, query*	ally	*enemy*
approval	*disapproval*	agree	*disagree*
approached	*receded, departed*		
abundant	*scarce*	bad	*good*
admit	*deny*	backward	*forward, onward*
advance	*retreat, retire*	bend	*straighten*

beautiful	*ugly*	close	*distant*
beginning	*ending*	clever	*stupid*
below	*above*	cold	*hot*
bent	*straight*	combine	*separate*
big	*small, little*	common	*rare*
blunt	*sharp*	clockwise	*anti-clockwise*
better	*worse*	correct	*incorrect*
best	*worst*	conceal	*reveal*
blame	*praise*	come	*go*
bless	*curse*	common	*uncommon*
bitter	*sweet*	comfort	*discomfort*
borrow	*lend*	courage	*cowardice*
bravery	*cowardice*	cruel	*kind*
build	*destroy, demolish*	courteous	*discourteous, rude*
bold	*timid, meek*	cunning	*simple*
bright	*dull*		
broad	*narrow*	dainty	*clumsy*
bury	*unearth, excavate*	danger	*safety*
busy	*idle*	dark	*light*
buy, or		deep	*shallow*
purchase	*sell*	decrease	*increase*
		definite	*indefinite*
clear	*vague, cloudy*	demand	*supply*
careful	*rash, careless*	despair	*hope*
calm	*troubled*	disappear	*appear*
capable	*incapable*	disease	*health*
captivity	*freedom, liberty*	discourage	*encourage*
cellar	*attic*	dismal	*cheerful*
cheap	*dear, expensive*	doctor	*patient*

299

dry	*wet*	expand	*contract*
dull	*clear, gay, bright*	expensive	*inexpensive,*
dusk	*dawn*		*cheap*

Here is another picture for which your child will find a suitable title from the similes listed on page 243.

early	*late*	fail	*succeed*
easy	*difficult*	false	*true*
ebb	*flow*	feeble	*sturdy, strong,*
East	*West*		*powerful*
economise	*waste*	foolish	*wise*
entrance	*exit*	fast	*slow*
employer	*employee*	few	*many*
empty	*full*	famous	*unknown*
excited	*calm*	forelegs	*hindlegs*
end	*beginning*	fat	*thin*

find	*lose*	hasten	*dawdle*
first	*last*	hate	*love*
freedom	*captivity*	healthy	*unhealthy, ill,*
fold	*unfold*		*diseased*
frequent	*seldom*	here	*there*
forget	*remember*	heavy	*light*
found	*lost*	height	*depth*
fresh	*stale*	hero	*coward*
friend	*enemy*	hill	*valley*
fortunate	*unfortunate*	horizontal	*vertical*
frank	*secretive*	hinder	*aid, help*
full	*empty*	honest	*dishonest*
		humble	*proud*
generous	*mean*	hunger	*thirst*
gentle	*rough*		
gather	*distribute*	imitation	*genuine*
glad	*sorry*	immense	*tiny, minute*
gloomy	*cheerful*	imprison	*free*
giant	*dwarf, pygmy*	include	*exclude*
granted	*refused*	inhabited	*uninhabited*
great	*minute, small,*	inferior	*superior*
	little	intelligent	*unintelligent,*
guardian	*ward*		*stupid*
guest	*host*	inhale	*exhale*
guilty	*innocent*	interior	*exterior, outside*
		interesting	*uninteresting,*
happy	*sad, miserable*		*dull*
hard	*soft*	internal	*external*
harmful	*harmless*	intentional	*accidental*

301

join	*separate*	loss	*find, win*
junior	*senior*	low	*high*
justice	*injustice*	loyal	*disloyal*
king	*subject*	mad	*sane*
knowledge	*ignorance*	magnetise	*demagnetise*
		master	*servant*
laugh	*cry*	mature	*immature*
lawful	*unlawful*	maximum	*minimum*
lazy	*industrious, energetic*	me	*you*
		merry	*mirthless, sad*
land	*sea*	minority	*majority*
landlord	*tenant*	miser	*spendthrift*
large	*little, small*	misunderstand	*understand*
last	*first*		
lawyer	*client*	narrow	*wide*
lecturer	*student*	near	*far, distant*
lender	*borrower*	neat	*untidy*
lengthen	*shorten*	new	*old*
left	*right*	night	*day*
less	*more*	noisy	*quiet*
light	*dark, heavy*	North	*South*
like	*dislike, unlike*		
likely	*unlikely*	obedient	*disobedient*
leader	*follower*	odd	*even*
little	*large, much, big*	offer	*refuse*
lofty	*lowly*	open	*shut*
long	*short*	optimist	*pessimist*
loud	*soft*	out	*in*

302

parent	*child*	polite	*impolite, rude*
past	*present*	private	*public*
patient	*impatient*	prudent	*imprudent*
peace	*war*	pretty	*unsightly, ugly*
permanent	*temporary*	punishment	*reward*

Here are a number of objects that are produced in different places; (number 1, beer, is made in a brewery). On a slip of paper write down the names of the other objects and state where they are made. (Answers at the foot of page 304.)

please	*displease*	pure	*impure*
plentiful	*scarce*		
poetry	*prose*	qualified	*unqualified*
possible	*impossible*		
poverty	*wealth*	rapid	*slow*
powerful	*feeble, weak*	regularly	*irregularly*

rich	*poor*	sense	*nonsense*
right	*wrong, left*	shopkeeper	*customer*
rigid	*pliable, soft*	singular	*plural*
rough	*smooth*	simple	*complicated*
satisfactory	*unsatisfactory*	slim	*thick, stout*

Can your child think of a suitable idiom as a title for this picture? (It is not given in the chapter on idioms.) Answers to this and other picture-questions on idioms, similes and proverbs in this chapter are all given on page 330.

304

security	*insecurity*	solid	*liquid*
scatter	*collect*	sober	*drunk*
serious	*trivial*	speaker	*listener*
secondhand	*new*	sour	*sweet*

Answers to quiz on page 303: 2. bread, bakery 3. portrait, studio 4. ship, shipyard 5. steel girders, foundry or steel-works 6. whisky, distillery 7. cup and saucer, pottery 8. oil, oil refinery 9. coke, gas-works (coke is coal with the gas extracted) 10. money, mint 11. wheel, wheelwright's.

sorrow	*joy*	truth	*untruth, lie*
sow	*reap*		
stand	*lie*	up	*down*
straight	*crooked*		
strong	*weak*	vacant	*occupied*
success	*failure*	valuable	*valueless*
sunny	*cloudy*	victory	*defeat*
		virtue	*vice*
take	*give*	visible	*invisible*
tall	*short*	voluntary	*compulsory*
tame	*wild*	vowel	*consonant*
teacher	*pupil*		
thick	*thin*	wax	*wane*
tight	*slack, loose*	well	*ill, unwell*
top	*bottom*	wisdom	*folly*
transparent	*opaque*	within	*without*

Some words form their opposites by *adding* a prefix (see also *Prefixes*, page 143):

advantage	*disadvantage*
common	*uncommon*

Other words form their opposites by *changing* the prefix:

ascend	*descend*
encourage	*discourage*
export	*import*
exterior	*interior*
external	*internal*
increase	*decrease*
inside	*outside*

305

20—H T.

Some words form their opposites by changing the suffix from *ful* to *less*:

careful　　　　　　　　　　*careless*

useful　　　　　　　　　　　*useless*

As a modification of giving common opposites, the child is sometimes given a choice of opposites to choose from;

lazy　(industrious, energetic, athletic, agile)

and is asked to underline the correct opposites:

lazy　(<u>industrious</u>, <u>energetic</u>, athletic, agile)

Another modification is to give a list of four or five words, and the child is asked to underline the two which are opposites:

come, here, go, where　　　　　　　　(come, go)

hurry, hinder, assist, pursue, chase　　　(assist, hinder)

suspect, innocent, guilty, accused, proud　(guilty, innocent)

Another similar test asks the child to find two words having the same meaning, from a list of four or five words. Sometimes one word is already underlined:

<u>end</u>, finish, length, empty, find　　　　(finish)

analogies

• •

306

Read these analogies to your child and make him guess the missing words:

A is to Z as first is to —— 　　　　*last*

A is to C as yesterday is to —— 　　*tomorrow*

A is to D as E is to —— 　　　　　*H*

arm is to body as branch is to —— 　*trunk*

arm is to wrist as leg is to ——   *ankle*

apple is to pip as plum is to ——   *stone*

arrow is to bow as —— is to rifle   *bullet*

artist is to —— as author is to book   *painting, or picture*

banana is to tomato as yellow is to ——   *red*

Ask your child to find a suitable title from the list of similes on page 242 to describe this lazy old tramp. (Not everyone who is as lazy as this is always quite as happy!)

bat is to cat as boat is to ——   *coat*

bird is to —— as fish is to sea   *air*

bedroom is to kitchen as sleeping is to —— *cooking*

birds are to nest as bees are to ——   *hive*

birds are to nest as people are to ——   *home, or house*

bird is to feather as sheep is to ——   *wool*

black is to white as wealth is to ——   *poverty*

strings are to violin as keys are to ——   *piano*

box is to lid as bottle is to ——   *cork*

bulb is to tulip as acorn is to ——   *oak*

break is to mend as lose is to ——   *find, or win*

bus is to road as train is to ——-   *rail, or track*

307

but is to button as gam is to —   *gammon*

car is to garage as aeroplane is to —   *hangar*

cat is to kitten as sheep is to —   *lamb*

cat is to — as dog is to wolf   *lion, or tiger*

chauffeur is to motorcar as jockey is to —   *horse*

clothes are to men as feathers are to —   *birds*

coming is to going as — is to departure   *arrival*

day is to time as yard is to —   *distance, or length*

You would not think that anyone would be quite so foolish as to try to cross the Atlantic in a bath! Ask your child to find a suitable title for this picture from the similes given on page 242.

308

desk is to wood as window is to —   *glass*

doctor is to surgery as artist is to —   *studio*

dog is to kennel as bird is to —   *cage, or nest*

dog is to puppy as fox is to —   *cub*

dog is to bark as horse is to —   *neigh*

dry is to moist as — is to few	*many*
egg is to bird as — is to plant	*seed, or bulb*
eye is to see as ear is to —	*hear*
father is to son as mother is to —	*daughter*
father is to son as king is to —	*prince*
finger is to hand as — is to foot	*toe*
foot is to boot as hand is to —	*glove*
food is to hunger as — is to thirst	*drink*
food is to man as — is to engine	*fuel*
fire is to hot as ice is to —	*cold*
fish is to sea as vegetable is to	*garden, or allotment*
fish is to swim as bird is to —	*fly*
funnel is to engine as — is to house	*chimney*
goodness is to reward as badness is to —	*punishment*
grass is to green as snow is to —	*white*
happiness is to joy as sadness is to —	*sorrow*
hate is to love as down is to —	*up*
here is to there as — is to that	*this*
him is to his as them is to —	*theirs*
hooter is to car as — is to train	*whistle*
horse is to cart as — is to lorry	*engine*
hot is to cold as sad is to —	*happy*
hotel is to room as zoo is to —	*cage*
ink is to pen as paint is to —	*brush*
I is to you as mine is to —	*yours*
inch is to foot as — is to shilling	*penny*
in is to out as entrance is to —	*exit*
king is to queen as prince is to —	*princess*
laugh is to happiness as tears are to —	*sorrow*

309

library is to books as greenhouse is to ——	*plants*
long is to short as far is to ——	*near*
lord is to lady as —— is to queen	*king*
lorry is to goods as bus is to ——	*passengers*
love is to friend as hate is to ——	*enemy*
milk is to cow as honey is to ——	*bee*
moth is to wing as fish is to ——	*scale, or fin*
mother is to child as hen is to ——	*chick*
moon is to night as sun is to ——	*day*
neighing is to braying as horse is to ——	*donkey*
nose is to smell as ear is to ——	*hear*
North is to South as East is to ——	*West*
one is to three as first is to ——	*third*
one is to single as two is to ——	*double*
orange is to peel as nut is to ——	*shell*
paint is to artist as ink is to ——	*writer*
pencil is to drawing as brush is to ——	*painting*
picture is to paint as drawing is to ——	*pencil-lead*
picture is to frame as field is to ——	*fence, or hedge*
pint is to gallon as 2/6 is to ——	*£1*
plough is to field as spade is to ——	*garden*
postman is to letter as baker is to ——	*bread*
pretty is to ugly as soft is to ——	*hard*
quick is to quickly as —— is to truly	*true*
right is to left as below is to ——	*above*
rich is to poor as ancient is to ——	*modern*
sad is to happy as hot is to ——	*cold*
seldom is to often as few is to ——	*many*
sheep is to flock as —— is to herd	*cow*

310

The man on the right of this picture is horrified at his neighbour's liking for frogs! Ask your child to pick out a suitable title for this scene from the list of proverbs on page 247. Now have him tell you what country he would be in if he saw this sight, and to give you his reasons. (Answers at foot of page 312.)

311

sheep is to lamb as —— is to calf	*cow*
sheep is to mutton as pig is to ——	*pork*
ship is to pier (or quay) as train is to ——	*platform*
ship is to sea as aeroplane is to ——	*air*
skin is to animal as bark is to ——	*tree*
soldier is to army as sailor is to ——	*navy*

soot is to snow as black is to ——	*white*
spider is to fly as cat is to ——	*mouse*
snow is to white as coal is to ——	*black*
stocking is to leg as hat is to ——	*head*
stop is to go as smooth is to ——	*rough*
straight is to crooked as full is to ——	*empty*
sugar is to vinegar as sweet is to ——	*sour*
Sunday is to Monday as first is to ——	*second*
—— is to cygnet as pig is to piglet	*swan*
tail is to fish as —— is to boat	*rudder*
tall is to short as fat is to ——	*thin*
tiger is to animal as cuckoo is to ——	*bird*
this is to here as that is to ——	*there*
three is to triple as two is to ——	*double*
train is to luggage as ship is to ——	*cargo*
truth is to lie as —— is to fiction	*fact*
twelve is to dozen as twenty is to ——	*score*
uncle is to aunt as brother is to ——	*sister*
up is to down as fast is to —— and as smooth is to ——	*slow, rough*
water is to air as fish is to ——	*bird*
water is to fish as air is to ——	*bird*
wet is to dry as inside is to ——	*outside*
window is to room as porthole is to ——	*cabin*
wireless is to sound as television is to ——	*sight*
woman is to womanly as child is to ——	*childish*
yolk is to egg as kernel is to ——	*nut*

312

Answers to picture-question on page 311: in France because you can see the Eiffel Tower, and because the French eat frogs' legs. "One man's meat is another man's poison."

Sometimes, as a modification of the above test, your child may be asked to underline the correct word to complete the analogy from a group of words:

> Yolk is to egg as kernel is to (army, nut, berry)   (nut)

Another variation is to have him underline the two words which are connected in the same way as the two words of the example:

> Tail is to fish (rudder, helm, boat, oar)   (rudder, boat)

series

. . . .

In this form of test each succeeding number or letter bears some arithmetical relationship to the preceding number or letter. Have your child discover what this relationship is, and then say what he thinks should come next. For instance, in question 1 each number is half the preceding one, in the next a quarter.

1. 4   2   1 $\frac{1}{2}$ —
2. 16   4   1   —
3. 1   2   6   —
4. 28 $24\frac{1}{2}$ 21   —
5. 12   24   36   —
6. 3 & 6   10 & 20   24 & 48   —
7. 1   3   7   —
8. KL   MN   OP   —
9. 34   31   28   —
10. 6   11   16   —
11. 13Z   16Y   19X   —
12. ab   de   gh   —
13. za   yb   xc   —

313

(answers overleaf)

Answers: **1** ¼ **2** ¼ **3** 24 (*first double, then three times, then four times*) **4** 17½ (*minus three-and-a-half each time*) **5** 48 (*add 12 each time*) **6** 52 and 104 (*the difference between the last number in one pair and the first number in the next pair is 4, and the last number in each pair is double the first one*) **7** 13 **8** *QR* **9** 25 **10** 21 **11** 22*W* **12** *jk* **13** *wd*

One number is wrong in the following:
    2 4 6 7 10 12

the 7 is out of place—it should be 8. Now do:

1. 17 15 13 10 9
2. 4 8 12 15 20
3. a c e f i
4. 4 9 14 10 24 29

Answers: **1** 10 *should be* 11 **2** 15 *should be* 16 **3** f *should be* g **4** 10 *should be* 19

odd man out

In question 1 there are the names of four months. The "odd man out" is *Spring*—being the name of a Season. Let your child write down on a piece of paper the "odd man out" in each of these.

1. June Spring May September October
2. pen pencil paper crayon brush
3. six eighth four two ten
4. breakfast dinner lunch food supper
5. apple lemon daisy pea orange
6. boot shoe clog glove slipper
7. red blue white dark yellow
8. goose duck turkey rabbit hen
9. bonnet hat cap tie helmet
10. apple plum carrot pear grape

314

11. daisy rose elm daffodil buttercup
12. cricket tennis soccer rugby chess
13. month year hour moon fortnight
14. dog tiger bull duck lion
15. butcher grocer baker ironmonger milkman
16. move watch walk run plod
17. colossal huge immense intense vast
18. green blue small large boys
19. France Belgium London Portugal India
20. hake cod trout salmon kipper
21. reap plough tramp sow thrash
22. evil bad wholesome spoilt nasty
23. cunning crafty disobedient sly wily
24. niece aunt baby son father
25. water ink pen milk petrol
26. mutton sausage beef veal pork
27. use eat munch drink chew
28. shrub bush branch tree
29. canary cat cow dog horse
30. turkey hen robin goose duck
31. coffee cocoa vinegar milk tea
32. cat mouse squirrel elephant rat
33. queen bishop knight king man
34. penny sixpence florin half-crown shilling
35. give take lend award bestow

315

Answers: **1** *Spring* **2** *paper* **3** *eighth* **4** *food* **5** *daisy* **6** *glove* **7** *dark* **8** *rabbit* **9** *tie* **10** *carrot* **11** *elm* **12** *chess* **13** *moon* **14** *duck* **15** *ironmonger* **16** *watch* **17** *intense* **18** *boys* **19** *London* **20** *kipper* **21** *tramp* **22** *wholesome* **23** *disobedient* **24** *baby* **25** *pen* **26** *sausage* **27** *use* **28** *branch* **29** *canary* **30** *robin* **31** *vinegar* **32** *elephant* **33** *queen* **34** *penny* **35** *take*

Sometimes as a modification of "odd man out", he may be asked to underline the "odd" word when it is the group name for the others in the list. Ask him for the "odd" word in the following:

1. lion tiger ass dog animal
2. uncle King man butcher bishop
3. rose daffodil violet flower lily

Answers: **1** *animal* **2** *man* **3** *flower*

correct order

Have your child arrange the following in their correct order (for example: poor, weak, fair, good, excellent, are correctly arranged) and write his answers (in numbers only) on a piece of paper:

1. 1 penny, 2 farthing, 3 sixpence, 4 shilling, 5 half-crown.
2. 1 walk, 2 run, 3 cycle, 4 motor, 5 fly.
3. 1 word, 2 paragraph, 3 line, 4 chapter, 5 page, 6 book, 7 letter.
4. 1 mouse, 2 bee, 3 dog, 4 horse, 5 elephant.
5. 1 more, 2 much, 3 most.
6. 1 speak, 2 shout, 3 whisper.
7. 1 King, 2 Emperor, 3 count, 4 commoner.
8. 1 hot, 2 warm, 3 cold, 4 boiling, 5 tepid.
9. 1 early, 2 late, 3 very early, 4 punctual, 5 very late.
10. 1 cruiser, 2 destroyer, 3 yacht, 4 canoe, 5 battleship.
11. 1 puddle, 2 pond, 3 sea, 4 lake, 5 ocean.
12. 1 farm, 2 market, 3 dinner table, 4 oven, 5 shop.
13. 1 house, 2 mansion, 3 room, 4 storey, 5 bungalow.
14. 1 penniless, 2 poor, 3 rich, 4 well-to-do, 5 millionaire.

15. 1 child, 2 boy, 3 youth, 4 baby, 5 man.

16. 1 short, 2 miniature, 3 gigantic, 4 tall, 5 average.

17. 1 handsome, 2 plain, 3 ugly, 4 beautiful.

18. 1 typhoon, 2 gale, 3 calm, 4 squall.

19. 1 trunk, 2 tree, 3 branch, 4 leaf, 5 twig.

Look at these ruffians; you would not expect to see them strolling along in the company of a policeman (unless he was arresting them !). From the list of proverbs on page 245 choose a suitable title for this picture.

20. 1 1966 A.D., 2 55 B.C., 3 300 B.C., 4 60 A.D.

21. 1 posted, 2 delivered, 3 collected, 4 stamped, 5 addressed.

22. 1 improbable, 2 possible, 3 impossible, 4 certain, 5 probable.

23. 1 town, 2 continent, 3 country, 4 county, 5 village.

317

Answers : **1** 2, 1, 3, 4, 5. **2** 1, 2, 3, 4, 5. **3** 7, 1, 3, 2, 5, 4, 6. **4** 2, 1, 3, 4, 5. **5** 2, 1, 3.
6 3, 1, 2. **7** 4, 3, 1, 2. **8** 3, 5, 2, 1, 4. **9** 3, 1, 4, 2, 5. **10** 4, 3, 2, 1, 5. **11** 1, 2, 4, 3, 5.
12 1, 2, 5, 4, 3. **13** 3, 4, 5, 1, 2. **14** 1, 2, 4, 3, 5. **15** 4, 1, 2, 3, 5. **16** 2, 1, 5, 4, 3.
17 3, 2, 1, 4. **18** 3, 4, 2, 1. **19** 4, 5, 3, 1, 2. **20** 3, 2, 4, 1. **21** 5, 4, 1, 3, 2. **22** 3, 1, 2,
5, 4. **23** 5, 1, 4, 3, 2.

There are fifteen things wrong with this picture: can you spot them all?
Write them down and then turn to the answers on page 320.

problems involving numbers

. . . .

These are not really arithmetic problems, since only simple numbers are used. It is your child's approach to the problem which matters.

1. $x + 5 = 14$. What does x stand for?
2. $y \div 4 = 6$. What does y stand for?

3. Instead of multiplying by 3, a boy divided by 3 and got 6 for his answer. What would the right answer be?

4. What is the smallest number that must be subtracted from 10 to make it divisible by 3?

5. My watch is 25 minutes fast. When it reads 10.15 what is the right time?

6. My watch is 5 minutes fast. I take 15 minutes to walk to the station. What time on my watch must I leave to catch the 8.30 train? (allow me also 2 minutes to spare).

7. It takes 3 minutes to boil 1 egg in a saucepan. How long will it take to boil 3 eggs in the saucepan?

8. 4 sisters each had 1 brother. How many were there in all?

9. If (a) 1 duck and 2 hens cost £2. 10. 0 and (b) 2 ducks and 1 hen cost £2. 15. 0 what is the cost of each?

10. If I had 16 marbles more, I would have 3 times as many as I have now. How many have I got?

11. How many miles does a car travel in passing 5 milestones?

12. How many times must you cut a ribbon 2 feet long to get pieces 6 inches long?

13. 12 trees are planted in a row 9 feet apart. How long is the row?

14. A clock takes 3 seconds to strike 4. How many seconds would it take to strike 6?

15. A box can hold 10 cigars. How many boxes do you need for 36 cigars?

319

16. If a shower of rain soaked 6 people in 3 minutes, how long would it take to soak 1 person?

17. When could there be 5 Mondays in the month of February?

18. A man, by mistake, was paid in half-crowns instead of florins. If he received 17/6d, how much should he have got?

19. 2 cars start going towards one another from points 140 miles apart. If one goes at 40 miles per hour and the other at 30 miles per hour, how long before they meet?

20. If a car going at 40 miles per hour follows a car going at 30 miles per hour which started travelling 1 hour earlier, how long will it take to catch up with it?

21. A man can walk uphill at 3 miles per hour and downhill at 6 miles per hour. He walks uphill for 1 hour and then downhill for another hour in the same direction. How long will he take to walk back?

22. A boat can be rowed 3 miles per hour upstream and 6 miles per hour downstream. What is the rate of the stream?

23. Write in figures eleven thousand, eleven hundred and eleven.

Answers: **1** 9 **2** 24 **3** 54 **4** 1 **5** 9.50 **6** 8.18 **7** 3 *minutes* **8** 5 **9** *A hen costs 15/– and a duck £1 (double* [a] *and we find 2 ducks and 4 hens cost £5. Take away item* [b] *costing £2. 15.0 and we find 3 hens cost £2. 5. 0. Therefore one hen will cost 15/–)* **10** 8 **11** 4 *(the distance between the first 2 stones is one mile. This is a common error which may also be easily made in calculating time,* e.g. *from Monday noon to Thursday noon there are 3 days: but from Monday to Thursday inclusive there are four days)* **12** 3 **13** 99 *feet* **14** 5 **15** 4 **16** 3 *minutes* **17** *When the first day of February comes on a Monday during a leap year* **18** 14/– **19** 2 *hours (for the cars approach one another at 40+30 miles per hour)* **20** 3 *hours (the slower car is being overtaken at 10 miles per hour [40−30 miles per hour] and it has thirty miles start)* **21** 2½ *hours (draw a diagram showing the distances covered)* **22** 1½ *miles per hour (the stream is helping movement one way and hindering the other way. Therefore 6−3 = twice the rate of the stream)* **23** 12,111

320

Answers to quiz on page 318: 1. The ceiling light has no flex 2. The lower part of the window should be on the inside 3. Although it is November the trees outside are in summer foliage 4. November has only 30 days 5. The picture on the right of the fireplace is upside-down 6. The clock has one of its numbers missing 7. The fire has no hearthstone 8. The hinges on the door are on the same side as the handle 9. The television screen is standing on end 10. The dog has a cow's tail 11. The hearthrug has a fringe at one end only 12. The armchair has one leg missing 13. The armchair has one wing missing 14. The table is laid for a left-handed person 15. The "Cook Book" has its title on the wrong side of the cover. How many did you get right?

"odd" questions

. . . .

1. What is the first day of the week?
2. Yesterday was Tuesday. What is the day after tomorrow?
3. What is wrong with, "The coin was marked 19 B.C."?

Here is another picture that illustrates one of the similes that your child learnt in chapter 11. Ask him to choose a suitable simile from the list on page 244 to describe this road.

321

4. What is the difference between:
   (a) theatre and cinema
   (b) pen and pencil
   (c) painting and photograph
   (d) pin and needle
   (e) nail and screw?

5. Draw the reflections of F N P R Z in a mirror.

6. Write down the letters (Capitals) in the alphabet which look the same in a mirror.

In each of these drawings there is one thing that is quite wrong; try to find each of them. (Answers at foot of page 325.)

7. A clock seen through a mirror reads 4.10. What is the correct time?

8. Should a salesman say, "This is a chair for a lady with Queen Anne legs"?

9. (a) If you were facing south and then turned right in what direction would you be facing?

(b) If you now turned right-round where would you be facing?

(c) Which way would you now turn to face north?

10. If someone said he had invented a liquid that could dissolve anything, would you believe him? Give your reason.

322

11. Which is heavier—a pound of lead or a pound of feathers?

12. Why is it impossible to put a bookmark between pages 9 and 10 of a book?

13. An article made of wood is wooden, one made of gold is golden, and one made of wool is woollen. What is it, if it is made of brass?

14. How many bars has a five-barred gate?

15. How can you tell a ½d from a 1/– in the dark?

16. On which side of a road with no footpath should a pedestrian walk, and why?

17. What does an inflated tyre contain?

18. What is a cul-de-sac, or a blind turning?

19. Which is the greater—half a dozen dozen, 6 dozen dozen?

20. Which would you rather have—half a ton of sovereigns or a ton of half sovereigns?

21. Who was the father of George V's son?

22. Mary lives next door but one to Jane, and Jane lives next door but one to Gwen. Helen lives next door to Mary and Jane. How many doors are there between Helen and Gwen?

23. John is taller than Peter but not as tall as Robin. Who is the smallest or can't you tell?

24. What is wrong with the following sentence?
The trio was made up of a pianist, a cello player and two violinists.

323

Answers: **1** *Sunday* **2** *Friday* **3** *when the coin was made Christ was not yet born* **4** *parent to explain* **5** *check with mirror* **6** A H I M O T U V W X Y **7** 7.50 *(check with mirror)* **8** *no* **9** (a) *west* (b) *east* (c) *left* **10** *no (for it would dissolve its container)* **11** *neither (they both weigh one pound)* **12** *pages 9 and 10 are always different sides of the same sheet* **13** *brass* **14** 5 **15** *the shilling has a milled edge* **16** *the right, so as to face oncoming traffic* **17** *air* **18** *a turning which you cannot go through (you have to turn around to get out again)* **19** 6 *dozen dozen* **20** *the ton of half-sovereigns contains more gold* **21** *George V* **22** 2 *(make a diagram and it becomes obvious)* **23** *Peter* **24** *a trio means 3 performers.*

Here are ten implements; write on a slip of paper the name of each one and state by whom it is used. (Answers on page 327.)

jumbled words

. . . .

324

Form words from the following (*example*; Number 1 makes *banana*):

1. nabana	2. aelpp
3. fgi	4. wsa
5. adet	6. tna
7. koclc	8. blate
9. aepr	10. acehp
11. rmoo	12. cmla

13. ilno	14. dlea
15. lkach	16. gerti
17. nbru	18. nru
19. lupm	20. aegpr
21. lwfo	22. psehe
23. richa	24. nkdi
25. binor	26. reosh
27. omeus	28. sked
29. sutj	30. aydis
31. mntou	32. tryso
33. zeise	34. isuptd
35. oughne	

Answers: **1** *banana* **2** *apple* **3** *fig* **4** *saw* or *was* **5** *date* **6** *ant* **7** *clock* **8** *table* **9** *pear* **10** *peach* **11** *room* **12** *calm* **13** *lion* **14** *deal* **15** *chalk* **16** *tiger* **17** *burn* **18** *run* **19** *plum* **20** *grape* **21** *fowl* **22** *sheep* **23** *chair* **24** *kind* **25** *robin* **26** *horse* **27** *mouse* **28** *desk* **29** *just* **30** *daisy* **31** *mount* **32** *story* **33** *seize* **34** *stupid* **35** *enough*

Correct these sentences:

1. The equator is a menagerie lion running round the world.
2. It was raining cats and dogs, so the road was full of poodles.
3. An optimist is a person who attends to people's eyes.
4. Your hair needs combing badly.
5. The plural of half is whole.

Answers: **1** *an imaginary line* **2** *puddles* **3** *oculist* **4** *your hair is badly in need of combing* **5** *halves*

325

Answers to quiz on page 322: 1. E and W on the compass should be changed so that W is on the left 2. The dots indicating the hours on the lower half of the clock face are unevenly spaced. 3. The man's shadow is falling the wrong way 4. There are only 30 days in September 5. The smoke and the flag are going in opposite directions 6. A newsagent would not sell eggs, wire or oil 7. The parting in the man's hair should be on the other side in the reflection.

other intelligence tests

· ·

GENERAL QUESTIONS

1. What do we mean by "an old salt"?

2. What do we mean by "to take it with a pinch of salt"?

3. What do we mean by "the weaker sex"?

4. What is meant by "filthy lucre"?

5. Why is it better to find a whole worm in the apple you bite into, than to find half a worm?

6. What is meant by having "one over the eight"?

7. To go "the way of all flesh" is to . . .

8. What do we mean by "elevenses"?

9. What do we mean by "to be someone's cup of tea"?

10. What do we mean by "God's Book"?

11. What is a "book-worm"?

12. What is a "wet blanket"?

Answers: **1** *an old sailor* **2** *to tend to disbelieve* **3** *women* **4** *money* **5** *you may have already swallowed the other half!* **6** *getting drunk* **7** *die* **8** *cup of tea* **9** *to be to someone's liking* **10** *The Bible* **11** *a person who reads a great deal* **12** *one who spoils other people's enjoyment*

QUESTIONS ABOUT FAMOUS PEOPLE

1. A man may be:

   (a) as proud as ——   (b) as wise as ——-

   (c) as patient as ——   (d) as old as ——

2. Who was the first woman?

3. (a) Who sat in a corner? (b) What did he eat?

4. Who could not tell a lie?

5. Who found a magic lamp?

6. Who was in trouble with a wolf?
7. Who said "Open Sesame"?

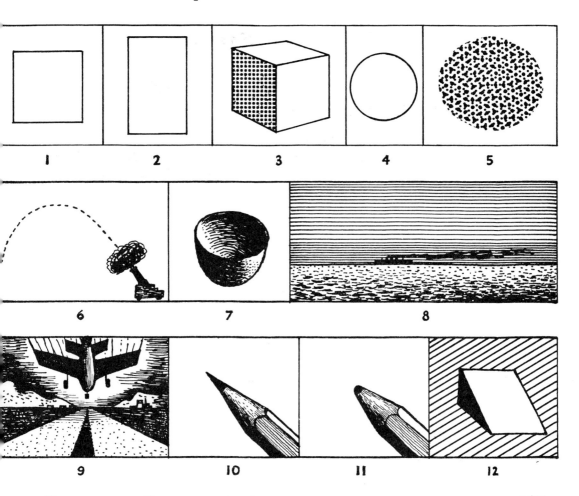

Here are some diagrams, each of which represents one of the following **327**
shapes: *flat, blunt, curved, oblong, oval, sharp, straight, hollow, circular,
cube, square, wedge.* Write on a slip of paper the number of the diagram
that goes with each shape—number 1 is a square so you write "1 square"
etc. (*Answers on page 328.*)

Answers to quiz on page 324: 1. brace and bit, carpenter 2. trowel, bricklayer 3.
paintbrush, painter or decorator 4. last, shoemaker 5. pitchfork, farmworker
6. anvil, blacksmith 7. blowlamp, plumber 8. pickaxe, miner or road mender
9. felling axe, lumberjack or forester 10. fork, gardener.

8. Who called for his fiddlers?

9. Who found an empty cupboard?

10. Who burnt the cakes?

11. Who tried again because of a spider?

12. Who ate no fat?

13. Who said "Elementary, my dear Watson"?

14. Who asked for more?

Answers: **1** (a) *Punch* (b) *Solomon* (c) *Job* (d) *Methuselah* **2** *Eve* **3** (a) *Jack Horner* (b) *Christmas Pie* **4** *George Washington* **5** *Aladdin* **6** *Red Riding Hood* **7** *Ali Baba* **8** *Old King Cole* **9** *Old Mother Hubbard* **10** *King Alfred* **11** *Robert Bruce* **12** *Jack Spratt* **13** *Sherlock Holmes* **14** Oliver Twist

QUESTIONS ABOUT MONEY

Have your child read the following passage and tell you the missing words.

Money is made in the ——. It is paid to a worker as ——, and to a professional man as ——. On a journey the money you pay for your ticket is called the —— and when you pay it the ticket seller may need to give you ——.

Answers: *mint, wages, salary, fare, change*

A few oral questions for your child:

What is a receipt?   (*an acknowledgement of money received*)

328 What do we call a thousand thousand?   (*a million*)

What do we call a dozen dozen?   (*a gross*)

The allowance sometimes made for the prompt payment of a bill is the ——   (*discount*)

Answers to quiz on page 327: 1. square 2. oblong 3. cube 4. circular 5. oval 6. curved 7. hollow 8. flat 9. straight 10. sharp 11. blunt 12. wedge.

REPEATING NUMBERS BACKWARDS

A bright 10½-year-old should be able to repeat five numbers back-wards. Say 7, 4, 3, 9, 8 slowly to him (one number per second) and have him repeat them backwards to you.

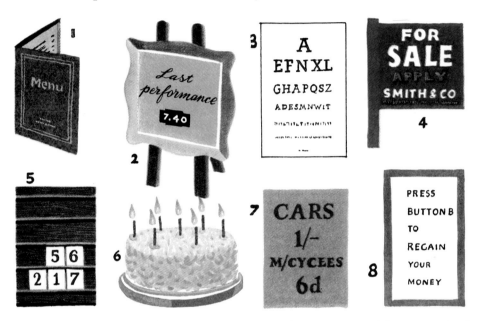

Where would you be if you could see each of these objects (for example if the first one was an oven, you would be in the kitchen). Write down your answers and then compare them with those on page 330.

MIXED SENTENCES

Your child may be given a number of sentences in which the order of the words is mixed, and he will be asked to state whether they are true or false.

Here is an example:

> Freezes it when ice water into turns.

The answer would be "true", for the jumbled words when rearranged make:

> Water turns into ice when it freezes.

GIVING WORDS AT SPEED

Ask your child to give you as many words as he can in one minute without repeating himself. Get a stop watch (or a watch with a second hand) ready, ask him if he is ready and tell him to start. Keep saying "good" to him. An intelligent 10-year-old should give you more than 30 words in the minute.

CODES

Success in code tests depends on how well the child can understand similarities and differences. Sufficient practice in these will be had by doing the tests in the specimen examination papers which are supplied with this book.

SENTENCE BUILDING FROM THREE WORDS

Your child may be given three words and asked to make a sentence from them; e.g. *England, people, Tuesday.*

"In England people work on Tuesday."

Answers to quiz on page 329: 1. in a restaurant 2. at a cinema or theatre 3. (eyesight test card) at an optician's 4. (estate agent's board) outside a building for sale 5. (hymn list) in a church 6. at a party 7. at a car park 8. in a telephone box.

Answers to the picture-questions on similes, idioms and proverbs in this chapter: page 298: bald as a billiard ball page 300: slippery as an eel page 304: lose one's shirt page 307: lazy as the day is long page 308: mad as a march hare or hatter page 311: one man's meat is another man's poison page 317: birds of a feather flock together page 321: straight as a die or an arrow. How many did your child guess correctly?

The Examination Papers

In the blue box accompanying this book you will find a set of Examination Papers, and on the following pages are set out the answers to them. The Papers are to be used in conjunction with the book. Do not allow your child to refer to any books while he is doing them; adhere to the time limit for each Paper and do not help him with the questions during the "Examination" time. Correct each Paper as soon as possible after he has done it, going over his mistakes with him and making sure that he understands the corrections and learns from them.

These Papers will give you, the parent, a good idea of your child's strengths and weaknesses. If, for example, you find that he is able to do all the questions on multiplication in the Arithmetic Papers correctly, you will know that you need not spend much of your study time on the multiplication section of the Course. Conversely, you will be able to make a note of the type of questions that he has difficulty in doing, and you can then revise them with him until he thoroughly understands the subject.

331

METHOD OF WORKING THROUGH THE PAPERS

Obviously we cannot give you a detailed time-table saying "Do Paper I when you have reached page 45 of the book, and so on." Each child develops differently and some learn faster than others; and were we to set down a rigid time-table for you, the whole object of this course would be lost.

We suggest that it is best not to touch the Examination Papers at all until you have really got into the swing of the Course with your child.

Once you think he is gaining confidence in himself and assimilating this new knowledge, let him start on the Papers. If he has an examination ahead of him, work out how many weeks you have before he sits for the exam. and try to give him the Papers at fairly regular intervals.

Keep a record of the marks he scores in doing the Papers. He will enjoy competing against himself and trying to gain more marks each time; but do not let him become discouraged if he fails badly on a Paper and scores low marks.

Do not give him a Paper to do if he is tired. After a full day at school he may well have had enough work for one day. Let him come to the Examination Papers fresh and relaxed; and one of the Papers will take the place of a session of coaching on the course.

Above all do not try to do too much with your child. Retain his enthusiasm and help him to build up confidence in himself. Self-confidence helps to spell success in every walk of life.

When a child does arithmetic and the problems involve detailed working or diagrams, he should be encouraged to use a ruler for neatness.

332 When comparing the results of the examination papers with the answers in the back of this volume, you must use a certain amount of common sense. If the child does not give the answer exactly as in the book but something which is just as intelligent and sensible, then you must allow him a mark. Depending upon the answer he gives so you will decide what mark to give him.

English 1 (*possible marks 100*)

PART 1 (*possible marks 57*)

Give 2 marks for each correct word

I (a) Where   (b) after   (c) their   (d) until, before   (e) How, off

2 (a) sobbing (*3 marks*)
(b) artful (*3 marks*)
(c) greedy (*2 marks*)
(d) spring (*2 marks*)
(e) distinguish (*3 marks*)

Give 3 marks for each correct answer

3 (a) toys   (b) games   (c) vegetables   (d) furniture   (e) liquids

4 beauty   cleverness   mighty   foolish   bravery

PART 2 (*possible marks 43*)

I cat (*2 marks*)

2 purring (*4 marks. Give 2 marks if any other good reason given*)

3 plenty of fish (*2 marks*)
plenty of milk (*2 marks*)
sat on hearthrug (*1 mark*)
curled her tail (*1 mark*)

4 white fur (*2 marks*)

5 "There, it is off now" (*4 marks*)

6 "might get the moth in it" or for words giving this idea (*2 marks*)

7 An adventure, or, what she had been through (*2 marks*)

8 (a) no (*2 marks*)
(b) suitable reason (*4 marks*)

9 Three of; fire, fish, milk, petting, liberty (*3 marks*)

10 *Give 2 marks for each correct answer*
(a) fine, wonderful, lovely   (b) thought   (c) happily   (d) freedom
(e) imagine

II *Give 2 marks for each correct answer*
(a) sees, or spies   (b) vain, or proud

333

Arithmetic 1 (*possible marks 100*)

Give no marks for incorrect answers except where otherwise indicated

PART 1

1	22 (*1 mark*)
2	45 (*2 marks*)
3	21 (*3 marks*)
4	66 (*3 marks*)
5	1 (*3 marks*)
6	33 (*3 marks*)
7	230 (*3 marks*)
8	86 (*4 marks*)
9	1,776 (*5 marks. Deduct 2 marks for each wrong figure*)
10	8, remainder 3 (*3 marks. Deduct 1 mark if no remainder given*)
11	45 (*4 marks*)
12	1/4½d (*3 marks. Give 1 mark only if the answer is left in pence*)
13	6/1½d (*4 marks. Deduct 2 marks for each wrong figure*)
14	2/10d (*5 marks. Deduct 2 marks for each wrong figure*)
15	1/4½d (*4 marks*)
16	6 inches (*4 marks*)
17	20 (*4 marks*)
18	4/5d (*4 marks*)
19	9 (*4 marks*)

PART 2

1	10·25 (*4 marks*)
2	15 years (*4 marks*)
3	32 (*5 marks*)
4	2/- (*6 marks. Give 1 mark for getting 14 pennies added, and 3 marks for getting 24 pennies in all*)
5	10½d (*6 marks. Give 2 marks for getting 15 × 1½d = 1/10½d*)
6	10d (*9 marks. Give 3 marks for getting father = 2 sons. Give 3 marks for: 5 sons cost 2/1d. Give 1 mark for: each son = 5d*)

Intelligence 1 *(possible marks 70)*

Give 1 mark for each correct answer

1   (a) P   (b) I   (c) E   (d) T   (e) O   (f) S   (g) AP   (h) 7
(i) 9

2   (a) NIP   (b) SAW   (c) NOT   (d) RUN   (e) PAT or APT
(f) MUG   (g) EAR or ERA   (h) SIT   (i) WHO   (j) ACT

Give 2 marks for each correct answer

3   (a) chair   (b) linen   (c) 5   (d) a   (e) learn

4   (a) Dick   (b) Tom   (c) one cannot tell

5   (a) Put on your hat   (b) Please shut the door   (c) How many goals did
you score?   (d) Many hands make light work

6   *Give 2 marks for the correct answer*

7   Wednesday *(3 marks)*

8   Thursday *(4 marks)*

Give 2 marks for each correct answer

9   (a) razor   (b) pin   (c) duck   (d) dull

10   (a)   (b)   (c)   (d)

English 2 *(possible marks 100)*

PART 1 *(possible marks 48)*

1   *Give 2 marks for each correct answer*
allow = permit   brave = courageous   be sorry for = sympathize
talk = conversation   unhappiness = misery   get in the way of = hinder

335

2   Speaking HIS loudest he asked THEM WHERE THEY WERE going. WAS
it to THEIR country house with ITS fine garden?
(1 mark for each word in capitals)

3   grieve *(2 marks)*
speech *(2 marks)*
sing *(2 marks)*
choice *(3 marks)*
addition *(3 marks)*

4	"Can I help you?" said the baker politely. "We have some fine cakes today." "No, thank you. I only want bread." (*6 marks. Deduct 1 mark for each error*)
5	*Give 2 marks for each correct answer* oxen geese sheep leaves

PART 2 (*possible marks 52*)

1	A plumber (*2 marks*)
2	Heads close together (*2 marks*) It had to be made larger (*2 marks*)
3	Sooty, or soot (*2 marks*)
4	Eyes elbow mouth nose (*1 mark for each word*)
5	Watering bruise taste sore (*1 mark for each word*)
6	Hammer (*2 marks*)
7	*Give 2 marks for a satisfactory answer*
8	Puffing panting red face (*2 marks for each correct answer*)
9	He got annoyed (*2 marks*)
10	Do not it is you have you are (*2 marks for each correct answer*)
11	(a) Looked hard into (*2 marks*) (b) Hole (*4 marks*) (c) Got on with the job eagerly, etc. (*4 marks*) (d) Excitedly, in great pain, etc. (*4 marks*)
12	Begged his pardon, or, apologised (*4 marks*)

Arithmetic 2 (*possible marks 100*)

Give no marks for incorrect answers except where otherwise indicated

PART 1

1	56 (*2 marks*)
2	103 (*2 marks*)
3	67 (*2 marks*)
4	48 (*3 marks*)
5	266 (*2 marks*)
6	682 (*2 marks*)
7	1,653 (*3 marks. Deduct 1 mark for each wrong figure*)
8	14, remainder 3 (*2 marks. Deduct 1 mark if no remainder given*)
9	5/7½d (*4 marks. Deduct 2 marks for each wrong figure*)

10	£12 2s 7½d (*4 marks. Deduct 2 marks for each wrong figure*)
11	2/1½d (*4 marks*)
12	£31 18s 3d (*5 marks. Deduct 2 marks for each wrong figure*)
13	£1 14s 3d (*6 marks. Deduct 2 marks for each wrong figure*)
14	35 (*8 marks. Deduct 2 marks for each wrong figure*)

PART 2

1	12 (*6 marks. Give 2 marks for knowing that there are 8 half-crowns in a pound*)
2	16, remainder 4 (*6 marks. Give 2 marks for division, 3 marks for 16 and 1 mark for getting the remainder correct*)
3	14/6d (*6 marks. Give 2 marks for multiplying by 12 and 4 marks if the answer is left in pence*)
4	9 feet 3 inches (*4 marks*)
5	1/6d (*8 marks. Give 2 marks for division by 5, and for getting an answer of 6d each give 2 marks*)
6	12 (*6 marks. Give 2 marks for 15/–, 2 marks for 15d*)
7	8 (*5 marks*)
8	2, 3, 4, 5, 6, 10, 12, 15, 20, 30 (*10 marks, 1 mark for each factor*)

Intelligence 2 (*possible marks 70*)

Give 1 mark for each correct answer

1	florist dentist archer jockey cyclist
2	duckling kitten calf boy kid
3	atlas, or gazetteer timetable directory diary cookery book
4	12 20 144 7 30
5	veal mutton beef pork lamb
6	(a) meat tame team mate (b) snip pins nips spin (c) arts rats tars star
7	These should be ringed: ounce farthing 156 consonant These should be underlined: ton half-crown 651 book
8	(a) NUY, GRNY *Give 1½ marks for each correct answer* (b) PARE, TRACE

337

22—H.T.

9	(a) − (*1 mark*) (b) × (*2 marks*) (c) + − (*2 marks*) (d) × (*2 marks*) (e) × + (*3 marks*)
10	*Give 2 marks for each correct answer* (a) woman (b) Friday (c) pen (d) pig (e) girl

English 3 (*possible marks 80*)

PART 1 (*possible marks 28*)

1
(a) neighbours (*2 marks*)
(b) blame, or accuse (*2 marks*)
(c) decide (*2 marks*)
(d) cost (*2 marks*)
(e) example (*2 marks*)

2   "Is that your ball ?" said John. (*10 marks. Deduct 2 marks for each error*)

3   *Give 2 marks for each correct answer*
(a) if   (b) while   (c) and   (d) after

PART 2 (*possible marks 52*)

1   In other old stories (*2 marks*)

2   "which applied all through the country" (*2 marks*)

3   They were made of "small bushes or else of stone" (*3 marks*)

4   Bad roads (*2 marks*)
Running into stray animals (*2 marks*)

5   Robbers, outlaws, etc. (*3 marks*)
Darkness (*1 mark*)

6   It was fenced all round (*2 marks*)

7   For the animal's keep (*2 marks*)
A fine for damage (*2 marks*)

8
(a) unfair (*2 marks*)
(b) wandering (*2 marks*) or lost (*1 mark*)
(c) pushing (*2 marks*)
(d) jump (*2 marks*)
(e) road (*2 marks*)

9   *Give 4 marks for each satisfactory answer*

10   rules (*2 marks*)

11   *Give 3 marks for each correct answer*
(a) silly, stupid   (b) big, bellowing   (c) chattering   (d) mischievous, meddlesome

Arithmetic 3 (*possible marks 100*)

Give no marks for incorrect answers except where otherwise indicated

PART 1

1   1,481 (*4 marks. Deduct 2 marks for each wrong figure*)

2   176 (*4 marks. Deduct 2 marks for each wrong figure*)

3   440, remainder 4 (*6 marks. Deduct 2 marks for each wrong figure*)

4   £43 5s 4d (*8 marks. Deduct 3 marks for each wrong figure*)

5   £85 12s 8d (*8 marks. Deduct 2 marks for each wrong figure*)

6   39 (*6 marks. Give 2 marks for multiplying gallons by 8. Give 1 mark for multiplying quarts by 2*)

7   £7 10s (*4 marks. Give 1 mark for dividing by 20*)

8   9/11 (*4 marks. Give 1 mark for dividing by 12*)

PART 2

1   4 tons 7 hundredweights (*4 marks. Give 1 mark for dividing by 20*)

2   6 feet 3 inches (*4 marks. Give 1 mark for dividing by 12*)

3   136 inches (*7 marks. Give 2 marks for multiplying yards by 3. Give 2 marks for knowing how to do the sum. Give 2 marks for multiplying feet by 12*)

4   77 pounds (*4 marks. Give 1 mark for multiplying stones by 14*)

5   6 yards (*5 marks. Give 2 marks for getting 18 feet. Give 2 marks for knowing how to do the sum*)

6   17 (*5 marks. Give 2 marks for knowing how to do the sum*)

7   28 ounces (*5 marks. Give 2 marks for knowing how to do the sum*)

8   £92 10s 6d (*8 marks. Deduct 2 marks for each wrong figure*)

9   £6 11s 2½d (*8 marks. Deduct 2 marks for each wrong figure*)

10   28,246 (*6 marks*)
The working should be as follows:

```
   487
    58
 ─────
 3,896
24,350
 ─────
28,246
 ─────
```

Even if the total is incorrect, you may give 2 marks for each correctly multiplied line

339

Examination 4 ANSWERS & MARKS FOR SPECIMEN PAPERS

Intelligence 3 (*possible marks 75*)

Give 2 marks for each correct answer

1   (a) abbbb abbbbb   (b) de ef   (c) 8 10   (d) 4d 5e   (e) //)))

2   (a) Mary   (b) cabbages   (c) John   (d) Tom   (e) Mary

3   (a) SAD   (b) YEAR   (c) HIGH   (d) TREE   (e) SOLID

4   *Give 1 mark for each correct answer*
    (a) 4   (b) Ⓐ   (c) West   (d) aunt, nephew   (e) ERIF   (f) LAZY
    (g) right   (h) dearer   (i) chemist or pharmacist

5   *Give 2 marks for each correct answer*
    (a) BLACK   (b) GOSLING   (c) THRONE   (d) LONDON
    (e) 4/–

6   C L A W
    L O B E
    A B L E
    W E E D

7   *Give 1 mark for the correct answer*
    Amber

    Give 2 marks for each correct answer

8   Postage stamps

9   Nine

10   South

11   (a) plumber   (b) an architect   (c) microscope   (d) monarchy
    (e) New Zealand

English 4 (*possible marks 100*)

PART 1 (*possible marks 46*)

1   Christmas (*3 marks*)

2   Holly and mistletoe (*4 marks*)

3   There was so much to buy (*4 marks*)

4   Fruit, flowers, sweetmeats (*3 marks*)

5   *Give 3 marks for each correct answer*
    (a) gleaming eyes   (b) equal distances   (c) shouted what they had for sale
    (d) was crowded   (e) according to how much money they had to spend

6   Entrancing (*3 marks*)

7 *Give 2 marks for each correct answer*
(a) looking   (b) sparkling or shining   (c) imagine   (d) piled
(e) bordered by

8 *Give 1 mark for each colour given that is not in the passage*

PART 2 *(possible marks 54)*

Give 2 marks for each correct answer

1 *Deduct 1 mark for each answer that is incorrectly spelt*
(a) artist or painter   (b) exit   (c) hero   (d) habit   (e) laundry
(f) miser

2 trumpets = blare   owls = hoot   monkeys = chatter
children = shout   bells = peal

3 (a) break   (b) open   (c) rough   (d) lie, falsehood or untruth
(e) praise

4 *Give 5 marks. 1 mark for each correctly placed capital letter*
Shall I see Prince Charles in London?

5 *Give 1 mark for each correct answer*
(a) were   (b) hate   (c) those   (d) what   (e) shall

6 *Give 2 marks for each correct answer*
caught   feel   wrote   called   sit   spoke

Arithmetic 4 *(possible marks 100)*

Give no marks for incorrect answers except where otherwise indicated

PART 1

1 69 *(1 mark)*
2 8 *(1 mark)*
3 28 *(2 marks)*
4 11/3d *(2 marks)*
5 534 *(2 marks)*
6 316 *(2 marks)*
7 £1 6s 6½d *(3 marks)*
8 7/– *(3 marks)*
9 10 *(3 marks)*
10 6 *(3 marks)*

11	5/– (*4 marks*)
12	17 (*4 marks*)

PART 2

1 1,149 (*4 marks. Deduct 2 marks for each wrong figure*)

2 556 (*4 marks. Deduct 2 marks for each wrong figure*)

3 23,031 (*6 marks*)
The working should be as follows:

$$\begin{array}{r} 853 \\ 27 \\ \hline 5,971 \\ 17,060 \\ \hline 23,031 \\ \hline \end{array}$$

Even if the total is incorrect, you may give 2 marks for each correctly multiplied line.

4 26 (*6 marks. Deduct 3 marks for each error*)
The working should be as follows:

$$\begin{array}{r} 26 \\ 13)\overline{\ 338\ } \\ 26 \\ \hline 78 \\ 78 \\ \hline \end{array}$$

5 £13 6s 4d (*6 marks. Deduct 2 marks for each wrong figure*)

6 £5 7s 10½d (*6 marks. Deduct 2 marks for each wrong figure*)

7 £2 6s 0½d (*12 marks. Give 5 marks for knowing how to do the sum*)

8 11,173 (*12 marks. Give 2 marks for knowing how to do the sum. Deduct 2 marks for each wrong figure*)
The working should be as follows:

£23	460	465s	5,580d	5,586½d
20	+5s	×12	+6½d	×2
460s	465s	5,580d	5,586½d	11,173 halfpennies

9 1,764 (*14 marks. Give 5 marks for 42 tiles each way. Give 4 marks for multiplying 42 by 42*)

342

Intelligence 4 (*possible marks 80*)

1   *Give 1 mark for each correct answer*

(a) D   (b) F   (c) W   (d) Wednesday   (e) April   (f) 7
(g) Helen   (h) quart   (i) four   (j) IV

2   *Give 1 mark for each correct word*
YOU ARE A GOOD CHILD

3   *Give 5 marks for each group of letters. Deduct 1 mark for each wrongly placed letter*
CADBE   EBDAC

4   *Give 2 marks for each correct name*
(a) John Dick   (b) Tom   (c) John James

5   *Give 1 mark for each correct pair*
(a) red yellow   (b) elephant cow   (c) six eight   (d) oxo axo, *or* oxo mug
(e) pint quart

6   *Give 4 marks for* (a) *and* (b) *but only 2 marks for* (c)
(a) Turn right up Broadway which is the road at the top of Mark Lane. Take the second on your right. The station is a little way up on the right hand side.
(b) Turn right as you leave the station. Turn down Bread Lane which is the first turning on the right, turn left at the crossroads into Beech Road, and we are on the left hand side of the road.
(c) No, on the opposite side.

7   *Give 2 marks for each correct answer*
(a) On Her Majesty's Service   (b) Before Christ   (c) Essex County Council
(d) General Post Office   (e) British Railways

8   *Deduct 1 mark for each word that is spelt wrongly*
(a) avenue   (b) island   (c) neighbours   (d) grocer's   (e) autumn

9   (a) LAD   (b) PET   (c) ONE   (d) HER or ERE   (e) SHE or HOE

English 5 (*possible marks 100*)

PART 1 (*possible marks 48*)

Give 2 marks for each correct answer

1   narrow   hard or difficult   failure or defeat   tame   evil

2   heroine   prince   doctor   manservant   hen

3   (a) since   (b) although   (c) and   (d) which   (e) if

4   ancient   hasten   labour   stroll   haughty

5 These words should *not* be crossed out:
(a) bare   (b) passed   (c) knew, did   (d) which, its *(give 2 marks for each word)*

PART 2 *(possible marks 52)*

1 Mary could not find her, etc. *(3 marks)*

2 There was no note for her, etc. *(3 marks)*

3 "to hunt everywhere for a piece of paper with her name on it" *(3 marks)*

4 Sitting-room and shop *(3 marks)*

5 Standing by the door of the shop *(2 marks)*

6 *Give 3 marks for each answer*
The steps had fallen down.
The rope was broken.
Aunt Molly had suggested that this might happen.

7 *Give 3 marks for each answer*
She soon stopped crying.
She realised what had happened.
She made plans to help her aunt by having tea ready.

8 She had seen his brass plate. *(3 marks)*

9 To make the kettle boil for the cup of tea. *(3 marks)*
To have the room cheerful, etc. *(1 mark)*

10 *Give 5 marks for each answer*
The kettle was boiled on a fire.
The station was across the green.

11 If the steps had been mended all the trouble resulting from the accident would have been saved. *For words expressing this give 10 marks*

Arithmetic 5 *(possible marks 100)*

Give no marks for incorrect answers except where otherwise indicated

PART 1

Give 2 marks for each correct answer

1 30,753

2 141

3 56

4 3

5	36

Give 3 marks for each correct answer

6	4/6d
7	15
8	12
9	10
10	$\frac{1}{5}$
11	14
12	24

Give 4 marks for each correct answer

13	1919 (*Give 2 marks for getting* $59-30=29$)
14	54 (*Give only 2 marks if the answer is not given in pints*
15	21 (*Give 2 marks for getting 20 as an answer*)
16	Thirteen minutes to two, or 1.47
17	1.15 p.m. (*Give 2 marks for 1.15 and 1 mark for 1.15 a.m.*)

PART 2

Give 6 marks for each correct answer

1	5 pounds 12 ounces or $5\frac{3}{4}$ pounds (*Give 2 marks for finding weight of half content; i.e.* $1\frac{3}{4}$ *pounds*)
2	15 (*Give 2 marks for getting the cost per article*$=4d$)
3	3 (*Give 3 marks for giving 160 as the answer*)
4	$6\frac{1}{2}$d (*5 marks. Give 2 marks for getting 1 pound extra. Give 2 marks for getting 8 halfpennies extra*)
5	4 feet 9 inches (*6 marks. Give 2 marks for half 4 feet 6 inches*$=2$ *feet 3 inches. Give 2 marks for subtraction*)
6	$\begin{array}{rr} 12s & 6d \\ 10s & 10d \\ 3s & 9d \\ \hline £1 \quad 7s & 1d \end{array}$

(*8 marks. Give 2 marks for each correct line*)

7	£1 6s 8d (*9 marks. Give 4 marks for giving the equivalent number of chickens as 6 Give 2 marks for dividing*)
8	20 (*3 marks*)

345

Intelligence 5 *(possible marks 80)*

1   *Give 1 mark for each correct answer*
Week   year   century   reign   year

2   *Give 2 marks for each correct group. No marks may be given if any of the numbers are wrong*
(a) 514263   (b) 51432   (c) 31524   (d) 23541   (e) 32145

Give 2 marks for each correct answer

3   calender   programme   menu   index or contents   directory

4   (a) A   (b) S   (c) S   (d) A   (e) N   (f) S   (g) A   (h) A
(i) S   (j) S

5   (a) Helen   (b) Charles   (c) James   (d) Doris   (e) Alan

6   (a) Post Office   (b) bank   (c) police station   (d) booking office
(e) aerodrome or airport

7   *Give 1 mark only for (a) but 2 marks for (b) and (c)*
(a) 1   (b) 1   (c) 12

8   *Give 2 marks for each correct answer*
(a) Dec 25th   (b) Nov 5th   (c) Oct 3rd   (d) Jan 1st   (e) May 28th

English 6 *(possible marks 90)*

PART 1 *(possible marks 40)*

Give 2 marks for each correct answer

1   (a) solid   (b) library   (c) afraid   (d) simpleton   (e) fish

2   (a) Were you calling me?   (b) He ran away at full speed.   (c) What did you say it was?   (d) We did what we were told.   (e) Go and lie down on your bed.

3   choice   arrival   speak   receive   attention or attendance

4   cherries   mouse   feet   shapes   penny

346

PART 2 *(possible marks 50)*

1   *Give 2 marks for each correct answer except where otherwise indicated*
(a) Vaughan
(b) Her parents were in India
(c) Major
(d) Walking, reading *(give 2 marks for each answer)*
(e) People of her own age, the bustle of school *(give 2 marks for each answer)*
(f) To find some books to read

(g) Such a lot of different things were in the attic
(h) Through windows in the roof
(i) Small print, history books (*give 2 marks for each answer*)

2 *Give 2 marks for each correct answer*
(a) thought   (b) (example only)   (c) bustle   (d) gather   (e) fine
(f) decorated

3 *Give 3 marks for each adequate expression*
(a) Crossed the sea to another country   (b) resounded as she walked
(c) over 200 years   (d) a nursery many years ago   (e) a picture of a person

Arithmetic 6 (*possible marks 100*)

Give no marks for incorrect answers except where otherwise indicated

1 2,405 (*3 marks. Deduct 1 mark for each wrong figure*)

2 4,693 (*3 marks. Deduct 1 mark for each wrong figure*)

3 179,524 (*6 marks*)
The working should be as follows:

```
    4,852
       37
    _____

   33,964
  145,560
    _____

  179,524
    _____
```

Even if the total is incorrect you may give 2 marks for each correctly multiplied line.

4 368, remainder 15 (*8 marks*)
The working should be as follows:

```
        368
   17/6,271
       51
       ___

      117
      102
      ___

      151
      136
      ___

       15
```

347

If the complete answer is incorrect you may give 2 marks for each correct figure in the answer.

5

```
 8s   9d
 1s   8d
 3s   7d
16s   0d
```
———
£1 10s   0d
———

(*10 marks. Give 2 marks for each correct line*)

6 1/6 (*4 marks. Give 2 marks for subtracting 1/9 and 2 marks for halving the remainder*)

7 $4\frac{7}{12}$ (*5 marks. Give 2 marks for giving $3\frac{19}{12}$ as the answer*)

8 $2\frac{3}{8}$ (*5 marks. Give 2 marks for giving $3\frac{3}{8}$ as the answer*)

9 $25\frac{1}{2}$ 5 marks. Give 1 mark for $24\frac{6}{4}$ and 2 marks for $25\frac{2}{4}$)

10 21 (*5 marks*)

11 10.5 a.m. (*8 marks*)
Give marks for these stages:

Time taken = $\frac{50}{12}$ hours	*1 mark*
$\frac{50}{12}$ hours = 4 hours 10 minutes	*2 marks*
2. 15 p.m. minus	
4 hrs 10 mins	*2 marks*
———	
10. 5	*2 marks*
———	
a.m.	*1 mark*

12 30 days (*8 marks*)
Give marks for these stages:

28 pounds = 1 quarter	*2 marks*
$7\frac{1}{2}$ hundredweights = 30 quarters or 840 pounds	*2 marks*
for trying to get number of days by division	*2 marks*

13 16 per day (*9 marks*)
Give marks for these stages:

one seventh of 84 = 12 sweets		*1 mark*
remaining	72 sweets	*1 mark*
lost	8 sweets	*1 mark*
remaining	64 sweets	*1 mark*
number of days = 4		*1 mark*

14 6 stones 11 pounds 12 ounces (*7 marks*)
Give marks for these stages:

stones	pounds	ounces		
8	1	4	minus	*1 mark*
1	3	8		*2 marks*
———	———	———		
6	11	12		

348

15	245 square feet (*14 marks*)

Give marks for these stages:

Area of lawn $= 28 \times 16$ square feet   *2 marks*

$= 448$ square feet   *2 marks*

Total length $= 33$ feet   *2 marks*

Total breadth $= 21$ feet   *2 marks*

Total area $= 33 \times 21$ square feet $= 693$ square feet   *2 marks*

Area of path $= 693 - 448$ square feet   *2 marks*

Deduct 3 marks for giving the answer in feet instead of square feet.

Intelligence 6 (*possible marks 100*)

Give 2 marks for each correct answer

1

(a)   (b)   (c)   (d)   (e)

G comes before H in the alphabet and not after.

2   hurriedly   straight   low   sad   silent

3   (a) E   (b) H   (c) L   (d) M   (e) E

4   A5   B4   C6   E1   F3

5   *Deduct 1 mark for each error in* (a) *and* (d)

(a) Clean shoes. Pull on. Lace up. Tie a bow.   (b) Tuesday   (c) Floor

(d) Sandra, Sara, sausage, Stephen, Susan.   (e) rash   (f) 53   (g) 13

(h) Helen   (i) One cannot tell   (j) Z

6   (a) boots and shoes   (b) pipes   (c) clothes   (d) machinery   (e) pots and pans

English 7 (*possible marks 100*)

PART 1 (*possible marks 45*)

Give 3 marks for each correct answer

1   pride   laziness   cowardly   heroic   splendour

2   (a) congregation   (b) audience   (c) team   (d) orchestra

3   (a) fragile   (b) inhabit   (c) ascertain   (d) naked   (e) cousin

4   What did John say to you?

(*Deduct 1 mark for each error*)

PART 2 (*possible marks 55*)

1 Food from the sea (*3 marks*)
The shipwreck (*1 mark*)

2 *Give 4 marks for each suitable answer*
(a) He noticed   (b) Very excitedly   (c) He saw   (d) Would sooner or later   (e) Felt grand   (f) the next month or two   (g) Something to take the place of a screwdriver

3 *Give 3 marks for each suitable answer*
(a) things   (b) quick or brisk   (c) fierceness

4 *Give 3 marks for each correct answer*
(a) He had to wait for the boxes and so forth to wash ashore   (b) They were in a tin and quite fit to eat   (c) There was a cottage on it   (d) They were partially dry   (e) The boxes were being washed onto the shore

Arithmetic 7 (*possible marks 100*)

Give no marks for incorrect answers except where otherwise indicated

1 £1 11s 6d (*4 marks. Give 2 marks for getting 4/6d per dozen*)

2 39 children (*4 marks. Give 2 marks for getting 13 pints*)

3 7 hundredweights $32\frac{2}{3}$ pounds (*8 marks*)
Give marks for these stages:

$87\frac{1}{2}$ hundredweights	*2 marks*
For dividing $87\frac{1}{2}$ by 12	*1 mark*
For getting 392 pounds	*2 marks*
For getting $32\frac{2}{3}$ pounds	*2 marks*

4 $1\frac{7}{12}$ (*5 marks*)
Give marks for these stages:

$\frac{6}{12}+\frac{8}{12}+\frac{5}{12}$	*2 marks*
$=\frac{19}{12}$	*1 mark*

5 $3\frac{3}{4}$ (*6 marks*)
Give marks for these stages:

$\frac{27}{8}\times\frac{10}{9}$	*2 marks*
$=\frac{15}{4}$	*2 marks*

6 $1\frac{13}{32}$ (*6 marks*)
Give marks for these stages:

$\frac{5}{8}\times\frac{9}{4}$	*2 marks*
$=\frac{45}{32}$	*2 marks*

350

7 | 3/6d (*6 marks*)
Give marks for these stages:

$\frac{2}{3}$ left — *2 marks*

$= 2/4d$ — *1 mark*

$\frac{1}{3} =$ half of 2/4d — *1 mark*

8 | 5 feet 8 inches (*5 marks*)
Give marks for these stages:

Outside measurements = 14 inches by 20 inches — *2 marks*

Total distance all round = 68 inches — *2 marks*

9 | £1 0s 10d (*5 marks*)
Give marks for these stages:

£$\frac{3}{8}$ = 7/6d — *2 marks*

£$\frac{2}{3}$ = 13/4d — *2 marks*

10 | 30 m.p.h. (*6 marks. Give 3 marks for getting 11.35 a.m. − 2.5 p.m. = 2$\frac{1}{2}$ hours*)

11 | 3 pounds (*9 marks*)
Give marks for these stages:

5 blocks weigh 10 ounces — *3 marks*

40 blocks weigh 80 ounces — *2 marks*

80 ounces = 5 pounds — *2 marks*

weight of box = 8 pounds minus 5 pounds — *2 marks*

12 | £2 15s 0d (*5 marks Give 2 marks for getting 22 yards = 1 chain and 1 mark for division by 8*)

13 | $\frac{9}{16}$ (*7 marks*)
Give marks for these stages:

Fraction slept $= \dfrac{10\frac{1}{2}}{24}$ — *2 marks*

$= \frac{7}{16}$ — *3 marks*

For subtracting $\frac{7}{16}$ from $\frac{16}{16}$ — *2 marks*

14 | 18 square inches (*6 marks. Give 2 marks for getting area of oblong as 36 square inches. If answer is given in inches, instead of square inches, deduct 2 marks*)

15 | David 3d, Charles 9d, Bill 1/– (*9 marks*)
Give marks for these stages:

Bill has 9d more than David — *2 marks*

Charles has 6d more than David — *2 marks*

Therefore 9d is left — *1 mark*

Shared between three boys 3d each — *2 marks*

3d + 6d = 9d — *1 mark*

3d + 9d = 1/– — *1 mark*

351

Intelligence 7 (*possible marks 90*)

Give 2 marks for each correct answer

1   (a) sister   (b) grandmother   (c) nephew   (d) aunt   (e) father

2   (a) Robert   (b) none   (c) none   (d) brown   (e) Charles

Give 1 mark for each correct answer

3   (a) Russia   (b) Germany   (c) Italy   (d) Ireland (Eire)   (e) Egypt
     (f) France   (g) Canada   (h) China   (i) Belgium   (j) Israel (Palestine)

4   *Give 2 marks for each correct answer. Deduct 1 mark for each letter omitted*
     (a) AKR   (b) R   (c) LT   (d) BR   (e) PC   (f) O

5   *Give 2 marks for each correct answer*
     (a) heroine   (b) authoress   (c) landlord   (d) mistress

6   *Give 3 marks for each correct line*
     (a) carpenter   wood   make a table
     (b) gardener   fork   dig the garden
     (c) teacher   chalk   write on blackboard
     (d) grocer   scales   weigh the tea
     (e) housewife   pen   write out recipe

7   *Give 2 marks for each correct pair*
     (a) feathers   tusks
     (b) fins   hands
     (c) wings   arms
     (d) fur   feathers
     (e) claws   fur

8   *Give 3 marks for each correct answer*
     (a) 2   (b) 3   (c) 1   (d) 2   (e) 3

352

English 8 (*possible marks 100*)

PART 1 (*possible marks 58*)

1   *Give 2 marks for each correct answer*
     (a) return   (b) occasionally   (c) attic   (d) fortnight   (e) abroad

2   *Give 1 mark for each correct answer*
     blew   stood   told   forgot   doing   ran   fell   could
     broken   taken   given   was   wrote   saying   had

3

17, Lake Walk,
Crofton.
14 March, 1956

Dear John,

Thank you for asking me to stay with you for a few days. Mummy says I may, and I am looking forward to seeing you at Easter.

Your loving cousin,
Timothy.

If your child has set out the letter as this specimen, give 11 marks. Otherwise give 7 marks for arranging the letter neatly; deducting 1 mark for each error of arrangement. Also deduct half a mark for each incorrect capital letter or punctuation mark.

4

Give 2 marks for each correct answer
graceful = dance   threatening = mob   peaceful = scene
quarrelsome = children   delicate = appearance   peculiar = fashion

5

Give 2 marks for each correct answer
(a) bough, etc.   (b) enough, rough, etc.   (c) through   (d) dough
(e) cough

PART 2 (*possible marks 42*)

1

It was holiday time (*1 mark*)
She was going on an expedition (*1 mark*)

Give 2 marks for each correct answer

2 By whistling incessantly

3 A servant

4 A horse or pony

5 Accept any adequate evidence taken from the passage

6 2 miles

7 The riders would be out from morning to afternoon

8 Help her to groom her pony, etc.

9 *Give 2 marks for each reason given*
Washed up   made beds   fed the poultry   made sandwiches

10 To suggest that Christina could not or would not look after her pony (*2 marks*)

11 *Give 2 marks for each correct answer*
(a) feels, has   (b) continually   (c) unable to, or cannot   (d) look
(e) looking after   (f) proud

12 *Give 3 marks for any suitable expression for example*
(a) I was sorry for my criticism   (b) The last insult hurt very much

353

23—H.T.

Arithmetic 8 (*possible marks 100*)

Give no marks for incorrect answers except where otherwise indicated

PART 1

1	152 (*1 mark*)
2	687 (*2 marks*)
3	17/10d (*3 marks*)
4	6/8½d (*3 marks*)
5	16 (*3 marks*)
6	56 (*3 marks. Give 1 mark for getting 1 stone = 14 pounds*)
7	42 minutes (*3 marks. Give 1 mark for getting 1 hour 52 minutes equals 112 miles*)
8	$5\frac{1}{6}$ (*4 marks. Give 2 marks for giving $4\frac{7}{6}$*)
9	$\frac{7}{8}$ (*4 marks. Give 2 marks for changing $1\frac{3}{4}$ to $\frac{14}{8}$*)
10	$4\frac{4}{5}$ (*4 marks. Give 2 marks for giving $3\frac{9}{5}$*)
11	$\frac{2}{5}$ (*4 marks. Give 2 marks for changing $2\frac{4}{5}$ to $\frac{14}{5}$*)

PART 2

1   11d (*4 marks*)
Give marks for these stages:

1/4d − 3d = 1/1d	*1 mark*
1d + 1/1d = 1/2d	*1 mark*

2   3 yards square, by 5 square yards (*Give 1 mark for stating that 3 yards square is the greater and give 3 marks for giving 5 square yards as the difference*)

3   ¼ quart (*4 marks. Give 1 mark for finding that twice half a half pint is half a pint*

4   8 (*4 marks*)
Give marks for these stages:

6 × 8 = 48	*1 mark*
for subtracting 40	*1 mark*

5   £1 14s 6d (*5 marks*)
Give marks for these stages:

7/6d = £$\frac{3}{8}$	*1 mark*
12/- = £$\frac{3}{5}$	*1 mark*
15/- = £$\frac{3}{4}$	*1 mark*

6

9s	2d
6s	3d
8s	9d
£1 4s	2d

(*8 marks. Give 2 marks for each correct line*)

7 | 76 tons 10 hundredweights 3 quarters (*8 marks*)
Give marks for these stages:

tons	cwt	qrs
5	17	3
		13

76	10	3

11	9	
65	51	4/39
—	170	9 r 3
76	20/230	
	11 r 10	

For correct working under "cwt"   *2 marks*
For correct working under "qrs"   *2 marks*

8 | $4\frac{1}{2}$ pints (*8 marks*)
Give marks for these stages:
10 gallons = 80 pints   *1 mark*
$17 \times 1\frac{1}{2}$ pints = $25\frac{1}{2}$ pints   *1 mark*
Total sold = $75\frac{1}{2}$ pints   *1 mark*

9 | $7\frac{1}{2}$ hours (*10 marks*)
Give marks for these stages:
8.28 a.m. to 9.13 a.m. = 45 minutes   *2 marks*
Travelling time per day = 90 minutes   *1 mark*
Travelling time per day = $1\frac{1}{2}$ hours   *1 mark*
$1\frac{1}{2}$ hours × 5 (times per week) = $7\frac{1}{2}$ hours   *1 mark*
For knowing how to do the sum yet failing to get the correct answer
                                                   4 marks

10 | $4\frac{4}{5}$ ounces (*11 marks*)
Give marks for these stages:
Total weight = 25 pounds   *2 marks*
$\frac{1}{25}$ is green vitriol   *2 marks*
$7\frac{1}{2}$ pounds = 120 ounces   *1 mark*
Therefore green vitriol = 120 ÷ 25 = $4\frac{4}{5}$ ounces   *3 marks*
For knowing how to do the sum yet failing to get the correct answer
                                                   3 marks

355

11 | 2d (*9 marks*)
Give marks for these stages:
Cost of petrol = 9/–   *2 marks*
Cost of oil = 1/6d   *2 marks*
Total cost = 10/6d   *1 mark*
For dividing 10/6d by 63   *2 marks*

Intelligence 8 *(possible marks 100)*

Give 2 marks for each correct answer

I (a) Répondez, s'il vous plaît (French, meaning: reply please)   (b) Master of Arts   (c) General Post Office   (d) Post Meridiem (Latin, meaning: afternoon) or Prime Minister   (e) Her/His Royal Highness   (f) Royal Air Force   (g) United States of America   (h) Pounds Shillings Pence   (i) Hire Purchase, or Horse Power   (j) Member of Parliament, or Military Police

2 (a) Thames   (b) Nottingham   (c) steel   (d) Brussels   (e) Prune   (f) left   (g) thistle, or lion   (h) Hastings   (i) Isle of Wight   (j) Sir Winston Churchill

3 (a) 5   (b) 11   (c) 100   (d) 113   (e) 1,000

4 (a) flock, or gaggle   (b) shoal   (c) pack   (d) hive, or swarm   (e) choir   (f) set   (g) crowd   (h) herd   (i) collection, or set   (j) fleet   (k) litter   (l) pride   (m) pack

5 *Give 5 marks for the correct answer*
It was impossible to know what he was dreaming if he died before he awoke

6 (a) Fred   Tom *(3 marks for each name)*
(b) Kate   Left *(3 marks for each name)*
(c) David   Eric *(4 marks for each name)*
Draw diagrams and the answers become obvious

7 *Give 1 mark for each correct set*
1a5c5d   4c4d4b5b   3d1c4b2a2b1b   3b5a3e3a   3e1a1c2e

English 9 *(possible marks 100)*

PART 1 *(possible marks 53)*

I *Give 2 marks for each suitable sentence*
Here are some specimen sentences:
As a result of our *encounter* in the High Street, I made a firm friend.
He did not want to be seen so he made a *cautious* approach.
He shut the door to *exclude* the draughts.
The boys were so loud and *unruly* that they had to stay in.
He broke off a *fragment* of bread for the ducks.

2 *Give 2 marks for each correct answer*
wife   uncle   lady   gander   sow

3 *Give 2 marks for each correct sentence*
(a) I shan't do *any* work today.   (b) Timothy is the *heavier* of the two brothers.   (c) Give me some of *those* apples for myself.   (d) He treated him very *spitefully*.

4 *Give 1 mark for each correct word*
beautify, beautiful   sympathy, sympathetic   fear, fear   agreement, agree pleasure, pleasing or pleasant

5 *Give 3 marks for each sensible answer. Deduct 1 mark whenever punctuation is wrong*
Here are some specimens of suitable answers:
     (a) "What time is it?" he enquired.
     (b) "Leave the slipper alone, Fido." the lady told her dog.
     (c) "Who would like to go swimming this evening?" asked teacher.
     (d) "You don't know how pleased I am." he said.
     (e) "I have bad earache." complained Mary.

PART 2 (*possible marks 47*)

1 How small birds are stolen from their nests (*3 marks*)

2 *Give 4 marks for each correct answer*
(a) friends of larger growth   (b) watch the progress   (c) plain traces of entry are visible   (d) his attention is otherwise engaged   (e) is a keen observer   (f) flight continually directed to one spot

3 *Give 1 mark for each correct answer*
boys   cats   crows

4 crows (*2 marks*)

5 early morning (*1 mark*) or, in the evening (*1 mark*)

6 their nests and babies (*3 marks*)

7 a collection of bushes (*2 marks*)

8 *Give 2 marks for each correct answer*
(a) leave   (b) pleasure, or glee   (c) need   (d) clear

357

Arithmetic 9 (*possible marks 100*)

Give no marks for incorrect answers except where otherwise indicated

1 180 (*2 marks*)

2 2,815 (*2 marks*)

3 | £13 5s 8d (*9 marks*)

There are two methods of doing this sum. By the first method £23 4s 11d is multiplied by 4. This will come to £92 19s 8d. £92 19s 8d is then divided by 7. The answer is £13 5s 8d.

By the second method £23 4s 11d is first divided by 7 and the answer (£3 6s 5d) is multiplied by 4 (£13 5s 8d).

Give 5 marks for knowing either of these methods but failing to get the correct answer.

4 | 17 feet 3 inches (*12 marks*)

Give marks for these stages:

8/7½d = 103½ pence	*3 marks*
8/7½d = 207 halfpennies	*2 marks*
8/7½d = 207 inches	*3 marks*
207 inches = 17 feet 3 inches	

5 | 1 pound 11 ounces (*9 marks*)

Give marks for these stages:

6/9d = 81 pence	*2 marks*
Dividing by 3	*2 marks*
For getting 27 ounces	*2 marks*
27 ounces = 1 pound 11 ounces	

6 | 160 hours (*14 marks*)

Give marks for these stages:

6 gallons = 48 pints	*2 marks*
48 pints = 96 half-pints	*2 marks*
For dividing number of pints by 1½	*3 marks*
For multiplying by 5	*3 marks*

7 | 14 square feet (*8 marks*)

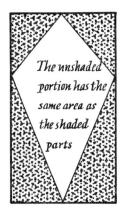

The unshaded portion has the same area as the shaded parts

The area of the rectangle surrounding the kite is 28 square feet. Because the kite is half this area it must measure 14 square feet.

Deduct 1 mark for not putting the answer in square feet.

8 | 5 hours 25 minutes (*14 marks*)
Give marks for these stages:

9.12 a.m. to 5.42 p.m.=8 hours 30 minutes	*4 marks*
For attempting the above, but failing to get the correct answer	*2 marks*
Travelling and lunch 2 hours 20 minutes	
+45 minutes=3 hours 5 minutes	*2 marks*
Time shopping 8 hours 30 minutes	
−3 hours 5 minutes=5 hours 25 minutes. For attempting this but failing to get correct answer	*2 marks*

9 | (a) 180   (b) 75 (*15 marks*)
Give marks for these stages:

$\frac{5}{12}$ of sweets remaining	*2 marks*
Difference between $\frac{7}{12}$ and $\frac{5}{12}=\frac{2}{12}$	*2 marks*
$\frac{2}{12}=30$ sweets	*2 marks*
Therefore total=180	*2 marks*
Therefore sweets eaten will be $\frac{5}{12}$ of 180	*2 marks*
$\frac{5}{12}$ of 180=75	

10 | £11 (*15 marks*)
Give marks for these stages:

Length=140 feet	*1 mark*
Number of hurdles=28	*2 marks*
Breadth=100 feet	*1 mark*
Number of hurdles=20	*2 marks*
Total hurdles=96	*4 marks*
96=8 dozen	*1 mark*
Cost=8×£1 7s 6d	*4 marks*
8×£1 7s 6d=£11	

Intelligence 9 (*possible marks 100*)

1 | *Give 2 marks for each correct set*
(a) WVRS SRVW   (b) LACK CLAK   (c) MRBY MBRY
(d) ALPS EHQU   (e) CUTO HAVE

Give 2 marks for each correct answer
2 | (a) editor   (b) mineral   (c) rash   (d) dramatist   (e) flax   (f) 2/–
(g) calf   (h) fish   (i) afraid   (j) strength   (k) butterfly   (l) hub
(m) vegetarians   (n) prism   (o) unmarried woman

3 | A3   C4   D5   E2   F1

4 | *Give 3 marks for each correct answer; except for (e), for which 5 marks should be given. Deduct 1 mark for each error*
(a) My mother   (b) Alice 10 Gwen 5   (c) At the end of nine minutes

359

(d) They were facing each other   (e) You are going to bed earlier
(f) Tuesday

5 *Give 2 marks each for (a) and (b), and 4 marks each for (c) and (d)*
(a) pound   (b) James   (c) despair   (d) fish

English 10 *(possible marks 90)*

PART 1 *(possible marks 40)*

1 *Give 2 marks for each correct answer*
A3   B5   C2   D1   E4

2 *Give 1 mark for each sentence in which the word specified is correctly used. Check with a dictionary if necessary*

3 Molly my sister, and I fell out.
And what do you think it was all about?
She loved coffee and I loved tea.
That was the reason we couldn't agree.
If this has been done without fault give 10 marks. Otherwise deduct 1 mark for each error

4 *Give 10 marks for doing these two sentences correctly. Otherwise deduct 1 mark for each error*
(a) The children were delighted to see the calves in the fields.
(b) The ladies sang solos.

PART 2 *(possible marks 50)*

1 To make it plain that it was very long *(2 marks)*

2 *Give 3 marks for each correct answer*
(a) not often visited by people   (b) as well as he could remember   (c) as far as was known   (d) what sort of creature he was   (e) lands where men live   (f) caused great anxiety or worry

3 *Give 2 marks for each correct answer*
(a) a man who makes statues or carves stone   (b) a hundred years (or a hundred runs in cricket)

4 *Any two of:*
He was the only one left.
He lived so far away.
People were frightened to go near him to tell him.
He had no mirror.
The streams were not smooth enough to see himself in
(2 marks for each correct answer)

5	A huge winged dragon, etc. (*2 marks. If "winged" is omitted give 1 mark only*)
6	He had flown so far (*1 mark*) He had not made such a long flight for a long time (*1 mark*)
7	Nobody had been near to tell him (*2 marks*)
8	He called in such a terrible voice (*2 marks*)
9	*Give 2 marks for each suitable word* (a) awful, or fearful (b) rough, or raging (c) decided (d) outskirts (e) ordered, or told (f) strange (g) workmen

Arithmetic 10 (*possible marks 100*)

Give no marks for incorrect answers except where otherwise indicated

PART 1

Give 1 mark for each correct answer

1	662
2	366
3	25,144
4	516
5	£8 13s 4d
6	£1 4s 10d

Give 2 marks for each correct answer

7	£1 12s 5½d
8	$3\frac{1}{3}$ (If the answer is given as $\frac{34}{12}$ give 1 mark only)
9	145
10	5/-
11	7·56
12	11 ounces
13	½ inch short (If the word "short" is omitted give 1 mark only)
14	45

Give 3 marks for each correct answer

15	2
16	120
17	31½ miles
18	½

361

19 | 11

20 | 26 inches

PART 2

1 | 12,099 (*3 marks*)
The working should be as follows:

$$
\begin{array}{r}
327 \\
37 \\
\hline
2,289 \\
9,810 \\
\hline
12,099
\end{array}
$$

Even if the total is incorrect, you may give 1 mark for each correctly multiplied line.

2 | 64 (*5 marks*)
The working should be as follows:

$$
\begin{array}{r}
64 \\
59\overline{)3,776} \\
354 \\
\hline
236 \\
236 \\
\hline
\end{array}
$$

Give 2 marks for dividing—even if the answer is incorrect.
Deduct 1 mark for each error.

3 | 226 yards 1 foot 1 inch (*6 marks*)
Give marks for these stages:

yards	feet	inches
7	2	5
		29
226	1	1
23	12	
203	58	12$\overline{)145}$
	—	12 r 1
	3$\overline{)70}$	
	23	

For correct working under "feet" — *2 marks*
For correct working under "inches" — *2 marks*

362

4 £3 16s 2½d (*7 marks*)

The working should be as follows:

pounds	shillings	pence	halfpennies
3	16	2	1
57/217	3	10	1
171	920	132	56
46	923	142	57
	57	114	57
46	353	28	
20	342		
920	11	28	
		2	
	11		
	12	56	
	132		

Give 1 mark for getting £3 correct and give 2 marks for each other item in the answer.

5 576 (*7 marks*)

Give marks for these stages:

Area of roof $= 16 \times 12 \times 12 \times 12$ square inches

Area of tile $= 6 \times 8$ square inches

Total number of tiles $= \dfrac{16 \times 12 \times 12 \times 12}{6 \times 8}$

(The above sum can be reduced by cancelling to $2 \times 2 \times 12 \times 12) = 576$

For finding area of roof · *2 marks*

For finding area of tile · *2 marks*

6 120 (*11 marks*)

Give marks for these stages:

Circumference of wheel $= 88$ inches · · · · · · · · · · · · · *2 marks*

Distance per minute $= \frac{1}{6}$ mile · · · · · · · · · · · · · · · *1 mark*

$\frac{1}{6}$ mile $\dfrac{(1760 \times 36)}{6} = 10,560$ inches · · · · · · · · · *2 marks*

Number of revolutions $= 10,560 \div 88$ · · · · · · · · · · · · · *3 marks*

363

7 | 11 hours (*12 marks*)

Give marks for these stages:

Flowers cost $5 \times 7/6d = £1$ 17s 6d	*1 mark*
Cabbages cost $4 \times 2/2\frac{1}{2}d = 8/10d$	*1 mark*
These two items total £2 6s 4d	*1 mark*
Labour cost £3 16s 7d − £2 6s 4d = £1 10s 3d	*2 marks for subtracting and 1 extra mark if the total is correct*
Number of hours = £1 10s 3d ÷ 2/9d	*2 marks*

8 | 4 pounds (*12 marks*)

Give marks for these stages:

8 glass blocks are equivalent in weight to 20 wooden blocks	*4 marks*
Therefore 25 wooden blocks would weigh 100 pounds (7 stones 2 pounds)	*5 marks*
Therefore each wooden block weighs 4 pounds	

Intelligence 10 (*possible marks 100*)

Give 2 marks for each correct answer

1 | Underline   contain

2 | Two

Give 1 mark for each correct word or letter

3 | U   E   I   O

4 | diet   tied   edit   tide

5 | *Give 2 marks for each correct answer*
(a) Tom   (b) carry   (c) bread   (d) pale

6 | *Give 2 marks for each pair*
(a) 21 19   (b) 46 57   (c) 128 512   (d) 04 05

Give 2 marks for each correct answer

7 | (a) USVNQFU   (b) LANTERN

8 | (a) Tom   (b) Toby   (c) Wednesday   (d) Thursday

9 | (a) sour acid   (b) under below   (c) climb ascend   (d) slumber sleep

10 | (a) underline James   (b) author   (c) 1/2

11 | Motor car £575   pencil 4d   cabbage 7d   gloves 21/–   butter 4/–

364

12 | *Give 3 marks for each correct pair*
(a) ○ × ○ ○ ○ ○   ○ × ○ ○ ○ ○ ○
                                 ○
(b) ○   ○
(c) × × × ×   × × × × ×
            × ×   × ×

English 11 (*possible marks 140*)

PART 1 (*possible marks 50*)

Composition.
    25 marks for ideas, taking into account both quality and quantity.
    14 marks for style and construction.
    6 marks for spelling and punctuation.
    5 marks for indefinable qualities.

PART 2 (*possible marks 46*)

1 Land (*2 marks*)

2 They had seen something like it on the previous evening (*3 marks*)

3 No bottom yet (*4 marks*) or
Nothing yet (*2 marks*) or
A scene of emptiness (*2 marks*)

4 Tears ran down his face, etc. (*2 marks*)

5 *Give 2 marks for each suitable answer*
(a) to and fro   (b) sounded sadly   (c) showing the two ships with us
(d) sea stretching everywhere

6 Yes, they go well together; lead is both dull and heavy; vacant means empty.
The words also have a slow, heavy sound (*4 marks*)

7 The East lightened (*2 marks*)

8 Senor (*2 marks*)

9 Anything reasonable, e.g. No Land, or A Disappointing Morning (*3 marks*)

10 *Give 2 marks for each correct answer*
pierced = broken   answer = reply   refrain = chorus, echo   revealed =
showing   vacant = empty   apathy = tiredness, listlessness   gazed =
stared, looked   unmoving = motionless, still

365

PART 3 (*possible marks 44*)

1 *Give 1 mark for each correct answer*
(a) fortify   (b) decide   (c) pliable   (d) penitent   (e) penetrate
(f) fragile   (g) discuss   (h) century   (i) extract   (j) inflammable

Give 14 marks if the passage is correctly punctuated, etc. Otherwise deduct 1 mark for each error. Permit a comma after Henry

2 "Help!" cried Henry from the ledge, "I'm splashed all over." "You'll have to go and get changed at once" said his mother sharply. "Why can't you keep out of trouble ?"

3 *Give 1 mark for each correct answer*
inhuman   nonsense   unreliable   dissimilar   illegible   misfortune
displeasure   unspoiled   unfortunate   unsocial or antisocial

4 *Give 2 marks for each correct answer*
I   is   Whom   It's   their

Arithmetic 11 (*possible marks 100*)

Give no marks for incorrect answers except where otherwise indicated

PART 1

1 699 (*1 mark*)

2 106 (*1 mark*)

3 203 (*2 marks*)

4 11,664 (*2 marks*)

5 £1 13s 4d (*2 marks*)

Give 3 marks for each correct answer

6 £1 7s 8d

7 £1 11s 1½d

8 £2 6s 3d

9 9 gallons 1 quart 1 pint

10 88

11 392

12 $5\frac{5}{6}$

13 $2\frac{5}{8}$

14 $5\frac{1}{5}$

15 $20\frac{1}{2}$

16	9·28
17	7·1
18	12.52 p.m.
19	63
20	8 inches

PART 2

1 3 minutes
Give 4 marks for each correct answer

2 $22\frac{1}{2}$ days

3 $7\frac{3}{4}$ stone

4 $3/- (16\frac{1}{2}+5\frac{1}{2})$

5 11 pounds 14 ounces (*10 marks*)
Give marks for these stages:

$\frac{1}{3}=7$ pounds 2 ounces 114 ounces	*2 marks*
since $\frac{1}{9}$ is $\frac{1}{3}$ of $\frac{1}{3}$, then $\frac{1}{9}=\frac{114}{3}=38$ ounces	*2 marks*
$\frac{5}{9}=(38\times5)=190$ ounces	*1 mark*

6 9 (*12 marks*)
Give marks for these stages:

Number of books at 2/8d $=\dfrac{168}{1}/-\div2\frac{2}{3}/-=\dfrac{168\times3}{8}=63$

Therefore saved 63 fourpences $=63\times\frac{1}{3}/-$	*5 marks*
Therefore number of extra books $=(63\times\frac{1}{3}/-)\div2\frac{1}{3}$	
$=\frac{63}{3}\times\frac{3}{7}$	*5 marks*
$\frac{63}{3}\times\frac{3}{7}=\frac{9}{1}$	

7 1,209,600 (*10 marks*)
Give marks for these stages:

$2\times60\times60\times24\times7$	*2 marks*
$=2\times3600\times24\times7$	*2 marks*
$7,200\times24\times7$	*2 marks*
$=172,800\times7$	*2 marks*
$=172,800\times7=1,209,600$	

367

Intelligence 11 (*possible marks 100*)

1 *Give 2 marks for each correct answer*
Here are some specimen words: level, eve, madam, ada, anna, redder

2 (a) flour   (b) 240 pence   (c) Japan   (d) solid   (e) uncommon

3	(a) the same as (b) Scotland (c) 22 yards (d) sister (e) licence (f) 3d (g) receipt (h) astronomer
4	(a) CCCAB (b) ACCAB (c) ACABA (d) CABCC (e) AACCA
5	(a) Nod (b) West (c) 7 miles (d) East (e) 3 miles

Give 2 marks for each correct word, etc.

6	(a) September 1st (b) ⎡⎯⎯⎯⎯⎯⎤ (c) milk, flour (d) Ass
7	(a) snail, slain (b) crate, react, trace (c) mates, tames, teams
8	(a) No. 4 (*2 marks*) (b) No. 2 (*2 marks*) (c) No. 5 (*2 marks*) (d) No. 3 (*3 marks*) (e) No. 5 (*3 marks*)

Give 2 marks for correct answer

9	"S" should be crossed out.
10	*Give 2 marks for each correct word or group of figures* (a) 63154 53127 (b) cart spare seat

English 12 (*possible marks 100*)

PART 1 (*possible marks 50*)

1	*Give 2 marks for each correct answer* (a) foreigner (b) knave (c) thief (d) coward (e) friend
2	*Give 1 mark for each correct answer* angry, angrily pain, painfully brevity, brief kindness, kindly desperation, desperate
3	*Give 1 mark for each correct answer* less, least beautiful, more beautiful drearier, drearier better, best bad, worse
4	The opposites are as follows: (a) tough or strong (b) wealth (c) wisdom (d) collect or gather (e) weakness or frailty *Give 2 marks for each sentence containing one of these words*
5	*Give 2 marks for each correct answer* (a) you will go to bed (b) I shall be late (c) his age (d) she was badly hurt (e) I shall stay at home

PART 2 (*possible marks 50*)

1	Some explorers have landed in a new country (*3 marks*)
2	They have never seen anything like the explorers before (*3 marks*)
3	*Three of these: (2 marks each)* Dancing Display of merchandise Playing at ball Offering a gift

4 They were brown-skinned (*2 marks*) and cleanshaven (*2 marks*)

5 Incomprehensible discussion (*4 marks*)

6 *Two of these:* (*2 marks each*)
Beards   Clothes   Armour

7 *Give 3 marks for each adequate answer. Here are some examples:*
(a) Were becoming brave and less afraid.   (b) To get it back again.
(c) After waiting a little.   (d) excited chatter.   (e) Looked at it carefully
(f) Got over their fear.   (g) Did not run away.

8 (a) goods (*2 marks*)
(b) silly (*1 mark*)
(c) serious (*2 marks*)

Arithmetic 12 (*possible marks 100*)

Give no marks for incorrect answers except where otherwise indicated

1 25 (*3 marks*)

2 18 (*3 marks*)

3 16 (*4 marks. Give 2 marks for knowing how to do the sum yet failing to get the correct answer*)

4 12/8d (*4 marks. Give 1 mark for getting 13/4d and 1 mark for subtracting 8d*)

5 (a) The boys (*3 marks*)
(b) by 3 (*1 mark*)
(c) 135 (*3 marks*)

6 2 tons 3 hundredweights 2 quarters (*7 marks*)
The working should be as follows:

$$
\begin{array}{ccc}
2 & 3 & 2 \\
15\overline{)32} & 12 & 2 \\
30 & 40 & 28 \\
\hline
2 & 52 & 30 \\
 & 45 \\
\hline
2\times & 7 \\
20 \\
\hline
40 & 7\times \\
 & 4 \\
\hline
 & 28
\end{array}
$$

Give 2 marks for correct working in each column
24+—H T.

369

7 $\frac{1}{9}$ (*7 marks*)

Give marks for these stages:

$$\frac{2 \text{ hours } 40 \text{ minutes}}{24 \text{ hours}} = \frac{160 \text{ minutes}}{24 \times 60 \text{ minutes}}$$

  1 mark

  2 marks

8   3·125 (*3 marks*)

9   6d (*8 marks*)

Give marks for these stages:

1 gallon = 8 pints   *1 mark*

8 pints = 4/–   *2 marks*

Therefore 8 ounces of butter will cost 4/–   *3 marks*

Therefore 1 ounce will cost 4/– ÷ 8 = 6d

10   (a) 23 feet (*9 marks*)

(b) $3\frac{1}{2}$ square yards (*8 marks*)

Give marks for these stages:

Length of cloth = 5 feet 10 inches + 1 foot 2 inches   *2 marks*

5 feet 10 inches + 1 foot 2 inches = 7 feet   *1 mark*

Breadth of cloth = 3 feet 4 inches + 1 foot 2 inches = 4 feet 6 inches   *2 marks*

Therefore distance all round = 14 feet + 9 feet = 23 feet

Area of cloth = 7 feet × $4\frac{1}{2}$ feet   *2 marks*

7 feet × $4\frac{1}{2}$ feet = $31\frac{1}{2}$ square feet   *2 marks*

$31\frac{1}{2}$ square feet ÷ 9(9 sq. ft. = 1 sq. yd.) = $3\frac{1}{2}$ square yards

11   £13 13s 0d (*7 marks*)

The working should be as follows:

52 × 5/– = £13

52 × 3d = 13s

Answer = £13 13s

12   1 ton 14 hundredweights (*15 marks*)

Give marks for these stages:

Van + 30 sacks = 3 tons 4 hundredweights

Van + 22 sacks = 2 tons 16 hundredweights   *3 marks*

Therefore 8 sacks = 8 hundredweights   *3 marks*

Therefore 1 sack = 1 hundredweight

Therefore 22 sacks = 22 hundredweights

22 hundredweights = 1 ton 2 hundredweights   *3 marks*

Therefore van will weigh

2 tons 16 hundredweights − 1 ton 2 hundredweights   *3 marks*

13   4.08 p.m. (*15 marks*)

Give marks for these stages:

8.15 a.m. to 10.07 a.m. = 112 minutes   *2 marks*

Therefore the train travels a mile in 2 minutes   *2 marks*

Therefore half that speed would be a mile in 4 minutes   *2 marks*
Time required from B to C=84×4=336 minutes   *2 marks*
336 minutes=5 hours 36 minutes   *2 marks*
Leaves B at 10.32 a.m.   *1 mark*
Add to this   5.36

Total=   16.08, which is 4.08 p.m.

Intelligence 12 *(possible marks 85)*

Give 1 mark for each correct group of figures

1   3833   545454   113311

2   6   S42   P3   B18

Give 3 marks for each correct answer

3   FORM

4   Z

Give 2 marks for each correct pair of words

5   (a) acute sharp   (b) intend mean   (c) fracture break

Give 1 mark for each correct word

6   Here are some specimen words: scar, care, cart, carp, card

7   purposely   pipe   paper

8   *Give 3 marks for correct answer*
Halfway between 2 and 3

9   *Give 2 marks for each correct answer*
(a) eager   (b) hazardous   (c) ancient

10   *Give 3 marks for (a), (b) and (c), and 4 marks for (d)*
(a) one cannot tell   (b) Tom Harry   (c) one cannot tell   (d) Helen

11   April *(3 marks)*   30 *(2 marks)*   March *(3 marks)*

Give 2 marks for each correct answer

12   (a) pear   (b) sixty   (c) Paris   (d) child (the others are all animals)
(e) four (the others are three-letter words)

13   (a) Will tomorrow be Friday?   (b) Each stick of rock costs twopence.
(c) I thought he was going to catch me.   (d) Susan and Mary were sisters.
(e) This test is not very easy.

14   *Give 6 marks for (a) (or 2 marks for each correct word); and 4 marks for (b)*
(a) 5+3*4*2* 1*3+2+ 4+2+1+   (b) FOREHEAD

371

English 13 *(possible marks 100)*

PART 1 *(possible marks 53)*

1   *Give 1 mark for each correct answer*
(a) tick   (b) tick   (c) cross   (d) tick   (e) tick   (f) tick   (g) tick
(h) cross   (i) cross   (j) tick

Give 2 marks for each correct answer
2   (a) would   (b) must, should   (c) was   (d) to worry   (e) I should not
eat so much, or I ought not to eat so much

3   (a) rotate, or revolve   (b) future   (c) minute   (d) everlasting
(e) industrious

4   *Give 2 marks for each sentence*
Here are suggested pairings:
     graciously, allowed   bitter, complaint   final, whistle   compose,
     letter   entertain, friends

5   *Give 1 mark for each correct answer*
(a) snow, or a sheet   (b) a fox   (c) an owl   (d) grass   (e) brass
(f) lead   (g) a pillow, or silk   (h) a pig   (i) a baby   (j) Punch

6   the queen's crown   the men's hats   a fairy's wand *(1 mark each)*

PART 2 *(possible marks 47)*

1   *Give 3 marks for each adequate answer*
Here are some examples:
     (a) were free to come and go   (b) knowing how vain they were
     (c) took no notice of   (d) took a good look at   (e) tried to get away
     (f) caused by their own foolishness

2   Beg, or ask *(1 mark)* petition *(2 marks)*

3   *Give 2 marks for each correct answer*
They were tired of doing what they liked   They wanted to be kept in order
They wanted to be made more honest

4   *Give 2 marks for each correct answer*
(a) noise   (b) tired   (c) gathered   (d) fright   (e) wonder   (f) dared
(g) eating
Accept any adequate word.

5   It didn't do anything *(1 mark)*

6   fable *(2 marks)*

7   To leave well alone, or to be content
For these or a similar expression *give 3 marks*

Arithmetic 13 (*possible marks 100*)

Give no marks for incorrect answers except where otherwise indicated

1 £218 9s 11½d (*5 marks. Deduct 2 marks for each wrong figure*)

2 9 hours 44 minutes 22 seconds (*6 marks. Deduct 2 marks for each wrong figure*)
360 hours 21 minutes 34 seconds (*12 marks*)
The working for the second answer should be as follows:

hours	minutes	seconds
9	44	22
		37
360	21	34

27	13	22
9	44	× 37
× 37	× 37	——
——	——	154
63	308	660
270	1320	60/814(13 r 34
——	——	60
333	1628	214
+27	+13	180
——	60/1641(27 r 21	——
=360	120	34
	——	
	441	
	420	
	——	
	21	

Give 4 marks for correct working in each column.

3 2 hundredweights 1 quarter 6 pounds (*12 marks*)
The working should be as follows:
  3 tons = 60 hundredweights
  60 hundredweights ÷ 26 =

2	1	6
26/60 cwt	32 qrs	168 lbs
52	26	156
——	——	——
8	6	12
× 4	× 28	
——	——	
32	168	

Give 4 marks for correct working in each column

373

4 | $\frac{3}{4}$ (*12 marks. Deduct 2 marks for each error*)
The working should be as follows:

$$\frac{\overset{2}{\cancel{16}}}{\underset{3}{\cancel{33}}}\times\frac{5}{8}\times\frac{11}{4}\times\frac{\overset{3}{\cancel{9}}}{\underset{2}{\cancel{10}}}=\frac{3}{4}$$

5 | 66 yards 2 feet 8 inches (*12 marks*)
Give marks for these stages:

12 yards 2 feet 10 inches × 2 = 25 yards 2 feet 8 inches — *3 marks*
20 yards 1 foot 6 inches × 2 = 41 yards 0 feet 0 inches — *3 marks*
25 yards 2 feet 8 inches + 41 yards = 66 yards 2 feet 8 inches

6 | 30·765 (*3 marks*)
8·858 (*4 marks*)
The working should be as follows:

```
    5·09
   18·3
    7·375
   ──────
   30·765
   21·907
   ──────
    8·858
```

7 | £1 14s 1½d (*14 marks*)
Give marks for these stages:

$14/7\frac{1}{2}$d = $175\frac{1}{2}$d — *2 marks*
$175\frac{1}{2}$d ÷ 27 = $6\frac{1}{2}$d
Therefore each packet cost $6\frac{1}{2}$d — *4 marks*
Therefore 63 cost 63 × $6\frac{1}{2}$d
= £1 14s 1½d
Give 4 marks for knowing how to do the sum.

8 | 120 (*10 marks*)
This requires finding the lowest common multiple:

$$\frac{4|8 \quad 12 \quad 20}{\quad 2 \quad \ 3 \quad \ 5}$$

4 × 2 × 3 × 5 = 120

374

9 | 60 miles (*10 marks*)
Give marks for these stages:

$$\frac{2}{15}+\frac{5}{6}=\frac{4+25}{30}=\frac{29}{30}$$ — *5 marks*

Therefore 2 miles = $\frac{1}{30}$ — *2 marks*
Therefore total distance ($\frac{30}{30}$) = 60 miles

Intelligence 13 *(possible marks 100)*

PART 1

Give 2 marks for each correct answer

1	chairman
2	mare
3	walks
4	aviary
5	calendar
6	farming
7	four
8	continent
9	1760
10	terminus
11	Trafalgar
12	China
13	fuel
14	elephants
15	30
16	artificial
17	knives and forks
18	sphere
19	laughing
20	avenue
21	hat
22	fifty
23	thank you
24	periscope
25	amazing

PART 2

Give 2 marks for each correct pair

1	(a) 45 56

(b) df eg
(c) sixpence shilling
(d) stone pound

(e)

2
(a) reign rain
(b) groan grown
(c) some sum
(d) bough bow
(e) fare fair

Give 2 marks for each correct answer
3 (a) foot   (b) Jane   (c) hasty   (d) president   (e) T

4 P6   R9   S4   T5   W8

5 C3   D4   E5   F2   G1

English 14 *(possible marks 100)*

PART 1 *(possible marks 53)*

1 *Give 1 mark for each correct word*
(a) to   (b) from   (c) on, in   (d) May or Should or Shall, can or may
(e) while   (f) During or In, about or over   (g) since

2 *Give 2 marks for each correct answer*
unhurried   misfortune   impatient   disarrange   illegal

3 *Give 1 mark for each correct answer*
consist = verb   and = conjunction   they = pronoun   sometimes =
adverb   black = adjective   diamonds = noun

4 *Give 1 mark for each correct answer*
Birds = subject   lay = predicate   eggs = object

5 *Give 3 marks for each satisfactory sentence. Here are some examples:*
(a) I cannot come at short notice.   (b) In order to escape, they agreed with one accord not to talk.   (c) Strange to relate, the cat was not afraid of the dog.
(d) They fought furiously, going for one another hammer and tongs.
(e) When he dropped the second catch he plunged into despair

6 *Give 1 mark for each satisfactory alternative word. These are the obvious words to choose:*
(a) boasted   (b) asked   (c) grumbled, or moaned   (d) explained
(e) recited   (f) proclaimed

7 (a) shortly, or soon   (b) fortnight   (c) can   (d) abroad *(1 mark each)*

PART 2 (*possible marks 47*)

1   A ship on fire (*1 mark*)

2   Owing to the reflection of the flames (*2 marks*)

3   *Give 2 marks for each correct answer*
(a) sinister   (b) ascended   (c) disc   (d) magnificent, glorious
(e) reward   (f) mournful   (g) laborious   (h) immense   (i) surrender
(j) charred   (k) stirring   (l) slim   (m) viciously

Give 2 marks for each correct answer

4   Coal

5   They were in the lifeboats

6   The stern

7   The paint had peeled off owing to the heat

8   Dawn

9   As the burning coal came into contact with the water (*3 marks*)

10   *Give a maximum of 5 marks for a good answer*

Arithmetic 14 (*possible marks 100*)

Give no marks for incorrect answers except where otherwise indicated

PART 1

Give 1 mark for each correct answer

1   81

2   22

3   1,176

4   73

5   £1 2s 6d

Give 2 marks for each correct answer

6   £3 2s 10½d

7   2/8½d

8   6/8d

9   3·01

10   42

11   288

12   10 ounces

24*

377

	Give 3 marks for each correct answer
13	$3\frac{11}{12}$
14	18 inches
15	$2\frac{1}{2}$ inches
16	15 yards
17	$67\frac{1}{2}$ miles
18	129
	Give 4 marks for each correct answer
19	32
20	$2/5\frac{3}{4}$d

PART 2

1   12,654 (*2 marks*)
The working should be as follows

$$
\begin{array}{r}
703 \\
18 \\
\hline
5,624 \\
7,030 \\
\hline
12,654 \\
\hline
\end{array}
$$

Deduct 2 marks for each error

2   109 (*3 marks*)
The working should be as follows:

$$
\begin{array}{r}
109 \\
27\overline{)2943} \\
27 \\
\hline
243 \\
243 \\
\hline
\end{array}
$$

Deduct 2 marks for each error

3   531 (*6 marks*)
Give marks for these stages:

£3 6s $4\frac{1}{2}$d $=66/4\frac{1}{2}$d	*1 mark*
$66/4\frac{1}{2}$d $=796\frac{1}{2}$ pence	*2 marks*
$796\frac{1}{2}$ pence $=1,593$ half-pence	*1 mark*
$1,593 \div 3=$ the number of $1\frac{1}{2}$d stamps	
$=531$	

4 | 2 stones 5 pounds 13 ounces (*8 marks*)
The working should be as follows:

```
        2        5         13 r 15
   23/55         8          10
     46       +126       +304
                         23/314(13 r 15
      9        134         23
     115
      9        ___         84
   × 14         19         69
   ___         19         15
    126      × 16
             ___
             114
             190
             ___
             304
```

Deduct 2 marks for each error.

5 | 2 miles 80 yards (*9 marks*)
Give marks for these stages:

120 steps = 180 feet	*1 mark*
180 feet = 60 yards	*2 marks*
number of yards walked in one hour = 60×60	*1 mark*
miles walked in one hour = $\dfrac{60 \times 60}{1760}$	*2 marks*

$$\frac{60 \times 60}{1760} = 2 \text{ miles } 80 \text{ yards}$$

6 | 81 square inches (*8 marks*)
Give marks for these stages:

Whole area = 216 square inches	*2 marks*
¼ area = 54 square inches	*2 marks*
⅛ area = 27 square inches	*2 marks*
54 + 27 = 81	

7 | 2/6d (*9 marks*)
Give marks for these stages:

Number of 3d = 45	*2 marks*
45 × 3d = 11/3d, so crocuses cost 11/3d	*1 mark*
Fare = 2/5d	
Expenses = 13/8d	*2 marks*
£2 16s 2d − 13/8d = wages of £2 2s 6d	*2 marks*
Hourly rate = £2 2s 6d ÷ 17 = 2/6d	

379

8 | Unbroken=112 (*4 marks*)
Broken=8 (*6 marks*)
Give marks for these stages:

$\frac{5}{8}$ are plates. Find $\frac{5}{8}$ of 320 for number of plates	*3 marks*
$\frac{5}{8}$ of 320=200	*1 mark*
$\frac{1}{25}$ of 200=8	
Therefore number of plates broken=8	
$\frac{3}{8}$ are saucers. Find $\frac{3}{8}$ of 320=120	*1 mark*
$\frac{1}{15}$ of 120=8 (number of broken saucers)	*1 mark*
Therefore number of saucers unbroken=112	

Intelligence 14 (*possible marks 100*)

1 | (a) 35 (*1 mark*)   (b) 6 (*2 marks*)   (c) 0 (*2 marks*)   (d) Either B+C or A+D divided by B (*3 marks*)

Give 2 marks for each correct answer

2 | (a) White   (b) Green   (c) Brown

3 | (a) right   (b) right

4 | (a) Jan 20th   (b) 5   (c) swing   (d) Monday   (e) NM

5 | (a) 4   (b) teenager   (c) stone   (d) $\frac{3}{4}$ (e) *chart* if it is done by length of words, and *cat* if it is done alphabetically

Give 6 marks for each correct group of letters

6 | (a) A   A   C   (b) B   A

Give 1 mark for each correct word

7 | (a) girl   man (or: man   girl)   (b) low   fat   (c) North   East Wales
(d) simple   Mary   (e) 1   pint

Give 2 marks for each correct answer

8 | (a) is worth two in the bush   (b) make light work   (c) A stitch in time
(d) gathers no moss   (e) Too many cooks

9 | (a) stars   (b) living things   (c) rocks   (d) plants   (e) medicines

10 | *Give 5 marks for each part of the answer*
(a) You know where you have come from so you can point the right arm in that direction.   (b) Three.   (c) Fill up the 5 pint jug and pour it into the 3 pint jug. Empty the three pints away and pour the two pints left in the 5 pint jug into the small jug. Fill up the 5 pint jug and then fill up the 3 pint jug from it. Four pints are left in the big jug.   (d) One pound.

380

Quick Examination *(possible marks 90)*

ENGLISH *(possible marks 23)*

1 That the dragon would be found and people would want to kill it *(2 marks)*

2 *Give 1 mark for each reason from this list:*
Had not harmed the fowls   Only lazed about   Only told stories   Only
enjoyed the sunshine   Only wrote poetry

3 Simply because it was a dragon; or words giving this idea *(3 marks)*

4 *Give 1 mark for each suitable word*
destroyed or killed   brave, heroic or gallant   tales or stories   thinking
or musing

5 (a) happened *(1 mark)*
(b) keep hidden *(1 mark)*
(c) a mark of distinction *(2 marks)*
(d) could not say he was not *(1 mark)*

6 fantastic *(2 marks)* queer *(1 mark)*

7 *Give 1 mark for each correct answer*
(a) Did you see him when he *came* to stay.   (b) None of us *has* done it.
(c) Mary is the *younger* of the twins.   (d) *Whom* do you want to see?

ARITHMETIC *(possible marks 33)*

Give no marks for incorrect answers except where otherwise indicated

1 9/4d, 1/5½d, 2/2d, 4/–, Total＝16/11½d *(9 marks. Give 2 marks for each correct item)*

2 4 yards 1 foot 9 inches *(7 marks)*
The working should be as follows:

$$
\begin{array}{ccc}
4 & 1 & 9 \\
\hline
23\overline{)105} & 2 & 9 \\
92 & +39 & +216 \\
\hline
13 & 41 & 225 \\
 & 23 & 207 \\
13 & \hline & \hline \\
\times 3 & 18 & 18 \\
\hline & & \\
39 & 18 & \\
 & \times 12 & \\
 & \hline & \\
 & 216 & \\
\end{array}
$$

Give 2 marks for correct working in each column.

381

3

(a) 6 pints (*3 marks*)

(b) 4 pounds 11 ounces (*6 marks*)

Give marks for these stages:

$\frac{2}{3}$ of $\frac{3}{4}$ [$\frac{2}{3} \times \frac{3}{4}$]=$\frac{1}{2}$

Therefore half a canful of water is poured away.

12 pounds 3 ounces minus 8 pounds 7 ounces=3 pounds 12 ounces

Therefore half a canful of water weighs 3 pounds 12 ounces   *3 marks*

Therefore a canful of water will weigh 7 pounds 8 ounces   *1 mark*

and the can itself will weigh 12 pounds 3 ounces minus 7 pounds 8 ounces

1 mark

12 pounds 3 ounces−7 pounds 8 ounces=4 pounds 11 ounces

Since the weight of a can full of water is $7\frac{1}{2}$ pounds and we have been told that a pint of water weighs $1\frac{1}{4}$ pounds the can will hold $7\frac{1}{2} \div 1\frac{1}{4}$ pints of water

2 marks

$7\frac{1}{2} \div 1\frac{1}{4} = 6$

4

3d (*8 marks*)

Give marks for these stages:

potatoes cost 21/– per hundredweight=$\frac{21}{112}$/– per pound   *2 marks*

$\frac{21}{112}$/–=$\frac{3}{16}$/– per pound   *2 marks*

4 pounds of potatoes cost $\frac{3}{16}$/–$\times \frac{4}{1}$=9d   *2 marks*

Therefore 3 bars of chocolate will cost 9d

and 1 bar of chocolate will cost 3d.

GENERAL QUESTIONS (*possible marks 34*)

1

Three (*1 mark*)

2

(a) Mr. Painter (*3 marks*)

(b) Mr. Baker (*3 marks*)

3

Give 2 marks for each correct answer

(a) ankle   (b) tomorrow   (c) piano   (d) medicine   (e) Ash Wednesday

4

Give 2 marks for each correct answer

(a) On Her Majesty's Service   (b) Royal Navy   (c) Greenwich Mean Time   (d) Royal Air Force   (e) Bachelor of Science

382

5

Give 3 marks for each correct answer. Deduct 1 mark for each misplacement

strange   stray   stream   stretch   strip   stroke

6

Give 1 mark for each word

EVIL   LIVE   VEIL   VILE

Intelligence 15 *(possible marks 74)*

1 *Give 1 mark for each correct item (total 10 marks)*

2 *Give 2 marks for each correct answer*
The following diagrams should have been crossed out:
(a) The 4th and 5th boxes which are in the wrong order   (b) The 2nd box which has only two strokes   (c) The 4th pair which is not completed

3 *Give 3 marks for each correct answer*
The following pairs should have been crossed out:
(a) The 4th   (b) The 2nd or 5th   (c) The 5th   (d) The 3rd

4 *Give 4 marks for each correct answer*
The following diagrams (counted from the line) should have been ringed:
(a) The 4th   (b) The 5th   (c) The 2nd or 4th   (d) The 3rd
(e) The 3rd

5 *Give 1 mark for each correct insertion (15 marks)*

6 The following diagrams should have been underlined:
(a) The 2nd *(3 marks)*   (b) The 5th *(3 marks)*   (c) The 1st *(2 marks)*
(d) The 5th *(3 marks)*

Intelligence 16 *(possible marks 94)*

1 *Give 5 marks for each correct answer*
The following diagrams should have been underlined:
(a) The 4th   (b) The 4th   (c) The 1st   (d) The 4th

2 *Give 4 marks for each correct pair*
The following diagrams should have been underlined:
(a) The 1st and 3rd   (b) The 1st and 5th   (c) The 3rd and 5th
(d) The 1st and 4th

3 *Give 4 marks for each correct set or 2 marks for each correct diagram*
(a) The 4th and 5th   (b) The 4th and 5th   (c) The 1st and 3rd
(d) The 2nd and 4th   (e) The 3rd and 5th

4 *Give 4 marks for each correct set*
The following diagrams should have been underlined:
(a) The 1st and 4th   (b) The 1st and 3rd   (c) The 3rd and 5th or the 2nd
and 6th   (d) The 1st and 5th   (e) The 3rd and 5th

5

(a) ⊘ ⊗ *2 marks* (b) ⊗ ⊗ *2 marks* (c) ⊡ ⊡ *4 marks*

(d) B B *4 marks* (e) ↘ ↗ *6 marks*

Intelligence 17 *(possible marks 94)*

1 *Give 2 marks for each correct crossing out and 3 marks for each correct underlining*
(a) The 5th should be crossed out. The 3rd should be underlined
(b) The 3rd should be crossed out. The 6th should be underlined
(c) The 4th or 6th should be crossed out. The 1st should be underlined
(d) The 5th should be crossed out. The 2nd should be underlined
(e) The 1st should be crossed out. The 2nd should be underlined

2 *Give 4 marks for each correct drawing*

(a)   (b)   (c)   (d)   (e)

3 *Give 3 marks for each correct letter*
R X W N D

4 *Give 3 marks for each letter placed in the correct position, except E, for which only 2 marks may be given*

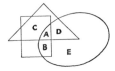

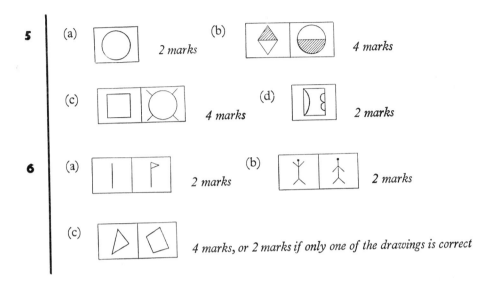

5 (a) 2 marks (b) 4 marks

   (c) 4 marks (d) 2 marks

6 (a) 2 marks (b) 2 marks

   (c) 4 marks, or 2 marks if only one of the drawings is correct

MADE AND PRINTED IN GREAT BRITAIN BY
WILLIAM CLOWES & SONS, LTD.,
LONDON AND BECCLES